D1564250

Rockin' the Free World!

Rockin' the Free World!

How the Rock & Roll Revolution Changed America and the World

Sean Kay

ROWMAN & LITTLEFIELD
Lanham • Boulder • New York • London

Published by Rowman & Littlefield
A wholly owned subsidiary of The Rowman & Littlefield Publishing Group, Inc.
4501 Forbes Boulevard, Suite 200, Lanham, Maryland 20706
www.rowman.com

Unit A, Whitacre Mews, 26-34 Stannary Street, London SE11 4AB

British Library Cataloguing in Publication Information Available

Library of Congress Cataloging-in-Publication Data

Names: Kay, Sean, 1967–
Title: Rockin' the free world!: how the rock & roll revolution changed
    America and the world / Sean Kay.
Other titles: Rocking the free world!
Description: Lanham: Rowman & Littlefield, [2017] |
    Includes bibliographical references and index.
Identifiers: LCCN 2016045405 (print) | ISBN 9781442266049 (cloth) |
    ISBN 9781442266056 (electronic)
Subjects: LCSH: Rock music—Social aspects—United States.
Classification: LCC ML3918.R63 K39 2017 |
    DDC 306.4/84260973–dc23
LC record available at https://lccn.loc.gov/2016045405

♾™ The paper used in this publication meets the minimum requirements of American
National Standard for Information Sciences—Permanence of Paper for Printed Library
Materials, ANSI/NISO Z39.48-1992.

Printed in the United States of America

Contents

Contents

Introduction and Acknowledgments

On November 13, 2015, Paris, France, was struck by a terrorist attack, which included mass killing at a rock and roll concert. Several hours later and thousands of miles away, in Columbus, Ohio, Bob Weir of the Grateful Dead took stage and shared the news from France. They were killed, Weir said, by, "… religious extremists who, if they had their way, would outlaw music in all the world. We should celebrate their lives and the joy that they found in music." Weir and his band, Dead & Co., rocked in defiance with songs of joy, defeating fear. The night ended with the band and the audience singing "We will get by, we will survive!" This is the power of rock and roll.

Rock and roll is more than a music form—it is an idea, an attitude, a way of thinking about the world. This book shows that rock and roll has renewed and sent American values rippling across the world—freedom, equality, human rights, and peace advanced via education and activism. The book also offers a warning that changes in the music business simultaneously expand and put at risk the rock and roll revolution. The central voices in this book come from interviews with people working across the spectrum of rock and roll, complemented by secondary sources. The list of people interviewed is not exhaustive but rather illustrative of the influence of artists and activists—and, the conclusions are the responsibility of the author.

Born in the San Francisco Bay Area during the Summer of Love, 1967, my family moved to Ohio in 1979—where I came of age to the soundtrack of America's heartland and where I began playing the guitar at age 12. In college at Kent State University, we made our own small contributions to the vibrant northeast Ohio music scene with our bands, the Good Rockers and the Flying Locomotives. While at Kent State University, I was privileged to perform at the annual May 4th commemoration. Since 1999, I have played with rock and roll groups around Central Ohio, even once opening for O.A.R

(Of a Revolution). From the 7th grade onward, I have worked with some of the best musicians one could hope to play with. I was inspired to do this book over pints at Grogan's Castle Inn in Dublin, Ireland, by my brother-in-law Des Mullan. I subsequently received funding from the Great Lakes College Association. I would not have been able to do this project without the advice of Tim Prindle—one of America's great historians and musicians. Tim, his wife Heather, and their children Colin and Liam are the best of friends. Same goes for Jim Breece, who offered extensive comments and who rocks away in Ohio on any given weekend. This project would not have been possible without the friendship of Mark, Deb, and Raven Tilford and Jarrod, Amanda, Dylan, and Caleb Owens, who, with the Prindles, Josh Anderson, and Brooke Bloom, have rounded out the "Michigan Crew." Thanks to Pam Laucher, Scott Calef, Ted Cohen, Mary Howard, Jim Franklin, Kim Lance, Deanne Peterson, Charles Stinemetz, and to Elaine McGarraugh, Jon Sisk and Chris Utter at Rowman & Littlefield. The author is appreciative of a number of artists who were able to meet but schedules did not allow for extended interviews including Jackson Browne, Joan Jett, Kenny Laguna, and Bob Weir. I am also appreciative to Nadya Tolokonnikova and Maria Alyokhina, from Pussy Riot, for fruitful exchanges on democracy and for their keeping the rock and roll spirit of freedom alive in Russia and beyond.

This book is a tribute to my grandmother, Anne Grimes. From 1942 to 1946 she was a music and dance critic for the *Columbus Citizen* in Columbus, Ohio. Also a performer, she recorded with Folkways Records. I am grateful for my parents, David and Jenni Kay, who exposed me to the power of rock and roll and to Matt and Anna Madigan for sharing Ireland with me. While interviewing, David Crosby asked if my daughter Alana (who was traveling with me) and I wanted to hear some new songs. Crosby performed just for us. I was thrilled to involve our children—Cria talking politics with Bob Weir, Siobhan hanging with Little Feat, Alana chatting with Joan Jett—and my lovely wife Anna-Marie, a teacher, meeting Graham Nash who wrote the song "Teach Your Children Well." *Rockin' the Free World!* is dedicated to Anna-Marie and our children–and to all the artists who have provided the soundtrack for our lives while making our world a better place.

Delaware, Ohio, November 2016

Part I

POWER AND PROGRESS

Chapter One

Bob Dylan's America

WITH GOD ON OUR SIDE

When inducted into the Rock and Roll Hall of Fame in 2004, *Rolling Stone* magazine founder Jann Wenner said: "Bob Dylan is the voice of my America." What did it mean—that Bob Dylan voiced a vision of America? From the first beats of Bill Haley and His Comets singing "Rock Around the Clock" to Dylan's "With God on Our Side" to the Beatles "Revolution" to the Clash rocking the Casbah to Joan Jett loving rock and roll to Kathleen Hanna championing a new feminism to System of a Down rocking B.Y.O.B. about war and to Pussy Riot championing freedom—the rock and roll revolution ripples across the world. Rock and roll affirms and spreads freedom, equality, human rights, and peace advanced via education and activism. As Irish rocker Sinéad O'Connor says: "The most powerful words in rock and roll is, " 'A whop-bop-a-lua—a whop bam boom,' Do you know what I mean?" "Although Little Richard's intention," she says, "may have been completely different when he authored those words, those were very political fucking words."[1]

TROUBADOURS OF TRUTH

Rock and roll is as much an attitude or an ethic as a music style. As Ice Cube said on N.W.A.'s induction to the Rock and Roll Hall of Fame in 2016: "The question is—are we rock and roll? And I say you God damn right we rock and roll!" He continued: "Rock and roll is not an instrument—rock and roll is not even a style of music. Rock and roll is a spirit. It's a spirit that's been going since the blues, jazz, be-bop, soul, R&B, rock and roll, heavy metal, punk rock—and yes, hip-hop. And, what connects us all is that spirit—that's what connects us all, that spirit. Rock and roll is not conforming to the people who came before you, but creating your own path in music and in life. That is rock and roll." Rock and roll's power has consistently taken what was once marginal and brought the mainstream to it. As bassist for Nirvana, Krist Novoselić (being inducted to the Rock and Roll Hall of Fame in 2014) explained: "Nirvana didn't go mainstream, the mainstream came to Nirvana." This revolutionary power exists in the interconnections that music creates between ideas and people. And, most of these rock and roll interconnections travel on the path laid down by Bob Dylan.

"It's Part of Our Job"

Bob Dylan articulated an enduring critique of the American experience blending folk traditions with rock and roll. David Crosby, co-founder of the Byrds and Crosby, Stills and Nash, and Young, says of his friend Dylan: "Often odd—but always interesting," he pauses, "because you really don't know where it's going to go—it could go anywhere."[2] Bob Dylan amplified durable changes in America in the 1960s, for example, in "With God on Our Side," Dylan exploded the myths behind the nation's heroes—"with guns in their hands, their God on their side." Jann Wenner recalls first hearing a Dylan song as a student at U.C. Berkeley in 1964:

There was this one rally that started where the students swarmed the main campus square and surrounded a police car where they were holding, they were trying to arrest a guy for demonstrating, I believe. They were surrounded by seas of people and they kept the police car hostage for a long long time. Joan Baez showed up at this rally, this event, and sang 'With God on Our Side.' I mean—what a setting to hear something like that. When you're in the middle of this energy-charged atmosphere of the event going down, where you are just at the center of this moment—that is electrifying. And then somebody gets up and starts to articulate a poetic and beautiful linkage of this event with all of the injustices of American society. You never ask questions with God on your side, and the civil war, the nuclear bomb and all that in one.[3]

Jann Wenner summarizes Dylan's impact:

It's profound in giving meaning to something that you're thinking and feeling. Then you go dig deeper into what he's written and he tracked, or led, this whole generation of people and artists by elaborating a vision of getting more sophisticated. And then getting more personal and taking out of the political world and into the more personal, philosophical level that was more intense than ever. When you get to 'Highway 61' and 'Desolation Row'—that's not a specific issue-oriented thing or specifically political. It's a powerful thought about bankruptcy of materialism and society and the craziness of it. His own stuff just got more and more intense than ever and you sort of follow along with it. It became your America. If you weren't thinking then about America obviously you saw it through new eyes, and that's how it becomes your America too. He defined in great part and gave meaning—a way of meaning, of looking at so much around you that you didn't quite understand. I mean, why are people possessing fucking nuclear weapons to blow up the world? You can talk about it in geopolitical terms. But you can just talk about it in terms of sheer fucking madness. There is a Dr. Filth that keeps his world locked up inside of a leather cup.[4]

Serj Tankian, of System of a Down, says of this legacy now, the artistic role is diverse: "You've got a lot of artists that are there to entertain—which has always been kind of like the mainstay of our industry. People want to be entertained. They want a mood change. On the cheezy side you've got elevator music. Then, on the more consumer side, you've got the big pop hits. But then you also have a cadre of artists that specialize in narration—telling stories and truths through what they do whether it's music or films or any of the above. It's an interesting difference, neither is wrong or right. I think both are necessary."[5]

In terms of global events, the Cold War that shaped a young Bob Dylan was nudged out with a rock and roll backbeat by Billy Joel (who with his band played the first major rock concerts in the Soviet Union in 1987), Crosby, Stills and Nash (who were at the Berlin Wall in November 1989, singing with the crowds as it came down), and Roger Waters of Pink Floyd (who performed the Pink Floyd masterpiece *The Wall* at the Berlin Wall in 1990). After the September 11, 2001, terrorist attacks on New York City and Washington, D.C., a concert in Madison Square Garden coordinated by Paul McCartney a month later lifted the spirits of a grieving nation. At that concert, Roger Daltrey's penultimate scream in "Won't Get Fooled Again" gave the song new context while Pete Townshend's guitar windmills were juxtaposed against British and American flags. The Who emboldened a nation to stay confident, not guided by fear. Two years later, however, America invaded Iraq on false pretenses. In 2006, Crosby, Stills, Nash and Young resurrected the legacy of music and protest with their "Freedom of Speech Tour 2006." Performing songs such as "Let's Impeach the President" in Atlanta, Georgia, many people were upset and about a third walked out. Yet, history shows Crosby, Stills, Nash and Young were right. Graham Nash says: "What I'd like to do is talk to those people that walked out—and say, 'O.K., in hindsight would you still have walked out? In hindsight—when you know what George

Bush and his cronies did—would you still walk out? And my God—holy shit—if you buy a ticket to a Crosby, Stills, Nash and Young concert—what the fuck did you expect?'" Nash adds that songs resonating decades ago remain vibrant:

> Because there's a certain anger when you realize—like for instance, 'Military Madness'—written about my father going off to World War II—has anything changed? No. So that makes me angry. So I have to deliver that song 'Military Madness' or 'Chicago.' It's still going on to this day. And so what happens is that you get angry that it's still the same—that we still haven't learned. And I get more intense on the delivery of those songs. Those songs aren't, 'Oh well let's do 'Chicago' because people love it.' I'm pissed off that I have to sing 'Military Madness.' I'm pissed off that I have to sing 'Chicago.'[6]

Even when, in the 2006 election, the Democrats won Congress, little changed. The Democrats were elected into a majority in Congress promising to end the war in Iraq. The war in Iraq, however, waged on until 2011 and then began again in 2014 under a Democrat, Barack Obama.

The vision of America that Bob Dylan offered stresses it is good to make the world a fairer place; it is heroic to champion freedom, equality, human rights, and peace. This vision came through in songs such as "Chimes of Freedom," "Oxford Town," "Only a Pawn in their Game," "A Hard Rain's A-Gonna Fall," and "Masters of War." Of course, Dylan also offered a soundtrack for the quest for a better world with "Blowing in the Wind." Dennis McNally, one of America's leading historians of rock and roll and culture, traces the roots of Dylan's America up and down the Mississippi River—building on traditions coming from ragtime, blues, and jazz—eventually finding their way via modern communications to Elvis Presley in Memphis, Tennessee, and the songs of young Robert Zimmerman upriver.[7] By the 1950s, this came to fruition with the art of Jack Kerouac, Jackson Pollack, and Charlie Parker. This improvisational freedom emerged alongside the tradition of the troubadour—travelers who sing songs or tell stories. Artists such as David Crosby and Graham Nash, for example, performed in 2011 at the Occupy Wall Street movement in New York City. They do it because, Crosby says: "It's part of our job. Part of our job is to be the town crier, the troubadour, and it always has been. We learned it from people like Pete Seeger and Woody Guthrie."[8] Crosby recalls: "We were at a time, when Bob showed up, where black people couldn't vote in their own country—in the South." Crosby reflects: "They were citizens. They were born here. They were being prevented from voting. The Civil Rights Act hadn't happened yet. Martin Luther King hadn't walked from Selma to Montgomery yet—with Harry Belafonte on his arm, by the way—and Joan Baez." Crosby observes:

Pete Seeger arrives at Federal Court with his guitar over his shoulder (1961). World Telegram photo by Walter Albertin. LC-USZ62-130860 (black and white film copy negative). Library of Congress Prints and Photographs Division Washington, D.C.

You can go back further than Woody. There was the folk tradition in this country and folk singers have always been partly the nightwatchmen—so to speak. Part of their job has been to take you on a voyage and tell you a tale. Part of their job has been to say, "Hey! It's 11:30 and all is well," or, "It's midnight and Congress just got bought by the Koch Brothers and you're in deep shit." It's part of the job. It's part of what we inherited from folk singers.[9]

"Troubadours," Crosby adds, "were the ones who carried the news from town to town in the Middle Ages, and if you look at the lineage it makes sense. It is something we inherited as part of the job if you were a folkie. That's where all of us came from. I mean, we went electric and became rock and roll, but our ethos was based in stuff that we learned as folk singers."[10]

Pete Seeger worked in that troubadour tradition using music to challenge society, furthered on by artists such as Peter, Paul and Mary and Joan Baez—who became activists in the civil rights and antiwar movements. Dylan and Baez performed together at the 1963 March on Washington organized by Martin Luther King Jr. And, on a freezing January day in 2009, Pete Seeger sang (on the same site) all the verses of his friend Guthrie's "This Land Is Your Land" for Barack Obama's presidential inauguration. As the song was popularized, controversial lyrics were often discarded, including: "In the shadow of the steeple I saw my people, by the relief office I seen my people; as they stood there hungry, I stood there asking—is this land made for you and me?" At a 2009 benefit honoring Seeger, Bruce Springsteen said: "He's gonna look a lot like your granddad that wears flannel shirts and funny hats. He gonna look like your granddad if your granddad can kick your ass. At 90, he remains a stealth dagger through the heart of our country's illusions about itself."[11] Months before he died there was Pete Seeger at the New York-based Farm Aid in 2013—on stage with Dave Matthews, John Mellencamp, Willie Nelson, and Neil Young, singing "This Land Is Your Land." Seeger added a new verse: "New York is my home—New York is your home—from the upstate mountains—down to the ocean foam. With all kinds of people—yes, we're polychrome. New York was made to be frack free!"

The influence of folk traditions on rock and roll shows up in diverse places. For example, Kate Pierson of the B-52s formed the Sun Doughnuts, a folk protest group, while in high school. Pierson says: "I wrote the song about Collie Lee [Leroy] Wilkins, who was a Klansman who shot a civil rights worker. I got interested in politics through these songs. It brought me into the civil rights movement. My father was in a union, so I kind of went into union songs. And, it also introduced me to blues." "It was in the air," Pierson adds, "everything in that era, because of the late '50s and '60s, things were happening, things were changing. I think the knowledge, the specific knowledge of a lot of those events kind of came through these folk songs. And also bringing in people like Oddetta, people of color, felt completely inclusive in that kind of group too—which weren't always included in the mainstream."[12] Billy Bragg was embraced by Woody Guthrie's family, who invited him to put Guthrie's unpublished lyrics to music. Bragg recalls Bob Dylan shaped his own approach to music, which began with Motown, led him to the Clash at a Rock Against Racism concert in 1978, and then found his way back to Dylan—and then to Woody Guthrie:

> You'd get to listen to the hits [from Motown, via various compilation records that worked their way to the United Kingdom, where he grew up]—but gradually as you would get from Vol. 3 to Vol. 4 to Vol. 5, something changed. Volume 5—after the Jackson 5, you get Edwin Starr singing 'War,' then you get the Supremes singing 'Stoned Love'—and then you get Marvin Gaye singing 'Abraham, Martin, and John,' and 'Ball of Confusion' by the Temptations. You're getting the feeling that something is changed in America. What you're hearing, I didn't realize it at the time, was the effects of the civil rights movement as it was filtering through Motown. I was hearing these songs that were saying something more than just standard love song lyrics. The other music

I was listening to at the time—since I was about 11, 12, 13, was Simon and Garfunkel and that pretty quickly led me to Bob Dylan. In fact, I exchanged my copy of the Jackson Five's *Greatest Hits* [with] a kid in my class who wanted to give that record to his sister for her birthday. I swapped it with him for his father's copy of *The Times They Are A-Changin'*—by Bob Dylan, which was undoubtedly the most political, most raw, most visceral music I'd ever heard up to that point.[13]

Bragg says: "There are certain times where music can play a role in that process by bringing people together to express their solidarity about an issue which is what happened to me at Rock Against Racism. So I think that's the thing that Woody and Dylan have in common with the Clash. Both, at certain times, important times, used their music for that role." Billy Bragg references Guthrie as being the first punk rocker and the last Elizabethian balladeer. "On the later of those two," Bragg says, "he recorded a song called 'Gypsy Davy,' which is a very very old English ballad that was first written down in my country during the reign of James I, who succeeded Elizabeth I. So, probably it was around before then. And, he learned that early from his grandmother. So he was at the tail end of that whole balladeer tradition. At the other end, he writes 'This Land is Your Land' because he's sick and tired of hearing on jukeboxes, after hitchhiking to New York in 1940, he's sick and tired of hearing Irving Berlin singing 'God Bless America.' So he's an alternative songwriter."[14]

"When People Are in Pain, You Go to Them"

The folk tradition remains embodied in the voice of Peter Yarrow of Peter, Paul, and Mary. In 2013, he traveled to Newtown, Connecticut, to perform for those who had lost 20 elementary students and six staff members in the December 2012 Sandy Hook school shooting. Yarrow led the audience through a heart-wrenching rendition of Bob Dylan's "Blowin' in the Wind." Francine Wheeler, a local music teacher and the mother of Ben Wheeler—one of the children killed—sang: "How many times must the cannon balls fly, before they're forever banned?" One of America's great contemporary songwriters and performers, Dar Williams, joined the stage asking: "How many times can a man turn his head—and pretend that he just doesn't see?"[15] Williams describes the event:

If Peter Yarrow had been Svengali, this world would have been in a lot of trouble. But he chose to use his sense of the power of a stage for the 'good.' I really admire him because he, at the last minute, changed who was going to sing which line when he suddenly understood that if Francine wanted to sing this line, she should be able to sing this line. And her community should be able to witness her singing this line of pure agony and frustration. That was Peter understanding that this was a historical moment, a communal moment to share—and I just love him for that. He's just so unafraid of looking at the theatrical beauty of a community event as it's unfolding.[16]

Dar Williams says she was nervous to perform. But she recalls Yarrow told her: "'When people are in pain, you go to them.'" Williams recalls: "There were a lot of tears, a lot of kindness, and it felt a little old guard—to be congregated, to use pure music as a way to be together and to heal."[17]

IN MY ROOM

Jann Wenner says rock and roll also gained influence through shared introspection: "Like Chuck Berry, just writing about how boring school was, 'ring ring goes the bell'—can't wait to get out of there! There's an expression of young people's frustration even in that limited area. Then as the '60s came into full swing you had artists like the Beach Boys, Phil Spector groups, sort of dealing with, you know, more 'grown-up' teen-age concerns." Wenner highlights the Beach Boy's song "In My Room." That song, Wenner says, is "…a real meditation about privacy and daydreaming and the need to be alone and find yourself. A series of issues that are within that song are part of the maturation process."[18] Kate Pierson elaborates about such common experiences and her band, the B-52s:

> When we started the band, we definitely had no intention of like, 'Let's write songs that uplift people.' I mean, unlike the folk movement where that was a conscious, 'Let's bring people together' and 'let's rally people.' This was like: 'Let's have fun! Let's just write these crazy songs.' It was totally unselfconscious, but, it had this incredible effect, years later of people telling us: 'Oh my God, your first album, and all your music, but particularly the first album, got me through high school, and helped me through hard times. I was this loner. I was the only one that liked your music and then I found someone else who did and it saved my life.' And how many people have told me that over and over—it's kind of amazing![19]

Kathleen Hanna, who spearheaded the Riot Grrrl movement of feminist punk rock in the early 1990s, recorded much of her 1997 album "The Julie Ruin" in her bedroom—noting that for girls, so much of who they are comes from that shared introspection.[20] Sini Anderson, who directed a documentary film on Kathleen Hanna says: "I'm so proud to see, 20 years later, real change has come in women's confidence—in the ability to voice what they feel is morally right or wrong. It's created empowerment in this way so that the art can be that much stronger."[21]

All You Need Is Love

The nexus between Bob Dylan's America and Brian Wilson's introspective meditations turned a liberating dance party into a socially conscious endeavor. This vision peaked with the Beatles, who took inspiration from the Beach Boys and the Byrds. The Byrds, meanwhile, were inspired by Dylan and Pete Seeger—with major hits covering Dylan's "Hey Mr. Tambourine Man" and Seeger's "Turn, Turn, Turn." David Crosby says of his band's ties to the Beatles: "I knew them, they were nice to me, they liked the Byrds—we were pushing the envelope. They made it very public."[22] The flow between Dylan, the Byrds, the Beach Boys, and the Beatles rippled fast and far. Graham Nash, with the Hollies, shared a bill in 1962 at the Cavern Club in Liverpool with the Beatles. Just five years later, Nash was an invited guest singing for the worldwide broadcast of "All You Need Is Love." "It was a very transformational moment," Graham Nash says: "That moment of realizing that the four kids in front of me that I'd known since November of 1959, who now were calling themselves the Beatles—were talking to over a billion people at once."[23]

Glen Ballard represents one of rock and roll's most successful interconnections among producers and song writers. He is a protégé of Quincy Jones and has production and songwriting credits including Aerosmith, Michael Jackson, Dave Matthews, Alanis Morissette, Wilson Phillips, Lisa Marie Presley, and Van Halen. He is credited with discovering Katy Perry. Growing up in the 1960s in Natchez, Mississippi, Ballard recalls: "The Beatles records were the thing that got me interested in all of it, really. I mean, I loved music. I'd been playing music—but their actual records were so astonishing to me on every level. I think I was hearing for the first time this sort of sonic—this next step in recorded music."[24] He says:

> The gulf between 2014 and say 1965—its light years, man! Its light years! The differences are as varied as the universe now. Hearing the Beatles records and hearing the George Martin produced records, I had no way of knowing at that moment that I was just kind of sitting there at the dawn of kind of a new art form. I also didn't realize that it was going to be over relatively quickly, too. I mean, that kind of golden age of people spending a year to make a record—that kind of investment in that art form. If it was really great you could expect people would listen to it for a year. I mean there was like this whole kind of relationship between what went into making a record and writing it and knowing it was so embedded in everybody's way of life and the Zeitgeist.[25]

Ballard says, "I mean, the *Sgt. Pepper* record—what's better than that? Just in terms of it being an indelible sonic masterpiece—for all time. I was having this conversation with Ringo this year and I said, 'When that record came out, I was in the 7th grade and I listened to it—my mother had to come and make me get out of my room because she thought there was something wrong with me.' So I probably listened to it like 50 times in a row…just mesmerized—no drugs, no nothing—that was the drug."[26]

It's not just harder to achieve now, Glen Ballard says: "It's impossible. It will never happen again." He argues:

> I don't think music will ever have the sort of same cultural weight, on every aspect of our lives, starting at the time of which we speak—in the '60s—where music—the sound of it changed; the intention of it and its purposes changed. The whole scope of what it could accomplish changed and expanded in ways that no one could even anticipate. You had everything, from the political commentary—obliquely—of Bob Dylan; who had ever really done that in sort of a serious way and in an unpremeditated way? A kind of real response to the moment. Music seemed to lead the charge in terms of our emotional response to everything at that time.[27]

Ballard notes of songs like "Ohio" by Crosby, Stills, Nash and Young: "They were meaningful in the political moment—hugely political—hugely important. Nixon had a lot of musicians and writers and singers on his fucking enemies list." He adds, "Nixon was not wrong to fear what was coming in terms of the awareness—and the music seemed to represent all of that—a new sense of awareness and possibilities." Ballard says: "The technical growth and the artistic growth happened at the same time. Those early records were made on four track, and they ended up with eight or sixteen tracks, which really was important. It cut down the amount of time they had to figure out how to multitrack. They hadn't got to the point like we are today where the technology is driving the process." Ballard recalls: "They were very efficient in the way they used that growth in these simple records from there, all the way to the end, that are these complex, sort of orchestrally influenced records—just genius sort of cinematic-like records. It was a huge arch, but it was not that long. It was—severe." Decades later, Glen Ballard found himself writing songs with Ringo Starr: "It's still about peace and love to Ringo, that's still his message, man. I've talked to him about it many times." Ballard adds, "Ringo's committed to it, without question, what else is there? He's seen everything. He's been among the most famous people in the world—and the perspective he has is that—if we're not striving for peace and love, then what the heck are we doing?"[28]

That severe arch of musical and social change was not limited, of course, to the Dylan–Beatles nexus. Few artists have been present at major moments of musical change as George Clinton, founder of the groups Parliament and

Funkadelic. George Clinton was there with his first record at the origins of rock and roll, in 1958, recording with the Parliaments from New Jersey. Then he went to Motown and served as a staff songwriter. From there, Clinton heard acid rock—especially Eric Clapton's band Cream. Clinton blended that with Motown to create funk, which eventually sowed the seeds of rap and hip-hop. "It's all," Clinton says:

> …funk, bass, blues, rhythm—funk, blues, and rock and roll. That's the tempos from the 40s and the 50s. That was the basis of it. Boogie woogie, a la Louis Jordon, and all of that instilled that element of dance. Boogie Woogie went into three different directions: the slow version of it becomes the blues, the mid-tempo—they don't say funk, but it becomes like the New Orleans mainstay, all this nasty stuff, which is also Motown. Motown spruced it up—they made it pretty with strings and things. We took the same thing and took it back into the blues and the rock and roll; loud Motown and psychedelic. We went in every direction you could possibly go in the '70s—with horns and James Brown and the African type of groove thing—which hip-hop basically sampled. The other side was sort of the loud, psychedelic music of Motown and R&B being played loud.[29]

Clinton says it was the kind of freedom you: "…could get at church, or any kind of ritual, but especially to do it on your own terms—not to get psyched into it, because you're still opening yourself up. But once you can be free enough—to do it—which is what rock and roll did to the '60s kids." It was an Englishman, Eric Clapton, who exposed Clinton to his American roots. When asked about the impact of Clapton's band Cream, Clinton says:

> Oh wow! That blew my mind. I felt real bad—before, we were doing funk. We were doing funk but we hadn't really named it, cornered it and got into it like that. I heard Eric Clapton talking about Robert Johnson—doing 'Crossroads' and a couple of other songs. I remembered those songs, well, with my mother—I had no idea. You know, the history of this dude that was writing these songs that all these new pop, the new Motown was coming in—these were songs that my mother listened to. I would pay attention to the history of what I'm doing and give more respect to it…The rock and roll, Jimi Hendrix had took me into it already. By the time I heard Cream, I'd heard Jimi Hendrix at the same time. When I heard their version of that beat that they had—there was no resisting that![30]

George Clinton hums a few notes from Cream's "Sunshine of Your Love" and says, "they were playing that sound like it was regular R&B, but when you pay attention, it's not. And they were playing like serious, heavy—from the Yardbirds on, Eric Clapton—and all of them."[31]

The ripples from the rock and roll revolution also spread across generations. Mark Karan was 11 in San Francisco in 1966. Two decades later, he
was playing with the Rembrants and Paul Carrack, becoming the lead guitar
player for the first post–Jerry Garcia incarnation of the Grateful Dead and
joining Bob Weir's band Ratdog. Karan reflects: "That ethic that I fell in
love with in the mid-60s in the Haight—even when I was doing the '80s,
when I had big hair and whatever the current clothing were and I was doing
new wave or whatever the hell it was, somehow at the core of my philosophical self, musically and otherwise I've always been connected to that
whole Haight thing." Karan adds the Beatles were key, saying in effect: " 'Be
whatever color you want to be. Paint whatever picture you want to paint. Say
whatever the hell you've got to say. Kiss, love, fuck—do whatever is real for
you—what's authentic, what's loving. Be that.'"[32] Michael Stanley similarly
gave voice to the Midwest ethic of his hometown, Cleveland, Ohio (with
national hits like "Lover" and "My Town") in the 1980s. Stanley graduated
from Hiram College, near Cleveland, in 1970:

> When I started at Hiram, 1966, women had to be in their dorms at 10:00. You
> couldn't hold hands walking across the campus. Dinner was sit-down—ties,
> dresses, this and that. By '70, when I got out of there, there were co-ed dorms,
> half the people were tripping, the offices and buildings had been taken over by
> the black student union or by this group or by that group. For some people, it
> completely freaked them out. For others, it completely opened up things. It was
> so completely different from the four years from when I went into college from
> when I came out. I think that sent a lot of us in whatever direction we ended up
> going. Whether it be right, left—or completely shell-shocked.[33]

This change in America's heartland resonated nationally when the government of Ohio killed four students protesting the Vietnam War at Kent State
University in May 1970. It was, Stanley says, "…unbelievable—it would
have been unbelievable if it had happened anywhere. Let alone for it to happen where I was at the time—from like 15 miles away."[34]

Today, it can be harder to get a "breakthrough" moment where an artist
transcends a moment in time—as Crosby, Stills, Nash and Young did with
"Ohio" following Kent State. To Graham Nash, "Every song that we write
needs a reason to exist. I did my share, with the Hollies, of writing my, 'moon
tune, fuck me in the back of the car song.' I've done my share of that. But, I
realized when I joined David [Crosby] and Stephen [Stills] and watched how
they wrote, and watched how Neil [Young] wrote, and watched how Joni
[Mitchell] wrote, it changed the way that I wrote."[35] There are risks, however,
for artists speaking out. In June 2014, a Columbus, Ohio, radio host attacked
Tom Morello of Rage against the Machine for being political, arguing that

people should walk out of his shows. Serj Tankian (who, with Morello, cofounded "Axis of Justice") says:

> Tom has been on the circuit and done those same radio shows and I've done some of those radio shows with him. I remember one in particular where we got on and we were talking about Axis of Justice. The first thing that the D.J. said is, 'Although I don't really agree with any of the things that you guys talk about, you are on this show because you are great musicians and we respect what you have to say.' And we looked at each other like, 'What the fuck?' It's kind of like pandering to the right. They do their numbers. They do their research. A lot of radio D.J.s play that right wing kind of thing that we've noticed. Some of them believe it, some of them don't.[36]

There can be severe professional costs to artists' protesting, as Sinéad O'Connor discovered after ripping up a picture of the pope on *Saturday Night Live* in 1992, at the time effectively ending her career in America. The Dixie Chicks were boycotted by conservative groups in 2003 for criticizing George W. Bush's plans to invade Iraq. O'Connor and the Dixie Chicks were proven right—and the Dixie Chicks returned with the hit "Not Ready to Make Nice" protesting the death threats that Maines had received.

Erin Potts heads RPM, a nonprofit advisory group for musicians engaged in social and political movements. She says:

> …there's an imagination process that happens in art for social change, meaning that we can envision a future. I think often times we get too stuck in reacting to the present and being negative. But I think that also helps energize and articulate frustrations that people are feeling. I think Serj [Tankian]—he may be preaching to the choir but, he's getting the choir really amped up. And that choir is hopefully going forward and fighting the good fight.[37]

Potts adds RPM's research shows that, as to the Dixie Chicks:

> They apologized for how they said it and that some people were angered by that. I think that's the key; they stuck it out. They didn't immediately say, 'Oh my God, I'm so sorry we shouldn't have said that.' They were like: 'We shouldn't have said how we said it, but we meant it. We really don't like this guy and we think his policies are awful.' And in that way, people respected them even in disagreeing with them.[38]

The other thing about the Dixie Chicks, Potts adds, "…is that they really cared about that. It wasn't just a flippant thing that they said. Same with Tom [Morello], he's not entering these really difficult issues just sort of off the tip of his tongue."[39] Jann Wenner acknowledges risks for activist artists: "You don't want to push it too far to the point where you get marginalized or your message gets marginalized." Referencing Sinéad O'Connor's *Saturday Night Live* appearance, he says: "I mean there's no percentage in attacking the pope. Or, if there is, choose your time and place."[40]

"Follow That Guy"

Shortly after Sinéad O'Connor's *Saturday Night Live* appearance, she was set to perform at a tribute for Bob Dylan in New York City. She was loudly booed when she walked on stage. This was ironic for O'Connor as exposure to Dylan, growing up in Ireland, shaped her introspective sense of purpose:

> At the time, between the age of 9 and 13, I didn't see my father—through no fault of his own. My mother excluded him. And perhaps I got to the age where you need a bit of a role model. So it just happened at the same time that Joe [her brother] came home with *Slow Train Coming* and that really was it for me. In some ways, Dylan became a bit of a godfather if you like, or a male role model; someone to follow spiritually. And also it was the coolest religious music I'd ever heard. It was right sexy—proper sexy.[41]

For O'Connor, Bob Dylan "…opened up a certain type of a priesthood for me. There was something in the presence of him in the sitting room when you're listening to that record—you're thinking, 'Well, follow that guy. He's going somewhere that I'm interested in going.'"[42]

"WE WON THE CULTURE WAR"

Inspired by the 1960s' revolution in music, literature, and psychedelic drugs, the Grateful Dead symbolized a countercultural wave that expanded exponentially. Jerry Garcia said in a 1968 press conference: "We're not thinking about any kind of power. We're not thinking about any kind of struggles. We're not thinking about revolution or war or any of that. That's not what we want. Nobody wants to get hurt. Nobody wants to hurt anybody. We would all like to be able to live an uncluttered life. A simple life, a good life. And think about moving the whole human race ahead a step, or a few steps."[43] Jerry Garcia, decades later, reflected that by 1967 when this countercultural community was noticed:

> It no longer had any power. I mean really. It did for the first couple of minutes—and then it went 'whoosh' and it was gone. It wasn't relevant anymore; not to the people who started there. As soon as that happened, everybody started to disappear—over to Marin County and other places—because nobody wants to

be in the center of the spotlight, not in your life. Maybe in your work, but not in your life. Those of us who were performers, like the Grateful Dead, we just performed and at that time we started going national. We started touring the whole United States. So it was no longer a community to us in the real sense. In the real sense, America became our community.[44]

Garcia noted he had some "…incredible psychedelic experiences that were so cosmic, so huge in scope that I knew that all the sudden I had to revise everything I thought I knew about anything. It doesn't matter to me whether it has any historical value or whether it's measurable in some objective way. I don't care. For me, the subjective reality is what counts." He added: "… that energy has gained enough momentum over the years. It's partly responsible for all the things that have happened historically since then—in some way—it's part of the gain in consciousness that the last half of this century has represented."[45]

We Will Get By

This American community resurged in the 1980s when the Grateful Dead had their first radio hit, "Touch of Grey." It celebrated that we're still here, "we will get by." Back in 1968, however, the "system" had left a generation saddled with the horrors of the Vietnam War and visionary leaders assassinated. So it was understandable if people wanted to "drop out." Jann Wenner asks: "Who would want to be a part of that political system which seems to leave its heroes in blood on the floors of hotels and motels?"[46] Cameron Sears, longtime manager of the Grateful Dead, now leads their charity foundation Rex. He recalls: "What made that San Francisco scene somewhat unique was that the notion of giving back was elemental to what it was all about. It started with free concerts." Cameron Sears says the Grateful Dead "…didn't want to use the stage as a holy pulpit. You never heard them say anything at a Rex benefit, or a Rainforest Action Network benefit. People were there to be entertained and have a good time." Sears recalls a key moment with Jerry Garcia who was doing a press conference in 1989 for a Save the Rainforest benefit that the Grateful Dead did at Madison Square Gardens in New York City. He says Garcia was asked: " 'How is it that you guys are the ones doing this?' and Garcia effectively said: 'Well, to be perfectly honest, it's really pathetic that it's up to us to be the messengers…We're not the experts. We're not the people who should be on the front line of this. But we're forced to do it, because there's a vacuum. It's ridiculous that it's up to us.' "[47] By 2008, however, the remaining Grateful Dead members went political—performing a concert in State College Pennsylvania for Barack Obama's presidential campaign.

Frank Zappa was nevertheless right that there are limits to the rock and roll revolution. In 1987, Zappa told a Danish television interviewer that: "Pretty much rock and roll has been reduced to a product itself whereas in the '60s there was a little bit more life to it. It was connected a little more closely to the lives of the people who made the music."[48] Yet, in 1985, there was Frank Zappa testifying before Congress as an expert witness on behalf of freedom of speech. At the time, there was a conservative backlash against rock and roll—waging a "culture war" to marginalize its impact. Entering the Rock and Roll Hall of Fame and Museum in Cleveland, Ohio, one is greeted by these artifacts of irrational fear. One woman tells a television audience about rock and roll, "We're talking about the kind of rebellion that can be so deadly." Another plays a rock record and says, "...someone sung this song for Satan." Another says: "There's anarchy, there's just blatant, raw sex." Rev. Jimmy Swaggart can be seen preaching: "...rock, sex, heroin, marijuana—four, five, six hours a day!" Defeated in part by generations of artists and fans embracing the rock and roll ethic, by 2016, it was clear the culture war had failed. Jann Wenner says: "It's not completely over, but yeah, we won the culture war."[49]

Alice Cooper represents a more skeptical view: "I go out of my way to be non-political. I'm probably the biggest moderate you know. When John Lennon and Harry Nilsson used to argue politics, I was sitting right in the middle of them, and I was the guy who was going, 'I don't care.' When my parents would start talking politics, I would go in my room and put on the Rolling Stones or the Who on as long as I could to avoid politics."[50] Perhaps, however, it can depend on what one means by politics. The Who's "Won't Get Fooled Again" challenged authority. The Rolling Stone's "Salt of the Earth" called on listeners to raise a toast to the working people "who need leaders but get gamblers instead." However manifested, with each subsequent generation, rock and roll has helped to advance and accompany progress—sometimes for individuals, specific communities, and for the nation and the world.

For Jann Wenner, advancing progress is largely what rock and roll is about. He points to a picture and says: "Look over there at that picture with Mick [Jagger] and Bruce [Springsteen] and Bono. Mick, though not directly involved in politics, has put out so much stuff about revolutionary, evolutionary attitudes and stood for such a questioning of the system." Bono, he says, "is on a full-out crusade" with his work in Africa. Wenner adds: "We have the power—and someone like Bono really consciously uses it. You know, I mean his Africa thing; all the wonderful things that they've done. Bruce has finally come around to doing benefit concerts and tours for presidential campaigns. That's revolutionary for a rock and roll star."[51] Internationally, groups such as Pussy Riot risked prison to advance freedom in Russia. In Iran, the Muckers were forced underground because people dance to their songs. Meanwhile, for every fun, but generic Pharrell-type "Happy," there was also a debate over Annie Lennox's and Beyoncé's definitions of modern feminism. There was Meghan Trainor, who in "All About That Bass" was telling young girls that confidence in oneself defines beauty. Taylor Swift's "Shake It Off" was a song of freedom—escaping people's hang-ups by dancing. George Clinton says, referencing his hit "One Nation Under a Groove": "Dance your way out of constriction, man. That's what 'One Nation' was about— and that's what people did. Funk—with or without drums, you can get into it like that. It's like church—whether you're into religion or not, you get caught up. With a good choir cooking—you're going. Those tones move you. They move the human spirit. Intent is there, intent is felt. We portray the intent to the audience, and they pick up—and do it for themselves, they get into the music."[52]

Rock the Sun: Leilani Munter, Sammy Hagar, Bob Weir, and Michael Franti—Modern Troubadours. Photo taken January 24, 2016, by Bob Minkin.

"This Is the Land of the Free"

In 2004, Bob Dylan was asked by *CBS* interviewer Ed Bradley if he ever looked back at what he had accomplished. Dylan said: "I don't know how I got to write those songs…Those early songs were almost magically written—'Darkness at the break of noon, the handmade blade, the child's balloon.' Well, try to sit down and write something like that—there's a magic to that." When asked why he changed his name—from Robert Zimmerman to Bob Dylan—he said: "You call yourself what you want to call yourself—this is the land of the free." To Dylan, "If you examine the songs, I don't think you're going to find anything in there that says I'm a spokesman for anybody or anything." At the time, Dylan viewed himself: "I'm a '60s troubadour, a folk rock relic—a wordsmith from bygone days. I'm in the bottomless pit of cultural oblivion."[53] Yet, in 1998, as with America—which has risen, crashed, and risen again—Bob Dylan won three Grammy awards for his record *Time Out of Mind.* By 2016 Dylan thrived, playing new music on an almost endless world tour.

POWER TO THE PEOPLE

As John Lennon suggested in his song "Power to the People," it is from the people that freedom advances, equality is gained, human rights are protected, and peace made real—and all are connected and amplified by rock and roll and secured via education and activism. Graham Nash says, "I have children. I have grandchildren. I've got to remain positive. I've got to think that I can help make the world a better place for myself and my family and my friends. Everything starts inside, doesn't it? How far can the ripples go once you throw that stone into the pool?"[54] Bob Dylan once said, "I think of a hero as someone who understands the degree of responsibility that comes with his freedom."[55] Then again, he also said: "If I wasn't Bob Dylan, I'd probably think that Bob Dylan has a lot of answers myself."[56] More than anything, Dylan captures the power of rock and roll. When inducted in 1988 into the Rock and Roll Hall of Fame, he thanked three people—Muhammad Ali (the legendary boxer), Alan Lomax (the legendary chronicler of folk songs), and Little Richard—"I don't think I'd have even started out, without listening to Little Richard."

Part II

VALUES

Chapter Two

Freedom—Revolution Rock!

YOU SAY YOU WANT A REVOLUTION

John Lennon warned in 1980 about the song "Revolution" that while we all want change, when talking about destruction, "you can count me out." Lennon insisted revolution be peaceful: "…you better free your mind instead." It can be revolutionary to get people dancing, be creative, and be expressive—to be free. Rock and roll amplified freedom in America—and rippled out to the Soviet Union, Eastern Europe, South Africa, and parts of the Islamic world. As the Clash sang in their 1979 song "Revolution Rock": "Revolution rock, it is a brand new rock. A bad, bad rock, this here revolution rock." As people triumphed over despotism, their efforts were often connected and amplified by rock and roll.

FLOWERS TO THE BARRICADES

While the government of Richard Nixon promised law and order in the 1970s, activists courted John Lennon. Abbie Hoffman, a radical leftist, said that Lennon and his wife Yoko Ono: "…made a distinct point to look us up before they met anybody in the United States…They wanted to show they had a political side." The U.S. Customs Service tried to deport Lennon—over an old drug charge. Hoffman said they wanted to kick Lennon out "…because he was getting involved with us, because he had a political side. He would say outright that he was a socialist and he maintained that right on through."[1]

Nevertheless, Lennon told *Playboy* magazine about the song "Revolution" in 1980: "The lyrics stand today. It's still my feeling about politics. I want to see the plan. That is what I used to say to Abbie Hoffman and Jerry Rubin. Count me out if it is for violence. Don't expect me to be on the barricades unless it is with flowers."[2]

The Times They Are a Changin'

While the US government was seeking to marginalize John Lennon, he and other artists inspired dissidents in the Soviet Union and Eastern Europe. Serj Tankian says: "Ultimately, you can call things as they are—be they real-politik, realist and whatnot and in the end, depress everyone to death. But, without telling them, 'Look, this is a choice'—that's very important—giving them the optimism to make that choice and saying that, '...it doesn't have to be this way: War is Over!' It's the power of visualization and saying that, 'It doesn't have to be this way. I choose for things not to be this way.' And if many people chose for things not to be this way, they will not be this way."[3] Graham Nash, who, with his bandmates, was at the Berlin Wall when it came down in 1989, believes: "That wall came down because of ideas. That wall came down because people in East Germany were overlooking the wall and seeing how the people in West Germany had better shoes, better cameras, better fashion, more freedom. They wanted that. Ideas brought down the Berlin Wall—no tanks, no wars, no armies—ideas. And I was thrilled to be there, actually chipping down that wall myself."[4]

In 1987, Yoko Ono traveled to Moscow and met with reformist Soviet leader Mikhail Gorbachev and his wife Raisa. Raisa Gorbachev sang some lines from a Beatles song and her husband said, quietly, "John should be here."[5] Artists like him helped inspire many people in the Soviet bloc who led peaceful revolutions—outcomes that could begin with the simple act of dancing. The 1965 hit "I'll Feel a Whole Lot Better" by the Byrds illustrates this dynamic of personal freedom. Released in spring 1965, the song was not overtly political. However, to watch a performance at its peak reveals young dancers around the band, embracing expressive freedom. "You can tell there's an innocence there that's really attractive," says David Crosby: "We were escaping from the '50s. We were escaping from Pat Boone and *Father Knows Best*—we were into, 'express yourself.'"[6] And, it's not a reach to imagine a dissident in Prague or Moscow in 1965 hearing these sounds coming from America and thinking, "This is how I feel about my dictatorship—I'll feel a lot better when it's gone."

As the Beatles grew into a global phenomenon, they occasionally conflicted with despots. They were harassed by the regime of Ferdinand Marcos in the Philippines over an apparent snub of the dictator's wife. George Harrison said, "I didn't even want to go that time...because we'd heard that it was a terrible place anyway. And when we got there, it was proved."[7] Plenty of people liked the Beatles in the Philippines and the insult was that they did not see the first lady, not that they had come. In the Soviet Union, however, disdain for the Beatles reflected a loyalty test. One young Soviet man, Kolya Vasin, described the dilemma saying that the Beatles's music provided "… all the adventures of my life," and that he had been arrested "many times, accused of 'breaching social order.' They said anyone who listened to the Beatles was spreading Western propaganda." He added, "When anyone said anything against them, we knew just what that person was worth. The authorities, our teachers, even our parents, became idiots to us." The sentiment of writer Art Triotsky was widely shared: "I'm sure the impact of all those stupid Cold War institutions has been much, much smaller than the impact of the Beatles."[8] Russian rocker Sasha Lipnitsky concluded: "The Beatles brought us the idea of democracy. For many of us, it was the first hole in the iron curtain."[9] Mikhail Safonov, an academic at the Institute of Russian History in St. Petersburg, writes: "In the 1960s you could not actually be imprisoned for changing the name of Lenin to that of Lennon, but trouble awaited anyone who blasphemed against the name of the immortal leader: problems dished out by the *Komsomol* (Communist Union of Youth) could wreck your career. And so, bit by bit, we Lennon fans became ensared in doubting the values that the system was trying to inculcate." "Beatlemania," Safonov concludes, "washed away the foundations of Soviet society because a person brought up with the world of the Beatles, with its images and messages of love and non-violence, was an individual with internal freedom."[10]

Thomas Shanker was a reporter working for the *Chicago Tribune*, covering the change that took place in the Soviet Union from 1985 to 1988. He eventually went to work for the *New York Times* as chief Pentagon correspondent and eventually became Assistant Washington Editor at the paper's Washington, D.C. bureau. Shanker arrived in Moscow in 1985: "I came in with Gorbachev, at a time really when nobody wanted that assignment." "When I got there," he says, "I was twenty-nine years old and at the time Gorbachev was viewed as simply a fresh face on an old product. It was a grim and dreary place." And then, "…just in a couple of years, with all of Gorbachev's changes *glasnost, perestroika*, it became simply the most important story in the world." Shanker thought:

> …why not as my kind of boutique side-theme of my Moscow years write about Soviet culture as a way to get *Tribune* readers to follow the story who might not really care about Gorbachev's latest speech on economic reforms? And that led really quickly to the whole 'underground cultural scene'—one because of my age, and one because underground artists and I shared similar tastes in western music. It was kind of just happenstance because, by becoming friends with this incredible group of underground rockers, I was able to write for *Tribune* readers

about Soviet life and culture and politics—not from the Kremlin out, but from the outside in.[11]

Within a few years, what was at the margins of that Soviet society broke through, transcended, and became something new, derived from aspirations for freedom.

Rock and roll was present in Soviet society, popularized by underground artist Boris Grebenshchikov whose music reflected realities of life under Soviet communism. But, as a rule, such music operated within serious political constraints. One study showed by 1972 there were over 50 cultural centers that had rock and roll bands just in one city in Ukraine. By 1978 there were 187 discos in Moscow. By 1984 there were an estimated 1,500 rock groups in the Moscow region of the Soviet Union, though many were "not recommended" by the state.[12] Indeed, in 1984, the Soviet ministry of culture suggested that several dozen Western rock artists be banned including: AC/DC, Black Sabbath, Alice Cooper, Elvis Costello, Depeche Mode, Nina Hagen, Pink Floyd, Kiss, the Sex Pistols, Patty Smith, the Talking Heads, and Van Halen.[13] Thomas Shanker notes that on traveling first to the Soviet Union, he brought cassettes of Vladimir Vysotsky —"their Woody Guthrie"—to give away. He recalls: "When I arrived there, at Moscow, for my first trip in August 1985, I had a bunch of Vysotksy tapes that my Russian teacher had given me. But I was too naïve to realize that they were actually contraband. The customs guard seized them from me, of course, as they were illegal. But, he pulled me aside afterwards and he thanked me—because he really wanted them for his collection."[14] A number of rock and roll artists performed in the Soviet Union as part of cultural exchanges, including the Doobie Brothers, Elton John, Bonnie Raitt, Carlos Santana, and James Taylor. Still for most of the early 1980s, Cold War tensions persisted and a series of aging Soviet leaders steadily died off while the economy collapsed. By 1987, the USSR embraced a reformist agenda of Mikhail Gorbachev and a new generation of Russians and Americans made peace. And, the Billy Joel Band came in 1987, performing Russia's first full-scale rock concerts.

Radio Liberty

Billy Joel's longtime drummer, Liberty Devitto, says the seeds of their concerts in the Soviet Union were sown in 1979– in Cuba. Their record label organized the visit:

> We played the Karl Marx Theater in Havanna, Cuba. For every American group that played, a Cuban group played. [It] started out with Weather Report being the first band to play and us, Billy Joel Band, being the last band to play, because

we were probably the most popular at the time. The kids would hear the radio from Florida. So they knew all our songs. It was great. We stayed at a hotel—it was really strange because when you'd turn the water on to take a shower, salt water came out. There was all these armed guards on the beach all the time, watching everything we did. In fact, a lot of the kids that came out to the beach to talk to us—we'd give them t-shirts and stuff like that and they had to turn them inside out.[15]

Liberty Devitto recalls: "We barely talked to anybody except for these young kids—teenage kids—that wanted to know about music." Devitto adds: "There are a few musicians that I know. [One's] father was a truck driver, and he came to the concert. He lives in the States now. I see him and he says it was because of that, when he saw me play, he started playing drums." He also recounts that later on they were playing a concert in California and a number of people who they had met in Cuba, and who subsequently fled the country, showed up. They said that some had been arrested, just for having spoken to the Billy Joel players.[16]

Billy Joel's shows in Russia were eight years later, yet a world apart. There was, to be sure, a residual effect of the Iron Curtain. At one show, Joel was upset that a film crew was lighting the audience. He halted "Sometimes a Fantasy" and yelled into his microphone: "Stop lighting the audience! Stop it! Let me do my show for Christ's sake." Then he tossed over his keyboard and slammed his mic stand on the stage. The camera lights were showing the Soviet-style audience just sitting there, rigid, as was custom. This might have made the show seem a failure. It might also have been that the audience needed a push as to how to enjoy a rock show. Billy Joel said, "…whenever they turned the lights on, anyone who was overreacting was being pulled out of the audience by a security guard. I wasn't yelling at the audience. I was yelling at the film crew. So I threw the piano, and that got their attention. Then they stopped lighting the audience and everybody started rocking out."[17] Thomas Shankar wrote: "After a trio of sold out shows in Moscow (each before an audience of 20,000), and three more in Leningrad (in a hall that holds 17,500), Joel has entered the Soviet pop pantheon. A near-mythology was created about the ability of American music to outgun even the local militia."[18]

Similar shifts happened to the artists who came to the Soviet Union. "The trip made me rethink my life," said Liberty Devitto.[19] "I'm getting on a German Lufthansa jet," he says, placing this visit in a sweep of history: "We'd already beat Germany in World War II. I'm flying to the 'enemy', right? Because I'd been told they're the enemy. And, my name is Liberty. I mean, I'm going to get arrested as soon as I get off the plane. It's all over for me!" Devitto adds: "I get off the plane thinking I am going to see the three-headed dragon breathing fire. I was totally blown away at what I met. Totally blown away. Now, I come from an Italian family and we used to do these big Sunday dinners and the family would just sit around; and the love, with the kids on the lap and the aunts and the uncles, and everything. It was *just like that.* It was just like that. It was unbelievable." The Billy Joel Band had more opportunity to interact with average people in the changing Soviet Union than just a few years earlier in Cuba. "We had guides that took us around," Liberty Devitto says, "and I went over there with one of our interpreters who came from the United States." The interpreter's grandfather had left the Soviet Union when things had gone bad there. "His dream," Devitto says, "was always to go back to the Soviet Union—to Russia. And he was getting too old. So when his grandson went with us, he actually brought icons to bring to the churches. Me and him went to these churches and kind of snuck these icons to these people. And to see them kissing these icons, the holy relics, was like—*unbelievable.*" They were also able to hang around with students and, Devitto says, "I remember once, they took me into a coffee shop. It was a government coffee shop but we went to another door and went down this long hallway, way into the back where it would be like the Village in the '60s where the poets and the musicians would hang out. And I can remember one woman sitting down across from me, and telling me: '… when the Soviet Union stops sending aid to Cuba—that's when we're going to fall.' That was like a year before it actually happened."[20]

Despite a quick drink with Boris Grebenshchikov, there was no jam session or opportunity for Billy Joel to highlight the artists who pioneered rock and roll in the Soviet Union. Thomas Shanker says, the experience was: "A breakthrough for your average apolitical Soviet concertgoer. After that, if you didn't rush the stage, it wasn't a successful concert. No one stayed in their seats anymore." Shanker stresses the overall intent and effect of Billy Joel's role was important and positive—but he explains: "In that specific experience, I think he did miss an opportunity. I remember so clearly, it was like a knife in the heart of all these young underground rockers who really did believe. I mean, Billy Joel sings about the redemptive power of rock and roll. Well these brave people actually lived it at the risk of poverty and jail. And they really thought that Billy Joel—the street brawler piano man—would understand their plight and do more with them than just have a beer."[21]

The Billy Joel concerts were unique because of the scale of the production and multicity tour. Two years of preparation was needed to perform in front of over 120,000 people at six concerts. That required 130 support people and gear. Liberty Devitto says: "Billy brought everything—lights, sound, stage—everything! It cost him a fortune to get over there. But that's what he wanted to tell his daughter when she grew up, that, 'This is what I did during the Cold

War to try to help relations.'"[22] Billy Joel said at the time: "We didn't know what was going to work—what didn't work. So we tried to pace it musically. It's going to be polite and reserved in the beginning, and after the halfway point, the show—it gets very rock and roll. And at the end of the show it's like an American concert. So it's great—it's a Russian and American concert."[23] Liberty Devitto reflects: "I believe it worked. I think people saw something that they never saw before. I mean, we stood in the parks where they all stood with their tape recorders all in a circle. They would put in a cassette and each one would tape a rock and roll album. And now here we are playing live for them." Liberty Devitto concludes: "I remember standing outside once and looking at the sky and thinking to myself: 'That's the same sky that's over us. We are definitely, like, one world.' And there was a poster on the wall of Uncle Sam pushing atomic bombs in a baby carriage and I thought, 'Oh my God, they're getting the same shit that we get. It's the government against the government; it has nothing to do with the people. The government is telling us to think one way—and we're buying it.' And I thought to myself, 'I'll never think like that again.'"[24]

"When we went there," Liberty Devitto recalls: "I really played up the American thing. I had a shirt that had an American flag on it. I had buttons on me—the American flag, Mickey Mouse. And I had flags on my drum set—American flags. "Billy Joel, he says, told him: "You've got to tone this down." Joel thought they were going to see an 'ugly American.' But that was not how it was perceived. Devitto says he was approached by the Russian-born comedian Yakov Smirnoff who said: 'When they looked at you and they saw the American flag on your chest, they saw a man who's able to think and create. They saw the ultimate "freedom in a drummer:'" Smirnoff told Devitto that he needed to come back and do drum clinics in Russia. "There are great musicians in Russia," Smirnoff told him, but, "there are no great drummers, because to be a drummer you have to think outside the box, and they still don't know how to do that."[25] In a nationally televised performance, Billy Joel introduced a song to his studio audience saying: "This song has been going around and around in my head since I've been here." The song was Bob Dylan's "The Times They Are a A-Changin.'" The Soviet audience responded with recognition and applause. Billy Joel said at the time, when asked if there was something "political" about what he was doing: "Of course I'm a political person. But I don't want to get up on a soap box and preach my politics to people. Just because I'm a musician, that doesn't mean I can tell people how to think or what to do. And in a situation like this, to spout a lot of politics would be counter-productive. They've heard it, we've heard it. What they haven't heard is the music. And what our people haven't seen is their reaction to the music."[26]

This Train's on Fire

Boris Grebenshchikov continues to rock in Russia, even enjoying a nationalistic embrace by the Russian government. In 2014, however, Grebenshchikov reacted strongly when state-run Russian television used his song "This Train's on Fire" with a video supporting Russian aggression in Ukraine. It selectively used the lines, "This land was ours 'till we got caught in the fighting. It's time for us to get it back." The song, however, is actually a story about how a military officer goes to the frontlines and tells his troops to stop fighting. Boris Grebenshchikov responded on Facebook: "I am touched that you decided to use a piece of my song…But since you are doing it, have the courage to publish it completely, including the words, 'I have seen the generals, they drink and eat our death.'"[27]

THE VELVET UNDERGROUND REVOLUTION

Many of the dissidents who championed reform in the Soviet bloc were artists. In particular, Vaclav Havel, a postmodern playwright, inspired peaceful revolutionary change—culminating in the 1989 "Velvet Revolution" in Czechoslovakia. Their path took a dangerous route in 1976 when activists, including Havel, worked to get an underground rock band—the Plastic People of the Universe—released from prison. The band idolized the Velvet Underground and took their name from a Frank Zappa lyric. Bill Payne, one of rock and roll's great keyboard players, cofounded with Lowell George the band Little Feat (in part) out of the Frank Zappa network of artists in the late 1960s. He says of Zappa: "One of the things that might have contributed to it getting beyond America's borders was [Frank Zappa's] use of classical music and jazz, based on his voice, his instrumentation of things, [their] chaotic nature, and quite frankly the theater that he created through his music and achieved through actions. These 'freak outs'—certainly would appeal historically more to a European sensibility of things. Particularly through a city like Berlin." Payne adds: "I think Europeans are particularly in tune with that. They embrace jazz, they embrace classical music, they embrace punk music. It doesn't matter what it is—if it's on that outside edge. They've lived dangerously for a long time."[28]

We Will Rock You

Rolling Stone summarizes what happened as Vaclav Havel had a meeting of the minds with Ivan Jirous, a poet and manager for the Plastic People of the Universe:

> In 1976…Havel and Jirous were brought together in a secret, 'highly conspiratorial' meeting that moved from a recording studio to a hotel wine bar. Havel and his fellow writers and academics had been harassed by the Communist

regime, but there had been few arrests. Jirous knew that the rock underground was on the verge of a major clash with the government; in a matter of weeks, 'a dragnet went out'…Almost two dozen musicians, including the Plastic People, were arrested as dissidents.[29]

Following the arrest, Havel and others organized a document and an associated movement called "Charter 77," which challenged the Soviet-backed Czechoslovak government to respect human rights. The result was further oppression and it was made illegal to disseminate the document. Havel, reflecting on music, said: "There was a strange magic in the music, and a kind of inner warning. Here was something serious and genuine…Suddenly I realized that, regardless of how many vulgar words these people used or how long their hair was, truth was on their side."[30]

Queen was among the first major Western rock and roll groups to perform in Eastern Europe. They played in Budapest, Hungary, in 1986—before the changes began to ripple across the Iron Curtain. Queen had tried for a more expansive presence in Eastern Europe. Freddie Mercury said: "They thought we'd corrupt their youth or something."[31] They were followed in September 1987 by Bob Dylan. Greg Mitchell, a filmmaker and concert promoter, summarizes how the East German secret police viewed the appearance:

> The Stasi didn't seem too worried that Bob, then in a down period in his career, would prove to be a rabble-rouser, as he was merely 'an old master of rock' with no particular 'resonance' with the youth of the day. In fact, the crowd, they predicted, would be mainly those in middle age or older. The Stasi expected Dylan to act in a 'disciplined' way and not cause undo 'emotions' among the crowd. Still, they took extensive security precautions and had plenty of their operatives on hand.[32]

Dylan showed up without incident, but when Michael Jackson performed in West Berlin in June 1988, the secret police in East Germany were worried that "youths will do anything they can to experience this concert, in the area around the Brandenburg Gate…certain youths are planning to [use the occasion] to provoke a confrontation with police."[33] *Der Spiegel* reports:

> As eyewitness, Alan Nothnagle, a translator living in Berlin, writes on his *Salon.com* blog: 'We noticed 'inconspicuous' men in civilian clothes, slouching on street corners in groups of three, eyeing the passers-by. The reason was no secret: somehow everyone knew that Michael Jackson was giving a concert in front of the Reichstag that evening, just a few hundred meters from where we were standing…Hundreds, soon thousands of young people congregated to hear the music. The Stasi agents also multiplied…We never heard a note of music that night, but soon voices arose in the crowd calling 'The Wall must go!' and 'Gorbachev! Gorbachev!' Now the plainclothes Stasi men came alive. They hurled the young people to the ground, shouting 'What did you say? What did

you say?' and hauled them off by the collar into side streets where police vans were waiting to bundle them off to Stasi headquarters.'[34]

Just a month later, in July 1988, with a post–Cold War idealism growing, Bruce Springsteen and the E. Street Band went to East Berlin.

When nearly 200,000 people turned out for the Springsteen show (and many millions more watched on a live state-run broadcast of the concert), it was a big deal. Into the concert, Springsteen said, in German: "I'm not here for any government. I've come to play rock'n'roll for you in the hope that one day all the barriers will be torn down." One concert attendee said: "It was gradually dawning on everyone between about 20 and 30 years old that things couldn't just continue in East Germany the way they had been going. Something had to change. And when Springsteen came, his concert fitted right into all that."[35] As Bruce Springsteen highlighted a performance of Dylan's "Chimes of Freedom," it became clear for the people attending the show, and those watching on TV, the Cold War was over. David Crosby, who in 1965 sang "Chimes of Freedom" with the Byrds, concludes: "That was a champion deal—ideas went over the wall. It wasn't a squadron of tanks, it wasn't artillery, it wasn't an army that knocked that wall down. It was ideas going over the wall…and the people, on the other side, seeing how it was on this side. That information knocked that wall down. Information destroyed that wall. That was a triumph. We won that one."[36]

The best, still, was yet to come when in November 1989 the Berlin Wall fell. It was the people of Eastern Europe who cast aside their chains and embraced freedom—they did not need rock stars to point out the difficulties of dictatorship. But, it clearly helped as a connection as the music had come to equate with freedom. And who was there, actually chipping away at the wall as it came down?—Crosby, Stills and Nash. Graham Nash recalls:

CSN was giving a concert in the United Nations building—in the actual hall where Khrushchev was banging his shoe, you know, in the General Assembly there in the United Nations. There had been rumors that the wall was coming down when we played that concert in New York. Stephen said to us, 'You know, we're here in New York—we're halfway there. Why don't we fly from New York—instead of going home to Los Angeles or Hawaii, why don't we go the other way? Why don't we go to Berlin?' And David and I thought that was a fucking fantastic idea. And that's exactly what we did. And I can't tell you what it felt like to actually be chipping that wall down myself. That wall came down because people in East Germany were overlooking the wall.[37]

Graham Nash recalled that on one of his albums he covered a song called "Chipping Away" written by Tom Fedora. "It was," Nash says, "about the Berlin Wall, it was about the walls around your heart, walls around your thinking." Nash adds: "When we went to Germany to deal with the wall, we got interviewed, of course, on the radio. We were going to attend a gathering of thousands and thousands of people opposite the giant [Brandenberg] gate. But there were no speakers. So during the radio interview, I had an idea. I said, 'Listen, why don't you [at the radio station] at 4:30 exactly, why don't you play 'Chipping Away', and we'll stand there and mime to it.' The guy from the radio asked how would people hear the song? Nash recalls saying: " 'Why don't we now, on the radio, invite everybody to bring their transistor radios and tune to your station?' " "I have a distinct memory of standing on that stage at the Brandenburg Gate." Graham Nash recalls, "and looking at all these kids holding their transistor radios in the air playing our song back to us. There's tremendous power in rock and roll, man."[38]

Eight months later, with Germany on the path to unification, Roger Waters presented Pink Floyd's classic record *The Wall* in Berlin. The show included performances from Bryan Adams, the Band, Paul Carrack, Thomas Dolby, Cyndi Lauper, Joni Mitchell, Sinéad O'Connor, the Scorpions, and Van Morrison. For the estimated 300,000 who watched the Wall built and come down, it was a coda to their peaceful revolution. Yet, contradictions inherent in the West also became apparent. Sinéad O'Connor, who sang the song "Mother" (with Rick Danko, Levon Helm, and Garth Hudson), says: "We were all there," at that gig, O'Connor says, "for the right reasons, [but] there are those that were there that were forced into an alarming situation, and the reason for that was it was all about the industry making a big TV show. They've got the lights all set, they've got this, that, and the other, they didn't give a flying fuck about the wall coming down or not coming down. It was a big fucking TV show for the industry to make a shitload of money." O'Connor adds:

> When I think of the wall coming down, I think more of actually the day it came down. I was actually quite emotional about it—not least because there was people passing music magazines over the wall—was one of the first things they were doing. That, for some reason, made me *really emotional* to think, 'My God, there are people my age, or younger—or even older—who had never seen a music magazine. They don't know what records have been on the radio for X amount of years.' You hear when you're younger about that separation—you wouldn't realize the just daily things that are gone.[39]

Sinéad O'Connor was upset that for her vocal, a rehearsal track was played without warning: "I don't like lying to the audience." O'Connor also recalls: "Musicians may have been part of that, but they weren't all of it. Do you know what I mean? It was people. It was *people*. It doesn't matter if they were musicians or not, or whatever. I mean, imagine a world where there was no music. That would still have come to pass at some point that the

Wall would have come down because of people's hearts."[40] Roger Waters's production of *The Wall* in Berlin cost about $10 million. Proceeds were originally slated for a British charity, although eventually the rights to the concert movie and recording reverted back to Waters. The intent was genuine—as Waters said: "If this concert is to celebrate anything, it's that the Berlin Wall coming down can be seen as a liberating of the human spirit."[41]

Vaclav Havel, on being elected president of the Czech Republic, asked Frank Zappa to serve as the nation's "Special Ambassador to the West on Trade, Culture and Tourism"—a symbolic gesture of respect for a person who Havel said was: "…one of the Gods of the Czech underground." This did not stand with America's Secretary of State, James Baker, who protested: "You can do business with the United States or you can do business with Frank Zappa."[42] The *Economist* reports that "…when Havel and Lou Reed met, Mr. Havel presented him with a handmade book of Velvet Underground lyrics. 'If the police caught you with that, you went to jail,' he explained. Mr. Reed, not easily impressed, was awestruck by Mr. Havel: a 'heroic, intellectual, music-loving amazing person.'"[43] On his role, Lou Reed said:

Lou Reed, left, former frontman of the legendary U.S. band Velvet Underground speaks with former Czech President Vaclav Havel, right, as they walk to attend a press conference in Prague on Monday, January 10, 2005. AP Photo/Petr David Josek.

I always thought the Velvet Underground, first and foremost, was about freedom. Freedom to write about what you want. Play it the way you want. Put it out anywhere you want. That was, I thought, the bottom line of the whole thing. And low and behold, it found a reception in Czechoslovakia. I even had that demonstrated to me in the sense of meeting all these people who said 'the music does this and this, I went to jail and I had this with me and these lyrics made me feel so-and-so.' The kind of repression you're talking about here—people, kids being told they couldn't play guitar on the Charles Bridge because they're worried that if kids get together they'll talk—and they would! And that's why people were afraid of rock and roll records in the first place. And, they were right to be afraid about that.[44]

Now, in Prague, a poignant remembrance of the path to freedom stands—the John Lennon Wall. Since 1988, people from around the world have been writing tributes on Lennon's wall. They write to celebrate not only the former Beatle, but also the spirit of freedom.

Is There Another Way? Can We Do It Differently?

Richard Combs is one of America's leading experts on Russia and ended a distinguished career as an American diplomat as the Deputy Chief of Mission in Moscow at the time of the Gorbachev revolution. Combs says, "U.S. artistic groups—musicians, dance troupes, etc.—had a different bridging effect, showing Soviet audiences the universal appeal of the arts. I remember clearly the enthusiastic Soviet reaction to the Alvin Ailey dance troupe, Dave Brubek, Vladimir Horowitz, Arlo Guthrie, and many other American artists." "I would say," he adds, "that by 1987, Gorbachev's *perestroika* and *glasnost* were well launched, and the attitude of Soviet youth was not central to those processes. Similarly, Yeltsin's eventual triumph over Gorbachev had little if anything to do with the popularity of American pop culture."[45] Of course, rock and roll, Thomas Shanker agrees, "didn't bring down communism." Rather, he says: "When the Soviet state collapsed, it collapsed because *it* collapsed. It was Gorbachev, it was the failed coup, it was the internal economic contradictions—economic failure that did it. But, all these other movements put in the minds of a broad section of the populace, 'Is there another way? Can we do it differently?'"[46]

SUN CITY

Just as rock and roll artists were venturing into the Soviet bloc, there was a growing international focus on South Africa. The government there was a minority white regime that, via Apartheid, brutally suppressed the majority black population and imprisoned freedom activists such as Nelson Mandela. South African artists like vocalist Miriam Makeba and others used music to bring international attention to combat Apartheid. In 1965, Harry Belafonte joined with Makeba to release the Grammy winning *An Evening with Belafonte and Makeba*, which used songs from South Africa to expose Apartheid's horrors. Belafonte spent years helping Makeba build her international presence. "We both had a chance to make history," Belafonte says.[47] Makeba subsequently had her South African passport revoked and could not return home for decades. On the death of Makeba in 2008, Nelson Mandela, who had toiled in prison for twenty-seven years, said: "The sudden passing of our beloved Miriam has saddened us and our nation...Despite her tremendous sacrifice and the pain she felt to leave behind her beloved family and her country when she went into exile, she continued to make us proud, as she used her worldwide fame to focus attention on the abomination of Apartheid...Her music inspired a powerful sense of hope in all of us."[48]

Artists United Against Apartheid

By the early 1980s, members of the African National Congress, which worked for political change in South Africa, allied with other groups at home and internationally to call for strong economic sanctions against the government. The United Nations General Assembly subsequently passed a nonbinding boycott of cultural visits to South Africa. Nonetheless, after the construction of a resort hotel and entertainment complex called "Sun City" in 1979, many artists took a big paycheck over principle and performed, including the Beach Boys, Elton John, Queen, Linda Ronstadt, and Rod Stewart. Guitarist Brian May of Queen said: "We've thought a lot about the morals of it…and it is something we've decided to do. The band is not political—we play to anybody who wants to come and listen."[49] Conversely, Peter Gabriel used his 1980 song "Biko" to celebrate South African freedom activist Steve Biko who died of head injuries after being beaten by police there in 1977. Then, in 1985, the British band Special AKA released a song titled "Free Nelson Mandela"—telling the world: "21 years in captivity, shoes too small to fit his feet, his body abused, but his mind is still free." Mandela (freed in 1990 as the Apartheid system collapsed) was a great fan of music. He had Ladysmith Black Mambazo, a popular South African vocal group, accompany him to receive the Nobel Peace Prize in 1993 and he was a self-described fan of the Spice Girls. Nelson Mandela also understood the power of the rock and roll stage. Speaking at the 2005 Live 8 concerts (put together by Bob Geldof to pressure global leaders to provide African debt relief), Mandela told his audience: "…as long as poverty, injustice and gross inequality persist in this world, none of us can truly rest. We shall never forget how millions of people around the world joined us in solidarity to fight the injustice of our oppression while we were incarcerated."[50]

Artists United Against Apartheid was established in 1985 by Steven Van Zandt (of Bruce Springsteen and the E. Street Band) along with producers Danny Schechter and Arthur Baker. The organization gathered prominent artists such as Jackson Browne, George Clinton, Bonnie Raitt, Ringo Starr, and U2, who agreed not to perform in South Africa. Central to the effort was a song, written by Van Zandt, called "Sun City." The recording was a video hit on *MTV* and earned over $1 million for various anti-Apartheid projects pressuring Congress to approve sanctions. Steven Van Zandt says: "It was completely successful, and that's such a rare thing. Issue-oriented events and records can be very frustrating, because you really don't see the results, whether it's feeding people in Ethiopia or raising money for AIDS research. Our goal was to stop performers from going there, and to this day no major artist of any integrity have played Sun City [commenting before the collapse of Apartheid]."[51]

Steven Van Zandt says that he had previously never read newspapers and was obsessed with rock and roll "until we broke through with *The River*, and at that point I said, 'Y'know, I wonder what's going on in the world?'" He adds that on his first trip to Europe, a child asked why he was putting missiles there—Van Zandt remembers:

> And it stayed with me for weeks. I couldn't get it out of my head. And it hit me—granted, late in life—oh my god, I'm an American citizen. It had never occurred to me before, y'know? And these people don't look at us as Democrats or Republicans or policemen or rock'n'rollers; we're all Americans over here. And I thought, 'Wow, I wonder what that means. I guess I *am* putting missiles in his country'...I thought, 'My god, I guess being an American citizen, even though we're not a democracy—we sort of pretend to be—with that goes some responsibility, and I wonder what *else* I'm responsible for.' So I started studying our foreign policy since World War II. And I was just so shocked to find that we were *not* the good guys everywhere; we *weren't* defending democracy everywhere...we were on the wrong side *most* of the time.[52]

Steven Van Zandt recalls: "...when I got down there twice in 1984 to do the research, it started to feel so—I started to witness the brutality. I remember the day I was in a taxi cab and a black guy stepped off the curb and [the white taxi-driver] swerved to hit him, [muttering] 'Fucking *kaffir*,' which means 'nigger' in Afrikaans. And I said to myself, 'Did I just witness that?'" While there, he perceived that the racist aspect of the regime was bereft with vulnerabilities—with ego being a key weakness. "And I thought," Van Zandt says, "Okay, if we can get the cultural boycott to take hold, we can communicate this issue to people through the media. We can then work towards the home run, which was the economic boycott."[53]

Steven Van Zandt had to address directly how he could use rock and roll to mobilize people for action—artists and average citizens. "I sat down and said [to myself], look, the art form of rock is not built for *information*-information. It's built for emotional information, usually. In this case, I gotta do information-information." The challenge was to: "...explain what's going on here as well as I can in the song itself, because it might be our only chance, y'know?...It was like, 'Okay, let me just tell their story as clearly as I can, because a whole education process is gonna have to take place here.'" He also had to grapple with a backlash at home, "...because we're naming Ronald Reagan in the song at the height of his popularity, which people don't remember right now, but this was like a *big* deal at the time. And every single artist who went on that record felt it could be the end of their career, and they still did it."[54] Van Zandt also had to grapple with the fact that Paul Simon had incorporated black South African artists into his top-selling 1986 record *Graceland*. Was Paul Simon exploiting African artists for his record sales? Or, was Paul Simon breaking down barriers?

Paul Simon says he only went to South Africa to record, not to perform, and thus was not violating the embargo. He recalls:

> Personally, I feel I'm with the musicians...I'm with the artists. I didn't ask the permission of the ANC. I didn't ask permission of Buthelezi, or Desmond Tutu, or the Pretoria government. And to tell you the truth, I have a feeling that when there are radical transfers of power on either the left or the right, the artists always get screwed. The guys with the guns say, 'This is important', and the guys with guitars don't have a chance.[55]

Steven Van Zandt asserts that either way, Paul Simon violated the boycott. Still, reflecting on the passing of Nelson Mandela, Simon noted the impact of music was huge in South Africa: "In fact, the music of the 'Graceland' album represented a unified black South African culture, even though it came from many different tribal heritages. 'The Boy in the Bubble' is an example of the modal accordion music of the Sotho people. 'I Know What I Know' is Shangaan in origin. 'Homeless' is Zulu choral music, while 'Diamonds on the Soles of Her Shoes', 'Gumboots' and 'You Can Call Me Al' were township jive songs, urban grooves that were straight from the streets of Soweto, where people of different ethnic origins coexisted under the boot of a racist South African government. 'Graceland' was united by the joy of shared music and the sorrow of apartheid."[56]

"It Was an Amazing Feeling"

Steven Van Zandt and the artists and activists he worked with were key agents of political pressure, especially in the United States where Congress overrode

Ronald Reagan's veto to impose sanctions. The isolation of the Apartheid regime succeeded. The South African government was left with little room to maneuver other than to free Mandela and others while letting democracy flourish. Rock and roll, of course, did not end Apartheid. It collapsed because of the weight of its racist immorality. Nevertheless, the effort of activists and artists to educate and hold colleagues accountable amplified change. Steven Van Zandt concludes: "I did a lot of politics in those ten years—international liberation politics. You gain an inch here, you lose a half an inch there—it's in inches. This was the only clear-cut victory we will ever see in our lifetime, and it was an amazing feeling."[57]

ROCK THE CASBAH

In their 1982 hit "Rock the Casbah," the Clash challenged social bans on music in the Middle East as a crisis of unchecked power. Rock and roll can flourish in parts of the Muslim world. Major international artists perform to packed halls in opulent oil-rich kingdoms such as the United Arab Emirates. At the same time, fear of Westernization is used by Islamic political movements to rally against moderate approaches to society. This does not mean that rock and roll is not heard and listened to, but in some countries there are significant constraints that can quash its potential. This tension came to a head in the 2011 Arab Spring movements across North Africa and the Middle East—and it had a soundtrack.

Walk like an Egyptian?

Rock and roll artists historically have not paid a lot of attention to the Islamic world. Ray Stevens had made light of the Arab life with his 1962 song "Ahab the Arab." Referencing it in 2010, Stevens said, "… you know, as a kid I read 'Arabian Nights.' I was a big fan of the whole culture. And so I wrote this song as a comedy song just for fun."[58] Conversely, rocker Warren Zevon provided his 1976 song "Mohammed's Radio." Zevon lamented how everyone was, "…restless with no place to go and meanwhile anger and resentments flow." Yet, the harmless Bangles 1986 hit "Walk Like an Egyptian" was dropped from some radio playlists after the September 2001 terrorist attacks on the United States. In 2011, the Arab Spring reflected a groundswell of popular discontent and, like the forces that brought change in Eastern Europe, people held the power. Bono of U2 offered context in a 2012 speech at Georgetown University: "What happened in Egypt was that the pyramid—the traditional model of power—got inverted. The people at the top got upended…and the base had its say…The base of the pyramid…the 99%…is taking more control.

The institutions that have always governed our lives: church, state, the mainstream media, the music industry—are being bypassed and weakened and seriously tested. People are holding them to account. Us to account. Demanding that they become more open, more responsive, more effective. Or else."[59]

While the rock and roll story is important in the Islamic world, its tributary hip-hop provided the main soundtrack of the Arab Spring. Hip-hop and rap emerged in the Arab world alongside communications technology facilitating rapid organization and mobilization for people to reclaim power. In Tunisia, where the Arab Spring first took root, a popular revolution was given voice by an artist known as "El General" (whose name is Hamada Ben Amor). In late 2010, he posted on Facebook a song and video titled "Rais Le Bld." The song detailed corruption and harsh economic conditions in Tunisia. He was detained and questioned by Tunisian authorizes for the production, but it was too late. As Martin Buch Larsen of Freemuse (an organization that advocates for musician's rights internationally) says, "His art and music became such a strong symbol of this revolutionary trend, that of course he became a target."[60] El General says: "Corruption was everywhere here. And it still is everywhere. You could see it every day. If you had money, you could do anything. Pay for whatever you want. The mafia family controlled everything. It was pure dictatorship. We were guests in our own country. We weren't landlords. The suffering of the people made me speak."[61]

One artist, Deeb, who provided a soundtrack for the revolution in Egypt's Tahir Square in early 2011, says: "A lot of [Egyptians] haven't heard about hip-hop before. So it was very interesting to see the crowd react with you and sing with you. Even in the square, when we meet up with people from an older generation—for example, like my father's generation or my grandfather's generation—they'd tell us, 'Listen, you've done something that we've never thought of doing."[62] Syrian-American rap singer Omar Offendum says: "The combination of hip hop and the Internet, and the ability to record it and put it up online immediately and bypass all these typical media outlets and typical industry outlets is what makes it so powerful."[63] The result was, according to Middle East scholar Robin Wright, that people like El General, "...captured the first real challenge—at a time when politicians didn't dare criticize the regime." El General, Wright observers, sang directly to the president: "'We're suffering like dogs, half the people living in shame—misery everywhere, people eating from garbage cans. Today I'm speaking for the people, crushed by the weight of injustice.'" The song asks how long must the Tunisian people live in dreams? Money, the song asserted "...was pledged for projects and infrastructure, schools, hospitals, buildings, houses—but the sons of bitches with people's money—they fill their bellies—they steal, they plunder—even a chair doesn't escape them." Robin Wright says, "That kind of challenge just wasn't found anyplace in Tunisia and in most other parts of the Arab world...It was sung by many of the protestors across Tunisia as the revolution spread—and then picked up in places from mighty Egypt to tiny Bahrain."[64]

While these Western art forms infiltrated the Middle East, there was tension that some policy makers in the West failed to understand—official American support for dissident music could endanger artists. Thus, when [then] Secretary of State Hillary Clinton said in 2010 that "hip-hop is America" she risked hurting those who had made hip-hop their own. Moreover, in some cases, artists were using the genre to advocate against regimes, like the one in Egypt, that the United States supported.[65] According to British rapper Lowkey: "Hip hop at its best has exposed power, challenged power, it hasn't served power. When the US government loves the same rappers you love, whose interests are those rappers serving?" Hip-hop artists and rockers are also as likely to be critical of America's role in the world. For example, global beat phenomenon Michael Franti sings of the F-16 being a "homicide bomber." Lil Kim was featured on a 2003 magazine cover in a burka and bikini and was quoted saying "Fuck Afghanistan." At the 2011 BET awards, the American artist Lupe Fiasco performed "Words I Never Said" draped in a Palestinian flag singing, "Gaza strip was getting burned; Obama didn't say shit!"[66]

Meet the Muckers

By 2016, Iran remained a keystone in the arch of the Middle East. Iran had a well-educated and young population growing tired of isolation from the world. Still, via religious and state censorship on television, radio and the Internet, Iran's ruling clerics set cultural guidance. Rock and roll is not illegal in Iran, but lyrics and public performances are heavily regulated and restricted. For example, in 2014, seven Iranian students were arrested for creating a video showing them dancing to the global Pharrell Williams hit "Happy." Each was sentenced to six months to a year in jail and to be lashed ninety-one times. Their sentences were deferred pending no additional "criminal" activity in the next three years. Pharrell said: "It's beyond sad these kids were arrested for trying to spread happiness."[67] The students took major risks. Two years earlier, in 2012, an Iranian rap artist living in Germany was perceived as singing songs offensive to Shiite believers and a $100,000 bounty to anyone who would kill him was published on an Iranian website. Iranians with influential voices were quick to create distance. For example, a columnist for the conservative state-run *Kahyan* newspaper said: "Just as Florida pastor Terry Jones, who last month burned Korans, does not represent the United States government, this *fatwa* does not represent the government of Iran."[68]

Rasoo, lead singer and guitar player for the Iranian band the Muckers, says, "Rock and roll music is legal in Iran. With my music, my kind of music, people are going to want to dance with it, or headbutt with it, or whatever, or jump with it…Everything's a little bit legal and a little bit not. It depends on how you play it. The biggest problem as a musician in Iran is that I wasn't able to play any shows—and you can't have fans, you can't promote your music."[69] A member of the Iranian band Hypernova said in 2007: "It's really dangerous to do what we do back home…We've come really close to [having our shows raided by police] a couple times. Every show we play we're putting our lives on the line. So it's intense, but that sort of fear adds to the rush."[70] Things worsened in Iran in 2007 when then president Mahmood Ahmadinejad banned all Western music from state-run radio stations. And, being heard outside of Iran, especially in the United States, can be difficult. The Muckers were slated to play at the industry festival "South-By-Southwest" in Austin, Texas, in early 2014. However, they were barred from entering the United States. Rasoo says after getting an invitation they went to an American Embassy and got: "…an FBI check and—actually just two of our members did because they went to the military service in Iran and they had to get checked. What happened was that took a really long time, and it passed the festival and they didn't give us a visa anymore."[71]

Rasoo brings unique perspective to Iranian rock and roll via the Muckers as he: "…grew up in at lot of different places—my dad worked for the Ministry of Foreign Affairs. So we were traveling every four years. I was actually born in London. I learned off YouTube and watching videos—I never took any guitar lessons. The first bands that made good music that I listened to were Placebo and lots of trash metal bands, too, like Megadeath and Metallica. I listened to everything. I listened to lots of the hits in the 2004 era—lots of Franz Ferdinand, lots of Arctic Monkeys, lots of Outkast." "When I was a teenager," Rasoo says, "I was growing up listening to music. It was just so interesting to me—how another person's feelings touches me so deeply. I started thinking, 'How can you do that?' How can you attract people's minds and souls with sound that you make?' And it feels pretty good when you listen to good music." In 2013, the Muckers staged a "secret concert" to make the point that rock and roll needs to be heard, not only played in the secrecy of one's home. Rasoo recalls: "The 'Secret Gig' that we did, we were pretty lucky. We had some friends—some embassy friends and when they have parties in Iran at their places, cops can't really knock on their door. They can knock on the doors, but they can't go on. We had a really, really good friend and she was a lot into music. She worked for an embassy and said: 'Let's do this, let's have a small gig at my place—just do it for thirty minutes and be really fast—like, invite people really secretly and tell them not to tell anybody.'"[72]

In Iran, Rasoo says: "You can make music. You can put it on Facebook, SoundCloud, everything—until the point that it's not really too political. There are some rap musicians in Iran that get into lots of trouble. They get into really, really, really big troubles and they get arrested. But it's because mainly they sing in Farsi and the stuff that they say, it's really obvious. Maybe if you just changed my lyrics into Farsi, translated them, maybe I would also be in a really big trouble. It's just because we sing in English, its not that obvious. It also depends on how famous you become. When you sing in Farsi you are going to have a lot more fans than a band like us because people like it more. And that's also going to make you more suspicious. There might be a chance that you get into trouble." For Rasoo: "We are just thinking about making music for the sake of music. I guess it's going to connect some cultures together, because every band is from different cultures. Somebody else is going to like it from another culture and from another country. Then you're going to dig into the band and see where they're from. And it can connect people a lot." For example, the Mucker's song "Analogy Between a Heart and a Pump," Rasoo says, symbolizes "…movement and not being at the same place—moving."[73]

The Muckers aspire to be appreciated for their music, not as the "band from Iran." Rasoo says: "It's because everybody, first thing people think about when you say you're a rock band from Iran, they say, 'Oh, it must be so hard.' But, really, like on a daily basis, when you go to the studio and you want to write songs, you can find so many studios in Iran. It's so easy to go and write music. The only thing people focus on is the political side of it. That shtick is getting old." At the same time, the Mucker's song "Guns" raises issues of justice and violence as universal problems for humanity. Rasoo believes, "Politically, I—all the ideas about the stuff that is happening to people in Palestine and Iraq and Afghanistan. That was really really hard for me. I'm really into it. I read about it all the time. I was, I think, writing about war, and that we are like human beings that are breaking and not human beings anymore—that there are guns on the way, and it's going to be downhill from now on." Rasoo adds: "Maybe I could enlighten somebody about all the political problems that he or she wasn't into before; but just came to listen to this kind of music—and, through the lyrics, gets another idea about politics. So that could happen, in every band. I think the role of artists has been, and is going to be really big."[74]

"We Have to Be Lucky"

The process of getting heard, Rasoo believes, can bridge Americans and Iranians. "There are people in Iran," Rasoo says, "who would love that to happen. That's why I'm saying it really wouldn't be a big problem—maybe [people] would be proud of us." "For everybody who loves music, it would be important to listen to us." The possibilities, Rasoo notes, are significant: "I think if people see that they have a band—an Iranian band—that is huge, that is getting to places—then they would be more interested in this genre of music. Worldwide, that would be also a big thing for Iran, because when people talk about Iran, they would talk about music in Iran." Rasoo concludes: "It is really hard to discover underground bands like us. How could they do that? We have to be lucky and people have to be lucky to discover us."[75]

A CHANGE IS GONNA COME

Sam Cooke's 1964 hit "A Change Is Gonna Come" gave voice to the growing aspirations of the civil rights movement in the United States. Yet, at a 2011 event discussing the impact of protest music at the Rock and Roll Hall of Fame and Museum in Cleveland, Ohio, with satellite links around the world, a 23-year-old woman participating from Baghdad, Iraq, suggested that the audience should hear Cooke's anthem in global terms. A summary of the event notes: "The woman's request was a compelling indication of the timelessness of certain songs, the cross-cultural appeal of music and how songs continue to be reinterpreted by generations and defy geographical boundaries in inspiring and shaping the events and culture that change our lives."[76] In effect, a change had come as freedom's march progressed—but only to reveal more work to be done for equality.

Chapter Three

Equality—This Land Was Made for You and Me

SHED A LITTLE LIGHT

"Let us turn our thoughts today to Martin Luther King," sings James Taylor in his 1991 song "Shed a Little Light." James Taylor speaks of recognizing the bonds that tie humanity together. Rock and roll artists frequently work to shine a light of transparency as the United States continues its long struggle with economic, racial, and gender inequity. Wealth has been consolidated among the rich, racial tensions stretched from Ferguson to Baltimore, and women confronted sexism and pay inequities. The quest for fairness is a value essential to America's declaration that all people are created equal and, as Martin Luther King Jr. said, they should be judged only by the content of their character. The rock and roll ethic has sustained this value of equality building on Woody Guthrie's premise that "this land was made for you and me."

THE NIGHTWATCHMEN

In 2015, Bernie Sanders launched an improbable campaign for president. A self-described "Democratic Socialist," Sanders championed a broad public sense that the government in Washington, D.C. had failed at one of its most important jobs—securing equal opportunity. Billy Bragg describes a new, populist "socialism of the heart":

> I think accountability is a key idea in the 21st century. If you don't have accountability, you don't really have freedom. I don't mean just holding politicians to account, I mean those in economic power also to account. And what is socialism

but a means to which we hold capitalism to account? This isn't a renege on the original ideas and the politics I still feel strongly about. It's just a less ideological way of articulating it. With 'socialism of the heart', I'm talking about compassion as opposed to ideology.[1]

There are many contradictions in the world of rock and roll, and as a music business it has far to go on the path to progress. But, some rock and roll artists are serving as—as Tom Morello puts it—Nightwatchmen.

"What Is Justice?"

By 2016, the United States had recovered from its deepest economic recession since the Great Depression. At the same time, both before the crash and after, many citizens were left behind. Billy Bragg observes: "The key players in growth are not entrepreneurs; they are consumers. And if consumers don't have proper wages, they can't buy shit." "I don't know why," he adds, "people think they can get away with stagnating wages like you've had here in the United States of America." In the United States, from 2009 to 2011, the mean net worth of the highest 7 percent of the upper-end of wealth distribution rose by 28 percent. The same measure in the remaining 93 percent of households fell by 4 percent. Although the stock market had doubled and employment had returned, wages remained stagnant, the middle class shrank, and the poor were increasingly left out of the American dream. Billy Bragg asserts: "We need to find a balance between an economy that has sustainable growth and an economy that is purely exploitative and has no other values than profit. We have to get back to putting people before profit."[2]

When opportunity is limited and the exercise of power done by the few, the battle over justice is engaged. Graham Nash explains that in his youth he came to understand justice as a commodity:

> My father went to prison for a year for having bought a thirty dollar camera from a friend of his from work. When the police came to the door and said that the camera had been stolen and, 'Who was it that sold him the camera?' My father wouldn't tell them. So immediately he's behind the 8-ball. I mean, you go to jail for a year? A fine upstanding man, for a year? For a thirty dollar camera? When you see George Bush and Donald Rumsfeld and Paul Wolfowitz and Dick Cheney walking free, having lied to the American people into the Iraq war for the oil? And convinced people that Saddam had weapons of mass destruction? Complete lies. So where is justice when Bradley Manning and Edward Snowden and Julian Assange are fugitives? Those people that tried to bring the truth about what the military was doing in our name, that we paid for—that they're in jail? They're fugitives and the people who lied us into the Iraq war which killed 5,000 Americans and wasted trillions of dollars? What is justice?[3]

Serj Tankian has also long championed justice: "Years ago I had the honor of meeting the Dali Lama one-on-one. I got to ask him, 'What was the intersection of justice and spirituality?' His response was basically: 'To follow a path of injustice would be, spiritually, extremely uncomfortable.' And that's an innate morality thing." "Justice," Tankian says, "is tied into our moral fabric. Justice is the only way to have an equitable democracy, whether it's a capitalist nation or otherwise. Without justice, none of the principles that we hold dear as a nation are going to last."[4]

Many rock and roll artists are empathetic because of their own experiences. As Michael Stanley rose to national success in the early 1980s, his sound reflected America's industrial heartland with songs such as "Working Again" and its lyric: "Put my time in, like my old man before me, died in dreamland, with the union by his side." Stanley says:

> If I had any intention, it was to get across the fact that we're all in this together. And even though we're on the stage and you're in the audience; once we walk out here, we're pretty much in the same circumstances. I may make more money than you, you may make more money than me. It doesn't matter in terms of where we've put down roots—and that sense of community. Be it a musical community, or the community in general.[5]

Stanley reflects he raised his children to understand: "'Don't think the plumber is less worthy than what I do. Probably more worthy because if the plumbing's not working, that song's not going to help you at all buddy. That songwriter's the last guy that you're looking for.'"[6]

Of course, that songwriter might also be Tom Morello of Rage Against the Machine—who performs solo as the Nightwatchman and is a political activist. In 2011, on the *HBO* program *Real Time with Bill Maher*, Tom Morello showed his eagerness to challenge President Barack Obama:

> Much like the president, I am half Kenyan. Much like the president, I'm a Harvard graduate. Like the president, I'm from Illinois. And like the president, I've been on the cover of *Rolling Stone* magazine. I've got a message for him, 'Dude, it's time to grow a pair, you know what I mean? A lot of people who put you in office, put you in office to fight for them; to fight against the Tea Party; to fight against this bullshit in Congress; to fight against those son of bitches who are attacking the working class and the poor in this country,' and he hasn't done any of that. Also, at the same time, I'm not waiting for him. I'm not waiting. I'm with the people in Madison. I'm with the people that are occupying Wall Street—that's what my music's about...When progressive, radical, or even revolutionary change has happened in this country, it's always come from below. When women got the right to vote, when lunch counters were desegregated. It was people you do not read about in history books who stood up in their place and their time for what they believe.[7]

Tom Morello says, "...it's been my job to weave my convictions into my vocation. My job is to steel the backbone of people who are on the frontlines of social justice struggles, and put wind in the sails of those struggles and people who are fighting on a daily basis, at a grassroots level for the things that I believe in." Tom Morello embraces the troubadour tradition, performing as the Nightwatchman: "I felt a visceral connection to the audiences—even on nights when no one was coming to see or hear me. When it went well, it really felt like everyone's soul in the room was at stake." Morello adds: "Sometimes it does seem like we are up against insurmountable odds." "But," he says, "during my lifetime, no one thought the Berlin Wall was going to fall or that Apartheid would be dismantled. Or, in days past, there'd be a desegregated lunch counter or that women would get the right to vote."[8]

At the same time, one or a few artists were not going to create massive social change given the structural inequities in the American economy. In a twenty-five-year period leading up to 2015, the American economy grew by 83 percent (after inflation) and corporate profits doubled as a percentage of the economy. In most of the country, median income was lower in 2014 than it was a decade and a half earlier even though workers were producing twice as many goods and services as they had in the late 1980s.[9] In 2011, these realities gained a voice from below: "We Are the 99 Percent!" rang out from Zuccotti Park near Wall Street where an "occupy" movement of loosely organized protestors gathered—Occupy Wall Street. "The goals of the occupy movement," Tom Morello said, "are as big as the goals of the 99 percent. The thing that the Occupy movement has done is that it has introduced into the national discussion, in the United States, the dirty, unspoken five-letter word-class."[10]

Tom Morello performed at Zuccotti Park, playing Woody Guthrie's "This Land Is Your Land" and also attended Occupy protests in Los Angeles, San Francisco, Seattle, Vancouver, and Nottingham, Newcastle, and London in the United Kingdom.[11] Morello showed up in troubadour fashion—as did Arlo Guthrie and Pete Seeger, David Crosby and Graham Nash. Other artists joining the Occupy protestors included Billy Bragg, Jackson Browne, Michael Franti, Katy Perry, Dar Williams, and Kanye West. Some, like Trent Reznor of 9 Inch Nails, used social media to show support. A website was set up called 'Occupy Musicians', where artists could sign on in support of the protestors—as did Laurie Anderson and Lou Reed. Still, the movement lacked a unifying sound. Peter Yarrow relates this to the nature of the music industry, which, he says, discourages artists from taking stands. "The bean counters took over...The bottom line is music has been destroyed by the all-mighty dollar."[12] The cultural shift also matters. Johanna Fateman of the band Le Tigre says: "If you thought about 'What is the culture?' of Occupy Wall

Street, unfortunately you thought about, like, these drum circles." Fateman adds: "I don't think that you can discount aesthetics and some cultural style—it's really important."[13] Dar Williams says, the Occupy movement "...didn't have a soundtrack and their sort of anti-hierarchical thing was sort of part of that. This was such a new thing." She says, "We were kind of ambushed on our own lack of ability to kind of sing, side-by-side when Occupy came along. We improvised a shitload of stuff that came much more naturally in the '60s."[14]

Christine Martucci is a well-known, New Jersey-shore rocker. Her song "Working Man" tells the story of Americans living in the shadow of Wall Street. Playing at the Wonder Bar in Asbury Park in 2011 she introduced the song, saying: "We've got a lot of people occupying Wall Street, occupying North Dakota, occupying Wyoming—everywhere, all over the country. We are the 99 percent. We really are."[15] The song tells of a man: "All he ever wanted, all he ever needed, was to be a working man—to feed his family. All he ever lived for, was a little dignity." Martucci recalls her inspiration:

> I did a gig in Detroit and I sat at a bar. There was a guy sitting next to me. He had an ashtray and a beer and a shot. I'd say he's probably like 45, 46—not shaven well and he's just sittin' there just looking, just staring off. In my head I'm like, 'This guy's got to go home and tell his wife he lost his job.' Probably not even what was happening, but I was painting this picture in my head. There he is, man, just trying to work, trying to be good. Especially in 2008, when the bailouts happened—it was a lot of bullshit.[16]

Martucci says: "I thought the artists, especially artists that have a lot of radio messaging—they can send it out all over the world. I was really surprised that they kind of just laid back. Maybe a little disappointed too. I thought maybe there'd be an anthem out there that would be like, 'Come on, let's bring these guys down!' And it just kind of fizzled out. I was like, 'Wow, are we that beaten down as a society, as Americans—that we just throw up our arms and just [go] like, 'We can't do anything anymore?'" "I just wish," she says, "we had a lot more balls. It seems like anybody who tries to stand up, to do something, they're ridiculed." She reflects there are: "So many positive messages out there that don't get there. I mean, Kim Kardashian is more important than people losing their jobs?"[17]

Money to Thieves

Reflecting on how billionaires can call the shots in America, David Crosby says: "They don't give a fuck what you think. They're power happy motherfuckers. Our votes do not matter. This is not a democracy. We didn't win this

one. Democracy has failed in the United States of America, as of right now."
Crosby however, found inspiration in the Occupy movement:

> I did, because there's people standing for what they believe in. They're saying,
> 'Hey! What do you think you're doing, bailing out the banks? We're hungry
> here. There are kids not getting an education. What in God's name are you
> thinking, giving money to thieves who just ripped us all off? And you want to
> bail them out?' They had the awareness to know they were being handed the
> short end of the stick—the balls, the courage, to stand up and say, 'I know what
> you're doing. I see it. I see what's going on here, and I'm not going to just roll
> over and put my paws in the air and shut up. I'm not going to take your hand
> out. I'm not going to buy your story. This is bullshit!'[18]

Bob Dylan offers his take, calling on the billionaires of America to invest
in jobs: "There are good people there, but they've been oppressed by lack of
work…Those people can all be working at something. These multibillion-
aires can create industries right here in America. But no one can tell them
what to do. God's got to lead them."[19]

WHAT'S GOING ON?

America's ongoing burden of race has tracked with the development of rock
and roll. From the first notes of Chuck Berry, Fats Domino, Little Richard,
and others—to integrated bands to Bruce Springsteen's protesting police
brutality against young African men in his 2000 song "American Skin (41
Shots)," rock and roll accompanied America's quest for racial equality.
In the early 1960s, *Stax* recording studio in Memphis, Tennessee, became
home to one of rock and roll's first integrated bands, Booker T. and the
M.G.s. The band included Booker T. Jones on keyboards and Al Jackson
on drums along with Steve Cropper on guitar and Donald "Duck" Dunn
on bass. *Stax* produced their many hits like "Green Onions" and "Time is
Tight." Jim Stewart, who cofounded *Stax*, recalls: We were sitting in the
middle of a highly segregated city. Highly hypocritical city. And we were
in another world when we walked in that studio and behind those doors. Yet
the reality hit us square in the face when we walked out. It was very trying;
I did not understand it. I could not understand why it had to be this way.
There was no reason for it. I had no other choice but to go home, after I got
out of the studio and they go home…But when we were inside, we were all
one. You could not feel any of the prejudices and hypocrisy that you felt
when you walked out that door.[20]

Journalist Larry Nager writes: "During the most explosive period of the
civil rights movement, *Stax* took that musical integration even deeper. The

heartbeat of *Stax* came from its half-black, half-white house band, its multi-racial songwriting staff, and the songs themselves, which mixed down-home blues and R&B with more than a little country music."[21] Liberty Devitto frames it like this: "I think racism is being perpetuated by hate, that it is being fed to people. I mean, if you went into the studio in *Stax* or *Motown*, you would never know that there was racism, you know what I mean?"[22] Lauren Onkey, of the Rock and Roll Hall of Fame and Museum, notes there was an early burst of African American access to the charts as the airwaves could not be segregated. It was, she observers, huge, "For Fats Domino to come out in the early 1950s and basically say: 'I am here! I am a man!'"[23]

One Nation Under a Groove

In addition to Booker T. and the M.G.'s, other bands emerged as integrated successes, including the Allman Brothers, the Doobie Brothers, the Jimi Hendrix Experience, Little Feat, Santana, Sly and the Family Stone, Bruce Springsteen and the E. Street Band, and Thin Lizzy. By the 1980s and 1990s, a new round of well-known integrated groups included Culture Club, Hootie and the Blowfish, Prince and the Revolution, and the Spice Girls. Today, the stage is diverse and there is a growing range of rock and roll forms from African to Asian to Latino to Native American. Bill Payne has played keyboards not only with artists like Jimmy Buffett, Eric Clapton, Pink Floyd, Bob Seger, and James Taylor—but also with James Cotton, Freddie King, Willie Dixon, Buddy Guy, Otis Rush, and Taj Mahal: "It is a rather fortunate part of what I've been able to do." He notes that during the forty-five years he was with Little Feat, it was a diverse group—including African American percussionist Sam Clayton—and members coming from Louisiana to Iowa to Hollywood. For Little Feat, being an integrated band was less significant than the music they made. Payne says, "The blues was important and designing what the blues was. It's getting people out of their comfort zone—[the idea] that the blues is strictly about black music. Then you point out to people, Steve Cropper—he helped Otis Redding on 'Sitting on a Dock of the Bay'. Steve is white. But, the sensibilities and that soul are something that's American. It's not black, it's not white—it's American."[24] As that promise often went unfulfilled in communities across the United States, the messaging in the music got more direct, for example, with Marvin Gaye's 1971 hit "What's Going On?" George Clinton, who had a direct role in these changes, says with his 1972 record "America Eats It's Young":

> The music went in all kind of directions. You know? Because with the war [eventually] being over, we was talking, you know, 'Maggot Brain', 'March to the Witch's Castle.' Then we did 'Chocolate City' also, we saw a black thing happening. Then the 'Chocolate Planet', you know, the Mothership

Connection. All of us understood that music was still that James Brown-based, Sly [and the Family Stone], which turned out hip hop. We talked about radio being that thing on our record 'Mothership Connection'—D.J. hip hoppers took that and literally became a new radio. Radio got restricted, but you got the talkers of that radio vibe on record. You got the Public Enemy, you got the D.M.C.s—those are the D.J.s in the clubs, making records, which is now electronic music.[25]

With his bands Parliament and Funkadelic, George Clinton had, he says, "...ten blacks on stage doing Jimi Hendrix-type music, rock was white, you know. They go crazy: 'Ten of them!'" "But," he adds, "for the people that liked us—they stayed, both black and white. It stayed diverse all the way through that. You go to L.A. and Detroit—everybody's there. It's like the circus."[26]

Some artists made advancing racial equality and justice central to their work. In 1966, James Brown was quick to perform at Tougaloo College, in Mississippi, at a march following the killing of James Meredith over his enrollment at the University of Mississippi. James Brown's 1968 hit "Say It Loud—I'm Black, I'm Proud" provided a burgeoning black pride movement an anthem. Brown put on a free concert in Boston, Massachusetts, after Martin Luther King Jr. was assassinated in 1969. The mayor of Boston wanted the show cancelled. However, James Brown argued they should play——and televise it. That way people stayed home and watched the show instead of going into the streets. In May 1970, Augusta, Georgia, erupted into rioting after a sixteen-year-old black boy with mental disabilities was beaten to death in police custody. The conflicts resulted in six deaths and more than sixty people were hurt. James Brown grew up in Augusta, and when the crisis erupted, he returned. Brown met with the governor and told the press: "We gotta respect each other, and we gotta sit down and talk about it as human beings" and that collaboration and cooperation was better than "people losing their lives." James Brown reflected: "My music was keeping pace with the changes in society. We were demanding our rights now—civil rights and human rights. People warned me not to get involved. I said, 'With all that's going on, I got to try.'" He was blunt in his assessment of the problem: "They whupped us all. Even the whites. They wouldn't (just) kill the blacks, they'd kill the whites for being a nigger lover. So I got to be concerned...I got to paint it real." "To me," James Brown said, "black power meant black pride and black people having a voice in politics——I now wanted to have something to say about the country I lived in."[27]

When the Beatles toured America in 1964, they entered a nation with deep pockets of resistance to national civil and voting rights legislation. When the band was told their concert at the Florida Gator Bowl on 11 September was in a racially segregated venue, Paul McCartney responded: "We are not going to play there." Days before the concert, the Beatles received notice that, for the first time, the Gator Bowl would accommodate equal access. Paul McCartney said: "I think it would be a bit silly to segregate people because I don't think colored people are any different, you know, they're just the same as anyone else…there are some people who think they're animals or something—I just think it's stupid—you can't treat other human beings like animals and so, I wouldn't mind them sitting next to me."[28] By 1965, the Beatles's contract for live performances included language that specified: "…the group not be required to perform in front of a segregated audience."[29] As racial tensions deepened in 1968, Paul McCartney offered the song "Blackbird." In 2003, he recalled in concert: "I was in Scotland playing on my guitar and I remembered this whole idea of, 'You were only waiting for this moment to arise,' was about, you know, the black people's struggle in the southern states." McCartney later teamed with Stevie Wonder to record the hit "Ebony and Ivory" in 1982. The duet used the analogy of the black and white keys on the piano working together, in harmony.

Paul McCartney and Stevie Wonder perform Ebony and Ivory at a concert honoring McCartney, recipient of the Gershwin prize, in the East Room of the White House. Photo courtesy of the White House, June 2, 2010.

Working behind the scenes, cultivating talent, and offering musical wisdom throughout has been legendary producer Quincy Jones. He was the first African American songwriter to work at senior levels of a major record label, Mercury Records. Across his career, Quincy Jones won an Emmy Award for his contributions to the landmark television show *Roots*; has seven Academy Award nominations, twenty-seven Grammy Awards and received seventy-nine Grammy nominations.[30] A protégé, Glen Ballard, says Jones is "... acutely aware of what function music had in the culture. He taught me that it's O.K. to entertain people. At the same time, you can still have a message. You can combine both of those things and you don't have to like, sort of, lecture people, but that you can inspire." Ballard explains:

> He's the ultimate teacher for me. I mean, I'm a white guy from Mississippi and he never thought that was anything weird, you know? I was doing a lot of R&B music and doing it successfully. He didn't care. Rod Temperton, an English guy who wrote some of the great R&B hits of all time—we were a couple of guys working with Quincy. And it didn't matter. He was colorblind about that shit. And in a funny way, I was the interloper. But it's like Quincy knows all kinds of music, every kind of music. And it was just a gift for me to be around somebody who has the musical education, first of all, that he has.[31]

Glen Ballard took the lesson to be that "I don't want to scare people, I want to inspire them."[32]

That spirit brought Glen Ballard to cowrite the 1988 hit "Man in the Mirror"—one of Michael Jackson's biggest hits. Ballard recalls:

> I wrote that with Siedah Garrett. I was staff producer for Quincy. I had written a couple songs for the Michael Jackson *Bad* record, none of which were right. This was the last one written for the record. We wrote it on a Saturday night and Siedah was so excited about it. She drove over to play it for Quincy the next day—which I would have never done, because I wasn't that confident, you know? But she was. She knew—and she was right, man. And I got a call from Quincy going, 'I love it', you know? He said, 'I'm going to play it for Michael on Monday,' and he played it for Michael and it was like: 'This is all a go.' It was one of those fantasy moments.[33]

Ballard is proud of a key moment in the song where: "I did this half-step modulation from G to Ab and everybody went for it. It was like, 'Yeah, let's do this crazy kind of 'change' where you go up a half-step.' I will take credit for that arrangement! But it was Quincy's idea to put the choir on, of course." "On every level, I had so many great people in that moment, who elevated my little song, which had been written very quickly, with great intention. I had this long thing at the end, you know. I kept thinking we're just going to fade it...and, man, he [Michael Jackson] just started working it out. It's like maybe my favorite moment of anything I've ever had associated with me, is what he did in the last two minutes of that record."[34] Performing the song at the Grammy Awards in 1988, Michael Jackson spun out the end—becoming airborne dancing and singing: "Come on everybody—black man gotta make a change, white man gotta make the change, black man gotta make the change. Change yeah!—Stand up!"

We the People

Gedeon Luke is an artist whose trajectory transcends the deep pockets of inequality in America. Known at the time as Gedeon McKinney, he captured the hearts of tens of millions of Americans with his strong performance on the 2005 season of *American Idol*. As a teenager from Memphis, Tennessee, Gedeon stormed the nation only to lose in closing rounds to talented entertainers like Jennifer Hudson. Now, after many years of hard work, Gedeon Luke has appeared on *Later with Jools Holland* and toured with Rusted Root. Luke says that he is glad that he did not win *American Idol*. Not winning allowed him, he says, to live free: "I'm free to grow, I'm free to learn things that I never knew before. I'm free to have control over who I am and what I think and what I do and what I write, what I post, what I say, what I think—I'm free. Had he won the show, at age seventeen: "I wouldn't have known a lot of things. Things would have been done behind my back. I don't feel like I probably would have been taken care of on the level of a human being, let alone an artist."[35]

Gedeon Luke comes from Memphis, Tennessee—where many African American youths experience inner-city realities. Memphis had a nine-percent unemployment rate among African Americans before the 2008 economic crisis. It skyrocketed to 16.9 percent versus 5.3 percent for white citizens after 2009.[36] Memphis was the poorest major city in the United States—and its population was 63.3 percent African American.[37] The city's newspaper, the *Commercial Appeal*, notes that in hardest-hit neighborhoods: "Block after block is dotted with abandoned homes and empty apartment buildings. The more fortunate ones have sheets of plywood nailed to the doors and windows, as if to seal hope of a rebirth inside."[38] Luke says of growing up in Memphis:

> I was raised in the projects. I was surrounded by a lot of gang violence, and drug abuse, and broken dreams and families. I always tell people, when I write music, I write from that place. I write from that place of pain, because I was taught that pain brings out joy. Pain makes you see the struggle, makes you accept the struggle, embrace the struggle, and from embracing the struggle, you can help other people. You can never get too high on your horse where you can think that you are so high that you can't be on the same level as other people.[39]

Gedeon Luke, who rose to national fame on American Idol, traces his roots from
Memphis, Tennessee, to a modern Soul Stew of rock and roll. Photo courtesy of
Gedeon Luke.

Gedeon Luke notes: "What goes on in places like Memphis, and Detroit, and Baltimore, I tell people all the time, this stuff has been going on." Luke says:

> In the hood, kids are brought up around violence. This is what they're seeing. It's like taking a child when they are twelve years old and training them to be something like Jihadist camp or something like that. Kids in these communities, they're seeing their parents get beat with bats and get stabbed with stuff in the house. So what do you expect for them to do when they grow up? It's by the grace of God that some people like me get out of places like Memphis. And I can go back to Memphis and tell them my story of how I was free, and how music set me free, and how the truth about all of this stuff set me free.[40]

Gedeon Luke recalls: "When I was in Memphis, what really took me from being on the streets—what kept me focused was the message in the music— not necessarily the music, because music speaks all kind of languages, but this particular message: the message of love, the message of peace, the message of real soul music coming from Memphis—waking up on a Saturday morning listening to my father play some Bobby Blue Bland and some Johnnie Taylor and some Al Green and some Isaac Hayes."[41]

As a teen, Gedeon Luke spent an hour on the bus each day to participate in "YO Memphis"—part of the Youth Opportunity Movement (a federal program funding youth community organizations): "They were getting paid to be involved in the community and to help build up the community instead of tearing it down. I joined the choir at age fourteen and at age fifteen I transferred to the YO Memphis Academy." This sense of community was central to his rise on *American Idol*. He was scheduled to audition at a local Memphis location. However, it was cancelled due to the impact of Hurricane Katrina. He could still audition in Chicago and so he asked his school's principal if he could have a concert to raise funds. "I set up my whole show," he says, "and the next day, I came to school and they were asking, 'How much is the show?' I said: '$2.00—just $2.00.' The whole school came and even after the show they started throwing money up on the stage to support me to go to Chicago. That right there alone, my faith was so strong going to audition, it was like, 'I know I'm not going home without a ticket.'" This was also the community that built a Habitat for Humanity home where Gedeon and his family lived after his mother wrote an essay for a competition: "When I was ten years old, we were evicted out of our house and moved back into the projects. We built our own house from the ground up. The day we built that house, we were just overwhelmed and filled with joy."[42]

Soul Stew

In 2014, Gedeon Luke performed his song "Gray" (cowritten with Charlie Midnight and Marc Swersky) on Martin Luther King Day at the Mount Pleasant Baptist Church in Albany, New York. He remembers:

> I'm singing this song because it is as relevant to today as it was when Martin Luther King was alive. I listen to 'What's Going On' because it's as relevant as today as when Marvin Gaye was alive. When I was singing that song, I was singing, and in my mind, I said, 'Ain't nothing changed. It's still the same.' See, it's so easy to end a so-called struggle with Dr. King, or with Malcom X. They never wanted this to end. They wanted us to keep the faith and keep on going and keep pushing for love, peace, and soul.[43]

Gedeon Luke's band is called the People and members hail from groups such as the Roots and Lenny Kravitz. "When we all come together, we're like one big family—the People," Luke says. And, he sees a peoples' movement coming from music: "When Marvin Gaye was singing about it, he wasn't the only one. You had Curtis Mayfield singing about it. You had the Beatles singing about it. You had the O'Jays singing about it. You had James Brown singing about it. Every artist you could think of at that time was singing about what was going on in the world." Luke says: "I put Bruce Springsteen, the Beatles, Jackie Wilson, Marvin Gaye, Otis Redding, Sam Cooke, Al Greene, Tina Turner—I put all these people in a pot and I stir it up. And I get what you call a 'Soul Stew'—which comes from a song called "Memphis Soul Stew." I put them in the pot with their message, with their sound. I stir it up and you get Gedeon Luke and the People."[44]

GIRLS TO THE FRONT

As rock and roll artists have been advocates for economic and racial justice, it would seem likely they also would advance gender equality. Yet rock and roll often lagged over women's equality. Rock and roll has also always had much to do with sex and there is often a blurred line between sexual liberation and objectification. Glen Ballard, who had major hits with Alanis Morissette and mentored Katy Perry, says, "…largely, the way women are viewed in the mainstream of pop is pretty degraded from, say, even twenty years ago. I have a real hard time with that aspect of it, because I've been involved with some artists like Alanis, who fought against objectification and who were really kind of crusaders, for female equality especially. I mean, women certainly have come a long way, but it isn't all the way. Certainly her message was, 'a strong, empowered female voice.'"[45]

Respect

Early women artists such as Martha Reeves and the Vandellas, the Ronettes, Shangri-Las, the Shirelles, and the Supremes passed a baton for the rise of songs like "You Don't Own Me" by Leslie Gore hitting No. 2 in 1963, eventually moving forward to Janis Joplin and Grace Slick (of the Jefferson Airplane). In 1967, Aretha Franklin achieved a breakthrough with the Otis Redding-written song "Respect." Franklin writes: "It was the need of a nation, the need of the average man and woman in the street, the businessman, the mother, the fireman, the teacher—everyone wanted respect. It was also one of the battle cries of the civil rights movement. The song took on monumental significance. It became the 'Respect' women expected from men and men expected from women, the inherent right of all human beings."[46] Yet, of *Rolling Stone*'s 2011 list of top 500 songs, only one in the top 20 is performed by a woman—"Respect." Of the top 100 songs, only six were performed by women artists. *Rolling Stone* also has ranked the top 100 greatest guitar players of all time with just two women represented: Joni Mitchell (75) and Bonnie Raitt (89). Kate Pierson, of the B-52s, says:

> I guess what's considered rock and roll is just a reflection of how society sees male and female. Suffragettes were never taken seriously. What suffragettes went through? They were beaten and jailed. But it's still like a joke, 'women's lib, ha ha' and women and rock. As far as *Rolling Stone*, you know, the 'Gods of Rock' all 'have to be men.' It's very hard to see a woman in that role.[47]

In the United States, by 2014, women were on average earning 78 percent of what men were.[48] While also in 2014, the highest earning artist was a woman (Taylor Swift)—among the top 40 highest paid musicians there were only eight women (Taylor Swift, Beyoncé, Pink!, Rihanna, Celine Dion, Miranda Lambert, and Carrie Underwood).[49] Of course, as with all workplaces, harassment in the recording industry also exists. Liz Phair recalls: "When I first met the people at Capitol Records, a woman who worked their press mentioned that a guy I was going to meet at a radio station liked cute women—and maybe I could change my clothes, and if he pawed me not to worry about it. I was aghast. I felt like someone was trying to fuck me after a handshake."[50]

Sinéad O'Connor summarizes a dilemma for women professionals with the title of her 2014 record, *I'm Not Bossy, I'm the Boss*. O'Connor borrowed the title to publicize a social media campaign called "I'm Not Bossy." The marketing undermined the idea that women should not be assertive. O'Connor says: "...for me, it's personal. If that translates to anybody else and they find that inspiring of whatever, that's fantastic." She notes that power is the main culprit for artists as, "…male and female, we're not encouraged to feel like we're the boss, or expect to be treated like we're the boss. At the time of the 'Ban Bossy' campaign, I was experiencing not being heard and not being respected and not being dealt with really in the manner that I fucking should have because I'm the boss. And, that's quite a common thing." O'Connor says: "I am the kind of woman who had the shit kicked out of her for being assertive…and that campaign directly began to take back some power, as a boss, as a female boss. I began to just eliminate anyone in my employ who had dealt with me disrespectfully on the basis of I'm a female." She also made a calculated decision to use sex appeal, with irony, to get attention to the "I'm Not Bossy" record. She underwent a makeover and wore a wig for a photo shoot and video. "It's astonishing, but it certainly did the trick," she says: "It did draw attention to the album, and that was the only purpose of it, to be honest."[51] The video for the song "Take Me to Church" begins with O'Connor playing the role of the stereotypical sexy woman with a guitar. As the song reaches its crescendo, she pulls off the wig revealing her true, bald, self, which has been her long-standing trademark of beauty, and sings "I'm the only one I should adore."

Men and women are both victims of sexism, Sinéad O'Connor notes, as men can suffer equally under a system based on unequal power dynamics. "It's real important," she says, "to have a different type of feminism where it's not necessarily all about women." In that sense, O'Conner believes:

> I think it's important to talk about women, and the empowerment of women. But, we're forgetting actually the empowerment of men also. That, in all this talk of the empowerment of women, we don't understand that men are the subject of the same mental slavery as women are within the system which has been created for us all to live in. As long as we only focus on women, we're also disempowering men. Men, generally, are not the ones who have created the system under which we're all, if you like, burdened to some extent, so I think its real important to have a different kind of feminism eventually where its not necessarily all about women.[52]

O'Connor suggests that men have a place in the discussion of how the music industry sexualizes them:

> The males are also sexualized. It's not just the women. Nobody would want to take the sex out of rock and roll. Rock and roll wouldn't be rock and roll if not for sex. It's that it's 100% of the time—if it were only a quarter of the time, but what's happened is that it's 100% of the time now, so all the other voices are being silenced. I mean, you can't go to the other extreme, where you say,

'Nobody can take their tits out ever,' you know? It's just that the other voices have been silenced. But it is the males and the females.[53]

In the music industry, she notes, there is a great amount of "...sexualizing young men who look like children...and so do the females." In 2013, Sinéad O'Connor got into a "twitter war" with Miley Cyrus. Cyrus, who had been a child star on Disney television, was breaking out and declaring her artistic independence celebrating sexuality. The discourse was prompted by comparisons made between the video for Miley Cyrus's song "Wrecking Ball" with O'Connor's 1990 breakthrough "Nothing Compares 2 U." In "Wrecking Ball" Cyrus appears naked on a large ball and chain and makes sexually suggestive gestures to a hammer. O'Connor penned several open letters to Cyrus, warning that she should, "...not let the music business make a prostitute of you."[54]

Sex does sell, and women artists have participated in that—some embracing it out of liberation and confidence. Debbie Harry, with Blondie, sang great songs while highlighting platinum blonde hair and sex appeal. Terri Nunn of Berlin sang about the pleasures of sex in "Sex (I'm a...)." Madonna sang about feeling "Like a Virgin." Sheena Easton invited the listener to climb inside her "Sugar Walls." Her other 1984 hit "Strut," however, declared: "Strut down, pout, put it out, that's what you want from women—come on baby what you taking me for?" Cindy Lauper, also in 1984, had a major hit with "She Bop," an allusion to female masturbation. Debbie Harry reflects: "Being hot never hurts, and ...regardless of what I say about trying to be better at what I do, I rely on looks a lot. Women's calling cards, unfortunately, are based on their looks. As far as aging goes, it's rough." She also said: "How can one be a woman and not be a feminist?"[55] Today, Beyoncé is widely praised for singing of empowerment—even employing an all-women backing band to provide access for female musicians. Beyoncé says: "Let's face it, money gives men the power to run the show. It gives men the power to define value. They define what's sexy. And men define what's feminine. It's ridiculous."[56] The nexus between empowerment and celebrating femininity coexists in her song "****ing Flawless" which declares: "Feminist: the person who believes in the social, political, and economic equality of the sexes." Still, a disconnect between words and imagery prompted Annie Lennox to challenge Beyoncé in late 2014. Lennox said she was "feminism-lite," explaining: "The reason why I've commented is because I think that this overt sexuality thrust— literally— at particular audiences, when very often performers have a very, very young audience, like 7 years old, I find it disturbing and I think its exploitative. It's troubling. I'm coming from a perspective of a woman that's had children." "Twerking is not feminism," says Lennox, "that's what I'm referring to. It's not—it's not liberating, it's not empowering. It's a sexual thing that you're doing on a stage; it doesn't empower you. That's my feeling about it."[57]

The debate about feminism and the conflict with sexualization as expressed by popular music artists is not new. Madonna explained the role of sex in her artistic growth:

> People have always had that image about women. And while it might have seemed like I was behaving in a stereotypical way, at the same time, I was also masterminding it. I was in control of everything I was doing, and I think that when people realized that, it confused them. It's not like I was saying, 'Don't pay attention to the clothes—to the lingerie—I'm wearing.' Actually, the fact that I was wearing those clothes was meant to drive home the point that you can be sexy and strong at the same time. In a way, it was necessary to wear the clothes.[58]

Yet, the singer/songwriter Jewell, who recorded major hits in the 1990s, said: "I think you have to be young and cute and sexy for *MTV* to want to play you. Whereas men definitely don't have that problem—they can be fat and hairy. And that's great, but it isn't that way for women. As much as Madonna liberated women in music, I think she also set the standard for sex selling music."[59] Bonnie Raitt said in a 1994 interview that she never felt she was a victim of sexism: "I haven't been, but in 20 years there still aren't any women executives in the record business to speak of. Men are reviewers and radio people, and women are still in publicity and public relations."[60] Kathy Kane, who by 2016 had been working with Bonnie Raitt for over eighteen years, and her manager for the last ten, notes that in rock and roll management:

> I definitely had some interesting experiences being in my thirties and female, managing Bonnie, working on a project or doing events with people that were managing artists of her stature—it was not always easy…I don't really care anymore and I didn't really care then or else I wouldn't have stuck with it. But, there would be times when I would get a call from someone twenty years my senior and it can be intimidating. And at the same time, it's invigorating because I work with someone who would back me up because what I was doing was on her behalf so she'd be fully aware of the situation.' She and I have the same philosophy on it. It is her career and she's the one making decisions about it… My role is to advise, weigh the pros and cons of any given situation or opportunity, and help navigate the waters. Ultimately it's her career and her decisions to make. But, that wasn't always the way the music industry operated. I think it has been refreshing to have a relationship of this nature with transparency. And a healthy dynamic because the first person I go to when I have a problem to address or a situation to resolve is always to Bonnie and together we figure out how to solve it.[61]

Ultimately, artists such as Bonnie Raitt, Joni Mitchell, and Cass Elliott suc-ceeded on their merits as artists, versus their merits and for their looks. Or, as Adele (one of the most successful modern women singers) says: "I don't make music for eyes, I make music for ears."[62]

Priestesses of a New Kind of Power

In the mid-1970s, the Los Angeles-based group the Runaways—which included Joan Jett—pioneered room for all-women rock groups. Cherie Currie of the Runaways says that, "We never had to push the envelope," to which Joan Jett adds: "We just had to show up—it was everybody else that was freaked out."[63] When she first went solo, twenty-three labels initially turned her down. Today, Joan Jett says:

> I think a lot of people have the image of feminism, they think of tough angry women who hate men, that's an image that is sort of left over from the early '70s. That is not at all what feminism is today. You might be able to find some feminists who are like that. I think it's more about saying, 'Look, we're more than 50 percent of the population, we deserve equality and to be looked at as equals.' Yeah, I'm a feminist, I'm glad that word's out there.[64]

Joan Jett established one of the earliest independent music labels (and the first woman-owned), Blackheart Records. Today, Blackheart Records is managed by Carianne Brinkman, whose father, Kenny Laguna (himself a songwriter and producer), was Jett's cofounder of Blackheart. Brinkman says that the label serves as a legacy for Jett's rock and roll ethic: "I think having an ethos at all is not just about dollars and cents; it's about carrying on what Joan started and my father started—beyond Joan being a woman. But because she's a woman she could really tell artists that we sign that they really had to come up with their own way of selling music."[65] Joan Jett was also instrumental in bringing Kathleen Hanna and her band Bikini Kill to a national audience.

Kathleen Hanna and the Riot Grrrl movement had a revolutionary impact on women in music and sparked change in American society. As a college stu-dent in 1990, Kathleen Hanna launched a new wave of feminism by changing the space for women in punk rock—in particular, groping and abuse that was experienced when moshing. Kathleen Hanna inverted this dynamic by insist-ing at Bikini Kill shows that girls go to the front, that men should give them space. Sini Anderson, Hanna's film biographer, describes going to all-women punk shows in the early 1990s: "There's a type of freedom that happens when you know that you could be in a sweaty environment in a punk music show and you could have a tank top on and you could be totally thrashing and slamming and you're not going to get assaulted." She says that she could not experience the freedom that punk rock symbolized until she had that unique experience among women: "Oh, this is the freedom! Oh this is the radical-ness! Oh this is the feeling of empowerment and change. And then you would leave that show and it would be like, energy, to go into the world and try to create change. You can't walk away with the same empowerment if you don't have a feeling of freedom."[66]

With the advent of the Riot Grrrl movement issues like violence against women, eating disorders, equality for not only women—but also gays, lesbi-ans, and transgender people were moved from society's margins into main-stream discussion. This movement was reflected in the punk scene's use of hand-printed "zines"—artistic fan magazines that facilitated a community of women sharing their feelings and thoughts. Social networking was exploding underground, years before Facebook. One zine listed the reasons to form all-women rock bands. First, "...cuz its fun"; second, "...it's a good way to act out behaviors that are otherwise deemed 'inappropriate'"; third, "...this is a refutation of censorship and body fascism"; fourth, "...this can deny taboos that keep us enslaved, ID, don't talk about sex or rape or be sensitive or corny"; fifth, "...to serve as a role model for other girls"; sixth, "...to show boys other ways of doing things and that we have stuff to say."[67]

Riot Grrrl zines provided information to help girls suffering from body image disorders—bringing what had been hidden and shamed into the open, paving the way for treatment and healing. This movement also challenged men to accept responsibility for sexism and violence in society. As one Riot Grrrl zine wrote, it: "...is not our responsibility to explain how boys/men are being sexist anymore than it is our responsibility to 'prevent ourselves' from getting raped. It is their responsibility Not to Rape Us and it is their responsi-bility Not to be sexist."[68] Kathleen Hanna offered a positive image of lesbians in her song "Rebel Girl." Hanna had a message for men who think women "ask for it" if they are raped or abused because of how they look or dress, in "White Boy": She sang of sexual abuse in "Suck My Left One." Riot Grrrl drew strength from marginalization and the goals were transformational. In one zine, Bikini Kill's mission is made clear: "Bikini Kill is a band and this our little thing to give out at shows etc...AND THEN THERE'S THE REVOLUTION." The statement goes on: "This society isn't my society cuz this society hates women and I don't. This society doesn't want us girls to feel happy or powerful in any way...Being a sexy and powerful female is one of the most subversive projects of all. (we are the priestesses of a new kind of power oh yeah)."[69]

The drummer for Bikini Kill, Toby Vail, wrote in one zine that part of the mission was to reclaim iconic women figures who had been attacked and marginalized. She described how the myth that Yoko Ono was responsible for breaking up the Beatles perpetuated a hierarchy of power. "You see," Vail wrote, "part of the revolution (GIRL STYLE NOW) is about rescuing our true heroines from obscurity, or in Yoko's case, from disgrace." Vail writes:

> So part of what your boyfriend teaches you is that Yoko Ono broke up the Beatles. As his girlfriend, according to this, you could easily do the same thing to him and he has to be careful that this doesn't happen. In essence, besides being completely unfair to both you and Yoko this works in a way that makes you into the opposite of his band and it's the whole western duality thing about women and also about the forbidden fruit and all that bullshit and when you are made into the opposite of his band you are sort of being relegated to the audience and it takes that much longer for it to become a real idea that you could participate instead of just watch...But besides being the victim of this girlfriend-is-distraction thing Yoko was so fucking ahead of her time. I mean in a lot of ways she is the first punk rock singer ever. What she was doing was so completely unheard of and she needs to be recognized for what she did— provide a true alternative to the corporate bullshit John Lennon was faced with in the Beatles at that time. Not to mention that the Plastic Ono Band was totally subversive politically, in form and content...those early records are absolutely incredible and name any other Asian woman in rock...[70]

This image of the horrible woman who had destroyed the Beatles eventually became a truism. Except as Paul McCartney insists, it is not true. "She certainly didn't break the group up, the group was breaking up," McCartney said in 2012. McCartney added that great John Lennon songs would not have been written were it not for Yoko's influence: "I don't think he would have done that without Yoko, so I don't think you can blame her for anything."[71] Kate Pierson, of the B-52s (which were influenced by Ono's stylings), says of Yoko Ono: "She's become, like a cliché: 'Oh you're being a Yoko, you're hanging around'—she just got such a bad rap. John Lennon was influenced, and saw what a creative, amazing artist she was. But, the world couldn't see that because it was just so obscured by the cliché of what women were in rock."[72] Johanna Fatemen says: "Certain things live on in the cultural imagination in a real toxic way. John and Yoko are like Adam and Eve—it doesn't matter what really happened or how preposterous and unbelievable the myth is—it's part of what our culture has latched onto as this archetypal relationship: 'the evil woman who ruined everything with her weird sexuality and greed.'"[73]

Just as Bikini Kill was on the edge of becoming a breakthrough national act, they split up. Hanna's work grew broader appeal, however, with the dance band Le Tigre. There was also at the same time growing interest in festivals featuring women artists, importantly the Michigan Womyn's Festival and the Lilith Fair tour featuring only top women artists. Today, Dar Williams (who performed for both) reflects: "The truth is when I turn the radio on and listen to classic rock stations I'll still hear only one woman every 12 songs or so. And a lot of modern stations too, you might have something similar. But generally you have the modern rock stations where women are in rotation more than they were because that was a big thing [learned from Lilith Fair]; don't be afraid to play two women back to back on your station."[74] Joan Osborne (also on the original Lilith Fair lineup), said at the time: "I think this concert tour is really blowing apart the notion that you can't have more than one woman on the same bill—because for a long time promoters really didn't want that. They didn't want a woman opening for another woman because they thought it wasn't going to sell any tickets."[75] Still, Carianne Brinkman of Blackheart Records says that in 2015: "In radio, there's still 'rules' that extend to certain formats where you can't play two women in a row—it's pretty amazing."[76]

There was also money to be made by embracing the theme of women at the front of rock and roll. Sara McClachlan, who has sold over 40 million records in her career, organized the Lilith Fair tours. She said in 1997: "I certainly think that women in the music industry are becoming very powerful—we're selling a lot of records and I don't think that can be ignored anymore. So we're having a lot more power, and I think that's a good thing—it's going to make things a little more balanced."[77] In that sense, power can also be equated with money and influence. Yet, Sini Anderson says as corporate interests take root: "Bikini Kill becomes the Spice Girls…it all gets coopted."[78]

It is possible now to take for granted that there always were people like Joan Jett or tours featuring only women artists. Carianne Brinkman says: "Woman were not, I don't want to say 'permitted'—but it was not the common place for women to be able to have attitude. There was a lot of walls to break down. I think anytime that there's something that's viewed as different you have that." Brinkman notes that when Joan Jett came along in 1980, the feminist movement was pretty well advanced. She says it was not just that these early women rockers were disliked—people would "…throw things at them, call them whores—I think people still struggle with that."[79] Joan Jett recalls that in the early days: "I figured we wouldn't have a problem because, to me, I thought rock and roll was freedom. I was really wrong about that. People started calling us names, you know…everything you could call a woman—a whore, a dyke, you know? I really don't understand where the hatred came from."[80] There are more bands, highlighted now on Blackheart Records and others, that feature talented women for their music and ethos first and foremost. "I just wish we could see more of them," says Carianne Brinkman.[81]

Johanna Fateman, who cofounded Le Tigre with Kathleen Hanna, was an active artist in the Riot Grrrl movement. Now, Fateman says reflecting on teaching university students today:

> My students weren't particularly like *avante garde* radical kids—but there's an openness—that they discuss things like eating disorders, body image, sexual assault—all these things that I don't recall at all from my college days. People did talk about those things, but they were the real radicals, the real rebels. And there was the sense of breaking silence and breaking taboos and discussing things openly. I do see that there have been changes. I would only add, with some humility, that all of those things really—the real shift, I think in terms of this country began with the consciousness raising groups of the early '70s. Although Riot Grrrl conceived of itself as kind of a rebellion, or overturning second-wave feminist asthetics and values, really Riot Grrrl is completely indebted to these very basic strategies that the personal is political and that sharing personal experiences was really key to making a political argument that, though these things happen to us in isolation, they're not ours alone.[82]

Fateman says: "I recall a real hunger for that kind of representation. I remember going to shows to see bands just because there were women in the band—even just one woman. I liked supporting the band even though I might not have been very into the music. I would get into the music just because I felt hungry for that. I don't know if growing up today (one would) necessarily feel that same need to support just any woman doing music, but that's how I felt in the early '90s for sure." Perhaps it was the case that the Riot Grrrl movement got blunted by groups like the Spice Girls, but without significant content. Johanna Fateman says, "Those acts filled the desire for some kind of representation on some level, but the content was not the same." Fateman adds: "What's interesting to me is that the Riot Grrrl idea of sexual liberation and sexual freedom and sexual empowerment was really about not so much the Beyoncé model of sexual power, but this idea that—in critiquing mainstream cultural values about conventional beauty, there was room to develop more positive body images, more open ideas about what beauty and sexiness was. Also, expanded notions of queer sexuality, ageism, all of these things which you don't see in the mainstream idea. Sexual liberation, in the mainstream sense is not about any of those things."[83]

"No One Can Call You a Crazy Bitch"

In November 2014, almost fifty years after Aretha Franklin made history calling for respect, Taylor Swift made history as the first woman to replace

her own hit as the number one record in the United States—"Shake it Off"
and "Blank Space." Then, in December 2014, Swift added to Meghan
Trainor's run at number one on the American charts (with her song celebrating all kinds of body images—"All About That Bass" so that a woman
topped the charts for 19 weeks in a row—a record. Along the way, Swift
used her newfound influence: "Why is it mischievous, fun and sexy if a guy
has a string of lovers that he's cast aside, loved and left? Yet if a woman
dates three or four people in an eight-year period she is a serial dater and
it gives some 12-year-old the idea to call her a slut on the Internet? It's not
the same for boys, it just isn't and that's a fact."[84] She also said: "My hope
for the future, not just in the music industry, but in every young girl I meet,
is that they all realize their worth and ask for it."[85] She added: "In order for
us to have gender equality, we have to stop making it a girl fight, and we
have to stop being so interested in seeing girls try and tear each other down.
It has to be more about cheering each other on as women."[86] Swift has also
said: "You have to maintain everyone's respect, especially as a woman in a
position of power. It's terrible to be at that kind of disadvantage, where if
you yell, people will talk about you behind your back much more than if you
were a man. Because of those social injustices we face as women, you have
to make sure that no one can call you a crazy bitch."[87] In December 2014,
Taylor Swift was honored as *Billboard*'s "Woman of the Year" and accepted
the award at a *Billboard* conference on women in the music industry. At a
panel discussion of emerging and accomplished women rock and rollers,
leading the audience in singing "Happy Birthday"—as Swift was turning 25
years old—was Aretha Franklin.

EQUALITY ROCKS

Prominent artists such as Taylor Swift and Beyoncé are giving new life to dis-
cussions on feminism. Artists such as Gedeon Luke are calling on a generation to embrace peace and love and soul in the melting pot of America. Tom
Morello and many others have led the way, warning America of the dangers
of economic inequality. They, and many more like-minded artists, built on
rock and roll's power as a force for advancing equality. As Kathleen Hanna
put it: "I have women come up to me and say, 'You helped me through my
adolescence,' or 'You turned me on to women's studies and I'm a women's
studies major now' and that is so much more gratifying than having somebody be like, 'Woah that guitar lead you did in the third verse was so awesome.'"[88] When asked in 2013 what was the biggest challenge for women she
said: "…poverty, because if you're just trying to put food on the table, you're

not part of the conversation. Everybody else is making decisions for you. And in terms of the feminist movement, if we don't hear from a huge, huge, huge segment of the population, and they aren't involved in creating the feminist movement, then the feminist movement dies."[89] Moving ahead, the quest for equality also reflected an even bigger agenda for human rights—in the world and in America.

Chapter Four

Human Rights—In the Name of Love

GET UP, STAND UP

In December 1948, in the shadow of World War II and the Holocaust, the United Nations General Assembly approved the Universal Declaration on Human Rights. The signatories promised: "All human beings are born free and equal in dignity and rights. They are endowed with reason and conscience and should act towards one another in a spirit of brotherhood." The Universal Declaration specifies all people enjoy basic human rights, i.e. life, liberty, security of person; not to be held as a slave or to be subjected to torture or to cruel, inhuman or degrading treatment or punishment; and all are entitled to equal protection under the law. Enforcement of these principles has been difficult and the world continues to see considerable abuse. Still, there is less suffering because of sustained efforts of rock and roll artists advancing Bob Marley's call to "Get up, stand up—stand up for your rights."

AMNESTY INTERNATIONAL

Amnesty International advocates for human rights and organizes campaigns against unjust prison sentences and prisoner's rights, poverty, women's rights, and against the death penalty. In 1979 with the "Secret Policeman's Ball" and then in 1981 with the "Secret Policeman's Other Ball" Amnesty International built momentum for progress via rock and roll. Reflecting on his 1981 performance, Sting said: "Amnesty, in my opinion, is probably the most civilized and civilizing of human organizations. It uses the writing of letters or the commerce of ideas and opinion to change the world rather than a gun or an army or an airforce."[1]

"We Are the Free, Helping the Un-Free"

In 1986, Amnesty International organized the "Conspiracy of Hope" tour of six major American cities. Headlining artists included Bryan Adams, Peter Gabriel, the Neville Brothers, the Police, Lou Reed, and U2. The tour was run by legendary concert promoter Bill Graham and Jack Healey of Amnesty International. Bill Graham was a giant among promoters—and a Holocaust survivor. Graham and his sister Tolla were placed in a children's home in Germany following *Krystillnacht*, then sent to Paris, eventually walking to Marseilles. He was forced to leave his ill sister behind in Lyon when he was sent to America, never to see her again. Graham's biography states, arriving in New York City in September 1941: "His only possessions were his *yarmulke*, a prayer book, and some photographs of his parents and sisters."[2] These experiences gave a tough businessman an equally generous heart. Journalist Michael Goldberg wrote after Bill Graham's death in a helicopter crash in 1991: "Graham never seemed happier than when he was harnessing the tremendous power of rock and roll for the good of a cause."[3] Graham's engagement with Amnesty International was facilitated by its U.S. director, Jack Healey. Healey grew up Irish-Catholic in eastern Pennsylvania coal country and spent time as a Franciscan monk before becoming a human rights activist in the 1970s. He recalls: "I got all of that sense of justice and fair play and 'fight for your rights' from my mother. I said to her one day, I was 12 or 13, 'Mom when will I be a man?' and the quick answer was, and I remember it well: 'You'll be a man when you've learned to walk the highways and byways of life and you've learned to listen to the weeping and wailing of the poor. Then and only then, you'll be a man.'"[4] Jack Healey eventually went to work as a director of the Peace Corps in Lesotho in southern Africa. Inspired by a Bob Marley visit to South Africa, Healey recalls: "When I first got back as Director of Amnesty my first call, practically, was to see Bill Graham." In either late 1981 or early 1982, he says: "I went to see Bill, and I got into a battle with him...he was a battler. He essentially said, 'You get the talent, I'll do the show,' and I felt that was a contract and, that's all I needed." Healey says it took prodding to secure the commitment he wanted out of Bill Graham. But, he persisted because, "I knew he had it in his heart because of his background in Berlin and all that," adding: "He was spectacularly and singularly important to what I did."[5]

The 1986 Amnesty International tour was the first major multicity concert tour designed to raise consciousness, membership, and money in a sustained way. According to Jack Healey, "We had to make a 'prisoner of conscience' understood in the United States, what it meant. We had to explain the disappearance (of rights activists), what it meant to Latin America, and we had to explain to Americans that the death penalty was a human rights violation." "I'm not saying we're causal," Healey says: "I'm saying the good hearts who joined us—Sting set up the Brazillians, Bono set up a number of organizations, Peter Gabriel set up Witness later. You know, they all went and changed the world and furthered their involvement. Sting wrote 'They Dance Alone' for the women of Latin America. They're great artists and they went and continued their human rights activities to this day."[6] Healey also credits *MTV*: "I got eleven hours of *MTV* free. I asked for the advertising—Bob Pittman gave it to me" and A&M records: "Herb Alpert and Jerry Moss literally would leave their offices when I came to town. They'd give me their whole office staff—everybody." The tougher sell was within Amnesty International. "Half of them were against us," he recalls: "They thought we were trivializing human rights, the *New Republic* attacked me, there was a lot of negativity against us." Getting the artist's buy-in was less difficult. U2 were relatively easy to get because, as Healey notes, this was still early in their careers. He adds: "Sting agreed, we met him in his apartment in New York—that was easy. I asked him to reunite the Police. He said he would if I kept it a secret. We kept it a secret. Gabriel was recruited by Bono. Lou Reed was recruited by Bono."[7] Announcing the tour, Bryan Adams observed: "To think that all we have to do is fill in a postcard we might help somebody out far far away seems like a great concept. And, I think it's a concept that we can endorse because it's so simple. We are the free, helping the unfree." Eventually, Peter Gabriel had a capacity crowd at Giants Stadium in New Jersey singing "Biko"—of which he said: "This is a song, written for a man of peace. Who was working for his people. Was arrested. Tortured for many months and killed in jail in South Africa. This song is dedicated to all the people in South Africa who've just been imprisoned in the last weekend. And dedicated to all the people in jail that Amnesty's now working for—with the help of your postcards. Steven Biko!" The song ends with the entire stadium singing Biko! with fists held in the air for justice.

These tours also impacted how the various artists and participants viewed themselves. When during the 1988 "Human Rights Now" tour, Bruce Springsteen saw the 50,000 people at the Felicia soccer stadium in the Ivory Coast, he observed, "It was a stadium of entirely black faces." His sax player, Clarence Clemons, said to him: "Now you know what it feels like!" Springsteen recalls: "The band came off feeling like it was the first show we'd ever done. We had to go out and prove ourselves on just what we were doing that moment on stage." Guitarist Nils Lofgren remembers at a performance in Africa, "…there was a moat around the entire stadium…It ran through the dressing rooms and we started to complain about it. We realized it was going to get much worse because it was the friggin' bathroom. There were no toilets and people were pissing and dumping into the moat. It just turned into a river."[8] Jack Healey says that: "Our first tour explained to the United States that the death penalty was not an oddball thing—it was a human rights violation." Healey remembers that when the artists were asked in Los Angeles if they were for or against the death penalty, the thought was that they would be split on it—but, "...all of our artists agreed they were against the death penalty...that was the battle that we had to fight." He also points out: "Remember, I was operating in an era of Reagan and Bush. Reagan did not give a shit about human rights. There were 300,000 people killed in Central America in my time at Amnesty." Healey recalls, "My government didn't care about human rights. So we talked about Central America all the time. We talked of prisoners of conscience, we got a new vocabulary for Americans."[9]

Jack Healey once asked a young person working for Amnesty International what he did. The person responded he was the president of Amnesty International at his high school. Healey says: "I thought, 'Man, I did my job.'" His job was not money—it was to "...reach into America and convince our young people to get active about a positive value." Healey also notes regarding the global impact: "Don't forget, when Sting writes 'You Dance Alone', when he got to sing that song in a stadium where those people were killed? No stadium's ever been turned back to the people with death and disappearances and torture in it. That stadium is still used by the Chilean people because Sting re-baptized that place with his music." Over two days, in concert, he adds: "Chilean kids understood what happened to them the last sixteen years. Because the press had been so oppressed they didn't know what was happening in their country. And they discovered in one concert, two days, what happened to their country. That's worth doing. [If] just one thing my whole life, that's worth doing."[10]

The Rock and Roll of Human Rights Movements

Amnesty International and its rock and roll alliance were celebrated in November 1991 as *SPIN* Magazine devoted an issue to the Amnesty International concerts, inviting Jack Healey to be the guest editor. *SPIN* declared:

> If music has a gut reason, it's to free the human spirit. Rock'n'roll liberated a generation in America, Europe, and then much of the rest of the earth. It's still doing that. Music drives tyrants mad. Why? Because music unchains minds. Those minds then work to free bodies, communities, and, finally, nations. Amnesty International is the rock'n'roll of human rights movements—courageous, unrelenting, and effective.[11]

Jack Healey reflects on these achievements, saying: "You have to have a vision. I took over Amnesty when it had everybody above [age] forty, there were less than 35,000 members. I left with a half-million members, and our budget had gone to between twenty-one and twenty-five million." He adds: "I wanted to unite our young with them. That was my goal. Money wasn't important to me, never has been. It was always to hook up our young with their young, to get the free to work for the unfree," Healey concludes.[12]

THE IRISH CONNECTION

Ireland has long been a hotbed for artists championing human rights—in part a reflection of the nation's experience with the history of oppression and conflict in Northern Ireland, and idealism about what is possible in the world. Artists are also given a special place of respect in Ireland. Bob Gross, who performed on several tours through the country, says: "They treat you like gold over there if you are a musician. Music is such a part of the culture. Numerous times we'd find ourselves after the gig at somebody's house playing music until the sun came up. And not just us—them too—so many of them are great musicians."[13] Today, Dublin-based artist Damien Dempsey translates this in concert, bringing his audience into a sing-along.

Damien Dempsey, pictured in Dublin, Ireland. Photo by Graham Keogh, courtesy of John Reynolds.

He says: "…when I was a child, one of the big things I remember is the sing-song, people singing together in houses. There was no instruments, just—a few drinks. You go to someone's house, or it might be at the pub—the closing time at the pub—and people singing. It was magical, you know?"[14]

How Long—To Sing This Song?

Irish folk-oriented groups, like the Clancy Brothers and the Dubliners, long inspired international artists and listeners. Jack Healey reflects on his heritage: "In the history of my faith and of my nationality, music and poetry have always carried us. You know—'Fields of Athenry' and rebel songs. We fought the British with music and poetry."[15] In 1972, Paul McCartney offered "Give Ireland Back to the Irish." The song was banned from radio play in Britain, yet reached number 16 on British and number 22 on American charts. It also hit number 1 in Ireland.[16] John Lennon added his voice, also in 1972, with "Luck of the Irish." Proceeds from his song went to support civil rights defenses in North Ireland. In the late 1970s, a new generation of Irish embraced Bob Geldof and his Boomtown Rats while the Pogues brought an irreverent attitude toward authority while updating Irish folk traditions. They also found a nationalist song, "Streets of Sorrow/Birmingham Six," banned in the United Kingdom.

From these tributaries, U2 embarked on an entirely new sound. Driven by the steady beats of drummer Larry Mullen and bassist Adam Clayton, the unique guitar styling of the Edge, and the passionate vocals of Bono, U2 became one of rock's most successful bands. Exploding onto the global scene, U2 evoked experiences in Dublin to make universal statements. For example, in the early 1980s, visitors arriving at Dublin airport would likely see the Ballymun Flats—seven tall towers in northwest Dublin, each named after a revolutionary leader from the 1916 uprising. These public housing slums became dens of crime, prostitution, and poverty. Since torn down, in the 1980s this blight on the Dublin skyline was immortalized in U2's 1987 song "Running to Stand Still." In it, Bono tells of a woman in Ballymun who seeks change but cannot find a clear way out. Bono sings: "You've got to cry without weeping, talk without speaking—scream without raising your voice." In the end, the young girl takes to the needle and heroin—the "poison, from the poison stream"—leading to pained screams of "Hallelujah!" in live renditions.

U2's early concerts featured Bono on stage carrying a white flag singing "Sunday Bloody Sunday." Songs like "40" asked existential questions about peace and love: "How long to sing this song?" they asked, hoping that humanity would, "sing a new song." Of "40," Bono notes the song's longing for social progress came from the Bible: "I had thought of it as a nagging question, pulling at the hem of an invisible deity whose presence we glimpse only when we act in love. How long hunger? How long hatred? How long until creation grows up and the chaos of its precocious, hell-bent adolescence has been discarded? I thought it odd that the vocalizing of such questions could bring such comfort—to me, too."[17] Bono says, "...there aren't enough minutes in the day, or days in the year, for us to approach every abuse of human rights, and because in the end, that isn't our job anyway. Our own way of dealing with it is to try to get at what is essentially behind all abuse of human rights, to go to the heart of the problem, to the kernel rather than the husk."[18]

Bono and U2 inspired countless people to charitable giving and activism. In September 2000, Bono met with ultraconservative senator Jessie Helms (R-North Carolina) advocating for debt relief for developing countries. Political scientist Joshua Busby documents Bono saying that Helms wept when they spoke. Bono says, "I talked to him about the Biblical origin of the idea of Jubilee Year...He was genuinely moved by the story of the continent of Africa, and he said to me, 'America needs to do more.' I think he felt it as a burden on a spiritual level." Helms, in turn, said: "I was deeply impressed with him. He has depth that I didn't expect. He is led by the Lord to do something about the starving people in Africa."[19] Later, in 2006 alone, the One Campaign (cofounded by Bono to end global poverty and preventable disease) inspired 500,000 people to join in action related to the campaign.[20] By 2015, the campaign claimed 6 million people taking action—including helping secure $95 billion in debt relief for poor countries."[21] Joshua Busby concludes of Bono's influence: "Celebrities compensate for movement weakness by drawing attention to the cause, but when they get in the room to talk to decision-makers, they have to be well-briefed. Bono succeeded in part because of his personality, but also because of initially low expectations that he would know anything about the issue. He has raised the bar for competence, but in the strategic sense about how to appeal to policymakers and substantive knowledge."[22]

U2 also reflect a dichotomy as they are hugely successful artists making a lot of money, yet by 2010 their home country lay in the rubbles of economic ruin of the failed "Celtic Tiger"—as its banking system collapsed and its economic sovereignty was abandoned in favor of massive European Union and IMF bailouts. U2 had been singled out in Ireland for moving their publishing operation from there to the Netherlands in 2006, thus avoiding paying what amounted to a 42 percent tax in Ireland. This made good business sense because most of what U2 earned was from outside Ireland. The *Sunday Times* nonetheless reported in July 2010 that the top-earning artists working to escape the tax were costing the nation 30 million a year in lost revenue, with U2 accounting for most of that. Meanwhile, in 2009, Larry Mullen had complained wealthy people in

Ireland were being badly treated. Mullen concluded: "We have experienced [a situation] where coming in and out of the country at certain times is made more difficult than it should be—not only for us, but for a lot of wealthy people." He added: "... how can I tell people, how can I fly the Irish flag and tell people 'come to Ireland because it's great?'"[23] U2's image took a further hit when bassist Adam Clayton filed a lawsuit against his bank for allowing his personal assistant to withdraw over 4 million euro from his personal accounts over a five-year period. Clayton argued the Bank of Ireland should be responsible because he "couldn't be bothered" to keep an eye on his millions.[24] The Edge set out well intended in Malibu, California, to build an environmentally friendly estate on pristine seashore. Yet, local commissions concluded the project would harm unspoiled seaside. In 2011, after four years, the plan was rejected. The head of the coastal commission said: "This is one of the most environmentally devastating projects that I've seen in the 38-year history of the Coastal Commission."[25] Compounding things for the band, a 2009 study concluded: "U2's CO_2 emissions are reportedly the equivalent to the average annual waste produced by 6,500 British people, or the same as leaving a lightbulb running for 159,000 years."[26] Subsequently, U2 found ways to offset the carbon footprint.

Today artists like Damien Dempsey give voice to the continuing Irish experience. He says, "I think it's the scam of all scams. The ordinary Irish people are paying back all these billionaire gambling debts, is basically all they are. I always thought if you made an investment in something and you lost it, then you lost it. But these guys [bankers] are demanding their money back on poor people, and disadvantaged kids, and disabled people and pensioners. It's just disgusting. It's like their socializing the debts and privatizing the profits."[27] In terms of music, Dempsey says it's tough: "I think we're being bombarded purposely with the radio stations playing pop, at the moment. They're not letting real artists on to talk about what's going on." He says, if you want to hear a protest song on one of the big stations in Ireland: "It never happens." It's all, "...computer music now and they can throw all the X-Factor music at young children." The result, he says being, "...to keep the music stations clear of any protest music, I suppose, music that's talking about what's going on at the moment." Dempsey warned of the economic contradictions in the booming years of the Celtic Tiger as early as 2001. "It was crazy," Damien Dempsey says, "it was like we were under a spell or something, the people." "A lot of people," he notes, "say we lost our hospitality and we lost our friendliness. I could see that happening—people getting arrogant. People in competition with each other." He remembers at the time: "People were saying, 'What the fuck is wrong with you? Look at this asshole. He'll always be complaining.'" Yet, many were working on assembly lines, with no union, for multinational corporations, and, he says: "...a lot of employment you could see, but was a lot of bollocks, it could be gone tomorrow. The hospitals were in shit, the national schools were falling down—some people were saying, 'Where's all this Celtic Tiger going?' You could smell the rot during the Celtic Tiger, definitely."[28]

Sunday Bloody Sunday

U2 were crucial to shedding light on injustice on both sides of the Protestant and Catholic divide in Northern Ireland. U2 traveled the world singing "Sunday Bloody Sunday," reinforcing the point that violence was not the solution. What began as a human rights campaign for minority Catholics in Northern Ireland had evolved into one of the world's most intractable conflicts. The toll was heavy—with Protestant majority discrimination and paramilitary recrimination against minority Catholics and brutal terrorism by the Irish Republican Army against British targets. More than 3,700 people were killed in the violence. Had a similar conflict consumed the United States, the equivalent death toll would have been 600,000.[29] The majority of people in Ireland wanted peace, but the barriers were difficult to overcome. As Bono said in 1989: "…with problems like Belfast's in Northern Ireland, or racism in the Southern states here in America, you're dealing with entrenched communities. When you're dealing with illogical views, the hells that are just deeper, the answer is not argument, often. They're not problems of the intellect." He recalls a Protestant friend in Northern Ireland who witnessed a murder, was wanted for questioning, and had to leave the country for fear of being targeted. "He's a Protestant," Bono says, "and he told me, even though he married a Catholic and he's a very right-on man, when he hears rebel songs, the hairs on the back of his neck stand up! He can't help it! He told me he couldn't explain it, it was like it was in his genes."[30]

The Troubles came to a head for Ireland when (in November 1987) a group of Catholic paramilitary forces detonated a bomb killing eleven and injuring sixty-three civilians at a Remembrance Day celebration in Enniskillen. The brutal murder of pensioners and their supporters marching to remember Irish and British sacrifices in World War I resonated when U2 performed that night in the United States. On stage, Bono spoke of why people left Ireland, and how "…some [ran] from the Troubles in Northern Ireland—from the hatred of the H-Blocks, the torture—others from wild acts of terrorism like we had today in a town called Enniskillen, where eleven people lie dead, many more injured, on a Sunday Bloody Sunday." The song by that name followed. Halfway through, Bono addressed the audience:

> I've had enough of Irish Americans who haven't been back to their country in twenty or thirty years come up to me and talk about the resistance, the revolution

back home, and the glory of the revolution and the glory of dying for the revolution. Fuck the revolution! They don't talk about the glory of killing for the revolution. What's the glory in taking a man from his bed and gunning him down in front of his wife and his children? Where's the glory in that? Where's the glory in bombing a Remembrance Day parade of old-aged pensioners, their medals taken out and polished up for the day? Where's the glory in that? To leave them dying, or crippled for life, or dead under the rubble of a revolution that the majority of the people in my country don't want.[31]

Bono then sang—even screeched—with emotion, "No more! No more! No More!"

In 1998, a peace deal created a new governance model for Northern Ireland guaranteeing minority rights and power sharing. A key part of this process came on May 19, 1998, when U2 appeared at a free concert in Belfast, appealing to Protestants and Catholics to vote in a referendum favoring peace. John Hume and his counterpart David Trimble, who negotiated the peace deal, joined them on the stage. U2 appealed for a "Yes" vote singing "Stand By Me"—broadcast live on the *BBC*. One of David Trimble's associates said: "We waited at the side of the stage for David to walk on with John Hume. DT was looking ill at ease and quite nervous as we listened to the screams of the hundreds of teenagers and the ear-piercing music. This was more nerve-wracking for him than anything else he had done so far on the campaign. The handshake was very stage-managed, but at the same time quite moving as the two stood on either side of Bono."[32] The handshake moved "No" images off of the television and papers—replaced with a "Yes!" image and a U2 soundtrack. The "Yes" vote prevailed by 71 percent. U2 set the stage in their show, covering the Beatles—"Don't Let Me Down" with a segue into "Give Peace a Chance."

Fight the Real Enemy

Sinéad O'Connor is one of the world's most recognizable singers, for her exceptional vocal talents and her iconic shaved head. She hit big in 1990 with the Prince-written song "Nothing Compares 2 U." It ranks as *Rolling Stone*'s number 162 on their list of greatest 500 songs and on *Time* magazine's (unranked) list of top 100 songs. She was the first female artist to win MTV's video of the year award, received multiple Grammy nominations, and won a Grammy for best alternative performance in 1990. She also performed one of the most controversial human rights protests in modern history. When Sinéad O'Connor went on *Saturday Night Live* in October 1992, she ditched her planned material, instead singing Bob Marley's "War." As she concluded, O'Connor tore up a picture of Pope John Paul II declaring: "Fight the real enemy!" Sinéad O'Connor intended to bring attention to the very real, but then unpublicized, sexual abuse of children in the Catholic Church, especially in Ireland. But tens of millions of American viewers had no idea what to think other than that she had disrespected Catholics.

Engineers at *Saturday Night Live* refused to turn on the applause sign following her song, and *NBC* censored her performance in its West Coast broadcast. *Saturday Night Live* music director John Zonars said, "I think that was the classiest move in the whole history of television—not cueing applause."[33] The show's producer, Lorne Michaels, however, reflects: "I think it was the bravest possible thing she could do...To her the church symbolized everything that was bad about growing up in Ireland, and so she was making a strong political statement."[34] Still, the next week's guest, actor Joe Pesci said if it had been his show, "I would have given her such a smack."[35] Ironically, while Sinéad O'Connor was widely condemned, Joe Pesci (also a Catholic) was not—although he apparently justified violence against a woman. Madonna also went after Sinéad O'Connor, saying: "I think there is a better way to present her ideas rather than ripping up an image that means a lot to other people." However, John Pareles, a *New York Times* music critic, wrote: "After Madonna had herself gowned, harnessed, strapped down and fully stripped to promote her album *Erotica* and her book *Sex*, O'Connor stole the spotlight with one photograph of a fully clothed man. But the other vilification that descended on O'Connor showed she had struck a nerve."[36]

In the decades since, the scale of sexual abuse of children in the Catholic Church was exposed to the world. In Ireland, investigations found persistent patterns of abuse and failure by the church and government to address the problem. Sinéad O'Connor reflects on those times: "I was born in a very religious country. I grew up to believe there is a Holy Spirit. I've felt since I was a kid that's important and that to nurture that relationship is the most important thing." She says, of the *Saturday Night Live* experience: "When I did that, I was doing it for that spirit. I wasn't actually talking, really, to anybody but that spirit because what I could see was that spirit had been totally misrepresented." She adds: "I was so inspired by the Church and everything growing up even though I could see there was negative shit about it, you know? So, when I came across the information that all of this had gone on, that this abuse was going on—and that the families were being silenced—I was just appalled." "I can't be included," she says, "in the line of musicians who would have consciously set out to talk to power." "That's why I've done the fighting," O'Connor insists: "It has been for victims, it has been how I identify with it because I came from child abuse myself and because I love the God character, or whatever. But it's also been really a keeping of a contract that I made with the Holy Spirit."[37] O'Connor argues that justice has not been done, because those in the church have lied in the presence of God, and that means they disrespect the Holy Spirit. "It matters so much to me that I'm prepared to embarrass myself constantly over it." "So," she says, "that's what I was in the business of when I'm ripping up pictures or when I'm doing any of that shit, or I'm fighting the Church."[38]

To Sinéad O'Connor, the "...scandal in the church is the biggest crisis in Irish history." She says: "I wanted to be sure that when I meet my maker, that it can't be said that the artists didn't care." O'Connor offers reasoned advice to the church: "It needs transparency or it won't survive—it has to become a twenty-first century institution." She says: "The essence of the church is beautiful," and that she has "...stood for what I knew is real."[39] By 2011, the views for which Sinéad O'Connor had long been marginalized became widely understood as the Irish Taoiseach (Prime Minster) Enda Kenny addressed the Dail (parliament) and said that a new report on children's abuse: "...excavates the dysfunction, disconnection, elitism—the narcissism that dominate the culture of the Vatican to this day. The rape and torture of children were downplayed or 'managed' to uphold instead, the primacy of the institution, its power, standing and 'reputation.'"[40] Sinéad O'Connor offers advice for change. First, she argues, "There has to be a regime change. There has to be a right to get rid of people." This can be achieved by making promotion within the church hierarchy open to public scrutiny, "...like when someone is nominated for the U.S. Supreme Court." Second, she suggested that priests should be allowed to marry. That priests cannot marry is a relatively new development in the church's history. Third, she said, there must be, "women in the hierarchy—women should be priests."[41]

"A Real Danger"

David Crosby says of Sinéad O'Connor: "I didn't even like her music, but I would have walked right next to her because I thought she was extremely brave." "I admire her from afar," Crosby adds: "She's like Joan Baez to me."[42] Still, in today's Irish experience, something has been lost as a consequence of the Church scandal. Damien Dempsey observes: "I know the church was very bad for us, in what they were doing, with people going to industrial schools and all. Horrendous—the depth of the state in collusion had done to the ordinary people of Ireland." But, he adds: "Since all the scandals, a lot of kids don't believe in anything anymore—and that's a real danger." For many Irish, during the rush of the Celtic Tiger, it seemed that greed replaced God. The dilemma, Damien Dempsey believes, is: "I go into the church when there's nobody there. The Catholic churches are great. They're open all day. They go in there, they say a prayer to all the good and the love in the world—and I encourage people to do that." Dempsey observes: "We've always been spiritual people, the Celtic people. And to have that taken away from us; I think that's why you're seeing a lot of suicide and a lot of mental health problems." In terms of spirituality, he says, "…you don't have to put a name or a face on it, but don't say there's nothing there because nobody fucking knows—atheist or a Christian. For me, it's the future, because it's [about] nature—and looking after nature, and looking after the planet. I think if we look to the indigenous people of the Earth and their teachings, we need to get back to what they were doing with the Earth. Because if we go on the way we're going us so-called civilized people are going to destroy this place. And we'll be fucked."[43]

"UNLIKE PUTIN, WE'RE NOT CHICKENSHIT"

Founded in 2011 as a feminist collective, performance art punk rock group, Pussy Riot became known worldwide advocating for women's rights, gay and transgender rights, and against abuses of power by the state and church in Russia. Russia's president Vladimir Putin had consolidated political, economic, and media power into the hands of his regime and oligarchs. Pussy Riot challenged this with membership including up to a dozen people who were anonymous, covering their faces with balaclavas. The most well known of the group are Nadezhda Tolokonnikova and Maria Alyokhina, who had done extensive study of Western political and feminist theory as university students. They drew heavily on existential European philosophy—especially the work of Julia Kristeva, who focused on intertextual relationships and how structures of power can determine human relationships. By challenging existing structural paradigms with artistic expression, Pussy Riot sought to change contextual thinking in Russia.

In February 2012, members of the group performed a song protesting the relationship between state and church at the sacred Cathedral of Christ the Savior in Moscow. Three, including Tolokonnikova and Alyokhina, were arrested and sentenced to seven years in prison for hooliganism. The intertextual inversion of power was on Vladimir Putin's register when he was asked by *Russia Today* in September 2012 about the sentence. Putin responded: "Can you please translate the name of the band into Russian?" The interviewer, in English, said he did not know the translation. Putin responded, "Can you translate the first word into Russian? Or, maybe it would sound too obscene?" Putin then said: "I know you understand it perfectly well. You don't need to pretend you don't get it. It's just because these people made everyone say that band's name, too many times. It's obscene—but forget it. Here's what I would like to say. I've always felt the punishment should be proportionate to the offense." Putin said: "I would rather talk about the moral side of the story," Putin said, referencing that members of Pussy Riot had videographed themselves in an orgy:

> Of course, people are allowed to do whatever they want to do, as long as it's legal. But this kind of conduct in a public place should not go unnoticed by the authorities. Then, they uploaded video of that orgy on the Internet. You know, some fans of group sex say its better than one on one. Because like in any team, you don't need to hit the ball all the time. Again, it's O.K. to do what you like, privately. But I wouldn't be that certain about uploading your acts on the Internet. It could be the subject of legal assessment too.[44]

On their sentencing in summer 2012, Amnesty International declared: "Today's verdict is a travesty…The decision to find guilty Maria, Ekaterina and Nadezhda amid global outrage shows that the Russian authorities will stop at no end to suppress dissent and stifle civil society." The official added: "From the initial unjustified arrest, to the questionable trial, to this outrageous verdict and sentencing, each step in the case has been an affront to human rights…It's a bitter blow to freedom in Russia. Amnesty International will not allow these women to be silenced. They will not be forgotten."[45]

One of the first artists to champion Pussy Riot was Paul McCartney. McCartney said in August 2012 just before the women's sentencing: "I would like you to know that I very much hope the Russian authorities would support the principle of free speech for all their citizens and not feel that they have to punish you for your protest…Many people in the civilized world are allowed to voice their opinions and as long as they do not hurt anyone in doing so I believe this is the best way forward for all societies," said McCartney.[46] In May 2013, McCartney sent a handwritten open letter to Russian authorities calling for their release: "In the great tradition of fair-mindedness which the Russian people (many of whom are my friends) are famous for, I believe that you granting this request would send a very positive message to all the people who have followed this case."[47] Performing in August 2012 in Moscow, Madonna advocated for Pussy Riot: "I know that everyone in this auditorium, if you are here as my fan, feels they have the right to be free."[48] Also performing in Moscow, Red Hot Chili Pepper's Anthony Keidis and Flea gave letters of support to Tolokonnikova's husband. Keidis wore a Pussy Riot shirt on stage. While touring Russia, Sting said: "Dissent is a legitimate and essential right in any democracy and modern politicians must accept this fact with tolerance. A sense of proportion—and a sense of humor—is a sign of strength, not a sign of weakness."[49] Also in Moscow, Franz Ferdinand's Alex Kapranos introduced their song "This Fire" saying: "This is for the girls in Pussy Riot…"[It] is dedicated to all of those musicians that end up in jail for just saying what they think." In a subsequent tweet, he criticized Putin, calling him a dangerous hypocrite for jailing artists while claiming "to be a fan of John Lennon."[50] In July 2013, a coalition of over 100 artists signed on with Amnesty International declaring the: "...shockingly unjust trial and imprisonment has spread far and wide, especially among your fellow artists, musicians and citizens around the world."[51]

Using Pussy Riot's imprisonment as a rallying cry, Amnesty International shed light on growing human rights violations in Russia: "Today most Russian media remains under effective state control, except for some outlets with limited circulation. Primetime national television is regularly employed to smear government critics." Meanwhile, new laws give the government power to, "...blacklist and block websites publishing so called 'extremist' materials or anything considered harmful to public health, morals, or safety." New laws were, "...significantly increasing sanctions for peaceful rallies, meetings, demonstrations and marches. Political protest is the primary target of this crackdown, but growing civic activism also suffers." The organization brought international media attention to Russian, laws which had undermined rights of lesbian, gay, and trans-identity people. They identified many "prisoners of conscience" in Russia (including Pussy Riot) and highlighted an incident in Moscow's Bolotnaya Square in 2012 in which 650 protestors of Putin's inauguration were arrested. The report concluded: "Since Vladimir Putin's return to office in May 2012 Russian authorities have intensified their assault on basic freedoms and undermined rule of law."[52]

"Pussy Riot Is a Mask"

The third member imprisoned, Ekaterina Smutsevich, was released on probation in October 2012 based on evidence that she had not sung her part. However, the other two were sent into harsh prison conditions. In December 2013, to deflect criticism in advance of the winter Olympics in Sochi, Russia. Alyokhina and Tolokonnikova were released. Maria Alyokhina said: "You know, I was always free, because I felt free. It's very important to be free inside. The most important thing is to feel free. You have the right to choose. Becoming conscious of that fact delivers a person." She said that she wanted to turn down the amnesty because: "I don't need it. I'm not guilty, I'm not a criminal. I don't consider it mercy."[53] On release, Tolokonnikova described being fed lard covered with fur. They were given massive workloads but paid only between one and forty Euro a month. And punishments were collective—that is, if one woman made a mistake, all were made to suffer. Basic necessities (like going to the bathroom in filthy toilets) were difficult. Alyokhina said that prisoners were sent to the "cold cage" where they had insufficient clothing and were left without heat.[54] Tolonnikova recalls: "... prison guards do their best to make sure that not only is a prisoner physically isolated but also isolated from news coming from the outside world. The news that did reach me used to work like magic on me. Any support [while one is in prison] is always like a miracle. People whose conscience cannot be bought is probably the most precious thing in this world."[55] The women from Pussy Riot stressed their release was not a victory for average Russians. Tolokonnikova said: "I'm grateful to those who supported us month after month, in Russia and abroad. I owe my release to the people, and not to our political leadership. That's why we must continue to apply pressure."[56]

Once free, the two women from Pussy Riot were often media cast as celebrities, not dissidents. Their first Western television interview after their release was with an Irish broadcaster in Dublin while en route to the United States in early 2014. The interviewer, Brendan O'Connor, repeatedly referred to them as girls and did not understand why Masha was willing to kiss him on stage, but Nadya was not. Nadya's husband Peter, also their translator, said that Nadya tried to explain that to avoid feminist misunderstandings, Brendan O'Connor should kiss Peter as well. Brendan O'Connor asked if they felt that Madonna, who had claimed Pussy Riot to be a "fellow freedom fighter," was in fact a "freedom fighter"—the two laughed at the premise. The two had also met that day with Sinéad O'Connor—and they put the Madonna question in that context. Tolokonnikova said: "The difference between them and us is that, in their societies, America and Ireland, they are forced to deal with the institution of religion, whereas in Russia, we have other institutions which basically utilize religion to get what they need from politics, from government."[57]

While the women were imprisoned, Sinéad O'Connor shaved "Free Pussy Riot" onto her head as a gesture of solidarity. O'Connor reflects: "I guess I have mixed feeling about the whole Pussy Riot thing, to be honest. At the point at which they were offered a deal in which they said they were sorry, or they went to jail; as a parent, I would say that it was a mistake not to just say sorry and go off to your kid. I don't think anyone on either side was think-ing of the small children. I don't think those children should have suffered the loss of their mother for anyone's political belief." O'Connor says: "Had I been there, I would have asked: 'Look, just say your fucking sorry, whether you're sorry or not is beside the point.'" She adds: "You can't go bursting into a church where there's a congregation full possibly of old people, where they get the fright of their fucking lives, not least because you're wearing balaclavas in a country where balaclava is associated with terrorism." Still, she insisted: "It's not something you should go to jail for, that's fucking ridiculous."[58] Pussy Riot nonetheless showed: "We couldn't even imagine that the authorities would be so dumb that they would actually legitimize our influence by arresting us. Sure, they tried to intimidate us constantly. But unlike Putin, we're not chickenshit."[59]

In February 2014, the women of Pussy Riot ventured to the United States. On meeting them, legendary rocker Patti Smith said:

This kind of oppression and misunderstanding goes back to biblical times, taking young girls who have families and have hopes and dreams and putting them in prison for issuing a teenage prayer...One of the things they were saying to me was: 'Everyone wants us to speak to them but what are we supposed to say?' And I said, 'You should say that we are all you because of our beliefs, our belief system or trying to say something new, to speak out against our governments or even our churches, or corporations. We are all potentially in danger. Speak to a younger generation to think for themselves.'[60]

The women of Pussy Riot were infants when Kathleen Hanna was doing Bikini Kill, and they were children during the Le Tigre work that Hanna did with Johanna Fateman and JD Sampson. Yet, the lineage of the Riot Grrrl movement was on display with Pussy Riot. Johanna Fateman (who, with JD Sampson, wrote a song for the women from Pussy Riot to perform on the television show *House of Cards* in late 2014) says: "It's definitely—talk about postmodern—I kind of feel like they are the ultimate neo-Riot Grrrl conceptual band, working with the post-Riot Grrrl band." She adds, "They are pranksters, but they're absolutely intellectuals."[61] The Pussy Riot members were eagerly sought out by celebrities during their first visit to America. They were even introduced by Madonna at a concert held in Brooklyn, New York (as a fundraiser for Amnesty International). They also met with the American Ambassador to the United Nations, Samantha Power, who officially "thanked them for their advocacy, particularly on behalf of those in prison whose voices cannot be heard, and their extraordinary bravery and pledged the United States' commitment to continue to advocate strongly on behalf of human rights and freedom of assembly and speech."[62]

At home, the remaining members of Pussy Riot were less impressed. Writing in the *Guardian* in February 2014, the remaining anonymous members wrote: "We demand real justice: that is the complete abolition of the verdict and the recognition that the entire criminal case against Pussy Riot was illegitimate." They added: "It is no secret that Masha and Nadia are no longer members of the group, and will no longer take part in radical actionism. Now they are engaged in a new project, as institutionalised advocates of prisoners' rights." They insisted: "The apotheosis of this misunderstanding was the announcement by Amnesty International of Masha and Nadia's appearance in Barclays Center in New York as the first legal performance of Pussy Riot...The event showed a man in a balaclava with an electric guitar, under the name Pussy Riot, while the organizers smartly called for people to buy expensive tickets. All of this is an extreme contradiction of the very principles of the Pussy Riot collective: we are an all-female separatist collective—no man can represent us either on a poster or in reality. We are anti-capitalist—we charge no fees for people to view our artwork, all our videos are distributed freely on the web, the spectators at our performances are spontaneous passersby, and we never sell tickets to our 'shows.'" They noted that: "We are anonymous because we act against any personality cult, against hierarchies implied by appearance, age and other visible social attributes. We cover our heads because we oppose the very idea of using female faces as a trademark for promoting any sort of goods or services." The remaining anonymous members concluded: "Since Nadia and Masha have chosen not to be with us, please respect their choice. Remember, we are no longer Nadia and Masha. They are no longer Pussy Riot."[63]

"Sometimes It's Hard to Show People Something New"

Back in Russia, Tolokonnikova says "a big apathy" had grown over the protest movement. "Now," she says, "the opposition movement is like a funeral…It's a ghost. Nobody smiles."[64] In a quickly staged performance outside the Sochi Olympics in early 2014, they were beaten by Cossacks with whips. Later in the year, they were assaulted in a McDonalds as blue paint was thrown at them. Meanwhile, Masha Alyokhina said about the international audiences they interacted with: "They want to listen to what they already know. And actually sometimes it's hard to show people something new, if this new thing doesn't have something bright or remarkable, something you can remember very fast." Moreover, the cases they sought to highlight as major human rights abuses did not involve celebrities, she says: "It's just common people—not, like, stars, or pretty women, or something—and they have already been in jail for two years, and nobody knows about it."[65]

DAMN RIGHT I SUPPORT IT

Dusty Springfield, famous for the hit "Son of a Preacher Man," was one of the first major rock and roll stars to hint at being gay or lesbian. In 1971, she said: "I couldn't stand to be thought of as a big butch lady. But I know that I'm as perfectly capable of being swayed by a girl as by a boy."[66] Later that decade, she and her partner were married in a private wedding ceremony in California—an act not recognized by the law. Also in the early 1970s, artists like David Bowie often appeared androgynous. An early breakthrough came with Jobriath, who was the first openly gay man to be signed by a major record label. Tragically, he died of HIV/AIDS in 1983. Two years later, Ricky Wilson, the B-52's guitarist, also died of HIV/AIDS—shocking the world that was only just beginning to understand the crisis. Kate Pierson remembers:

> Ricky died pretty early on in the sort of ravaging period of the AIDs disease and we weren't even realizing Ricky was sick. Cindy [Wilson, Ricky's sister and bandmate] didn't know and Ricky was a very very private person and didn't want anybody to be hovering over him. So really it was a complete shock. We kind of knew, sort of near the end, that he was ill. But he kept denying it. In any case, it was a total devastating shock and we didn't think we could go on. And for a while there, a decision was made not to say anything because of his family. It turned out, for maybe a year we were deniers in a way."[67]

The band regrouped, eventually to record their biggest hits, and became AIDS activists. By the 1980s, artists like Madonna embraced and celebrated gay culture and "out" artists like Melissa Etheridge advanced cultural acceptance. Some artists took longer to declare their sexuality—like R.E.M.'s Michael Stipe or Elton John—but by the time it was publically acknowledged, they were long accepted. Others, like Freddy Mercury of Queen, became iconic figures in the gay community—with Mercury tragically lost to HIV/AIDS in 1991. By 2014 times had changed. Macklemore and Ryan Lewis won a Grammy for their song "Same Love" celebrating marriage equality. While they performed "Same Love" at the Grammys, Queen Latifa presided over a mixed gay and straight marriage ceremony. A sea change culminated in a July 2015 Supreme Court ruling making a marriage license a right for all Americans.

"Gay Marriage Is Punk Rock"

Elton John was widely understood to be gay but did not come out until 1988. In a 1976 interview with *Rolling Stone*, he hinted: "There's nothing wrong with going to bed with somebody of your own sex. I think everybody's bisexual to a certain degree."[68] When asked why he had not come out sooner, he said he figured most people knew. "I've been waiting for people to ask me this. It's not exactly a secret. I live with my manager. I'm openly gay outside. I don't have a girlfriend...I just thought it was common knowledge." He said he did not think it would hurt his career, but it did: "In America, people burned my records for a second and radio stations didn't play me."[69] For artists to "come out" in the 1980s was difficult as HIV/AIDS was creating a major scare and gays and lesbians were often stigmatized and marginalized. Some religious conservatives maintained that being gay or lesbian is a lifestyle choice and antigay sentiment could be wielded as a powerful political tool in many conservative circles. With time, however, artists helped to spark a gradual but certain shift in attitudes. In the 1990s, Melissa Etheridge "came out" as a lesbian at the first gay and lesbian inaugural ball, which was held after Bill Clinton was sworn in as president in January 1993. Almost two decades later, Henry Rollins, a prominent punk rocker declared: "Gay Marriage is Punk Rock…When we all got into punk rock, we learned we had all kinds of people in our scene; gay was part of it. I thought it was really cool. We were a crew of social misfits of all stripes and it was music that brought us together." Writing after Washington State legalized marriage equality in 2012, Rollins argued: "I am elated as much as I am frustrated by why this country refuses to wake up and smell the 14th Amendment of the Constitution."[70] Dar Williams reflects on groups like the Westboro Baptist Church, which advances a bigoted view toward gays and lesbians, saying: "If you can't share music, side by side, it's hard to march side by side. So now I do 'Somewhere Over the Rainbow' and I talk about how that's what we should sing every time the Westboro Baptist Church shows up. We should serenade them. Obviously they're a bunch of angry, frustrated, terrified people. So why not serenade them and say, 'Come over the rainbow with me?'"[71]

During the 1990s, a ban on gays and lesbians serving in the American armed forces became a significant issue as Bill Clinton instituted a compromise—"don't ask, don't tell." It meant that the government would not ask if one was gay, and it would not be reported. This, however, made it difficult for harassed or abused gay or lesbian soldiers to report to their superiors. It also forced soldiers to break the oath of integrity that the military command structure requires. Reflecting major changes in social attitudes, Chairman of the Joint Chiefs of Staff, Adm. Michael Mullen, said in Senate testimony in 2010: "I cannot escape being troubled in the fact that we have in place a policy that forces young men and women to lie about who they are in order to defend their fellow citizens."[72] Christine Martucci, the Jersey Shore rocker, is lesbian and married. And, Martucci served for nine years in the U.S. Army during the "don't ask, don't tell" experiment. She recalls: "Honor, duty, country—everything. How can you be honorable when you have to lie about who you are?" Martucci explains:

> Growing up, I always knew I was gay. But in those times you didn't discuss it. It was easy to live a double life, because if you did dare come out you were met with major hate and opposition from your own flesh and blood. So when I decided to join the military it was pretty much to have some sort of direction or new family. When they asked me if I was a homosexual—they did back then when you sign up—I of course lied and said no. There was a part of me, a very small part, that stung a bit when I lied. But for the most part lying about who I am was normal. I didn't think about gays or lesbians in the military, to me that was secondary.[73]

She adds: "I didn't see it was being dishonest to my unit or my country. I saw it as a woman and a lesbian that I am willing to give my country my life—'I earned my right to be here,' I never felt less of a person or soldier, because when it was time to do my job I did it well." "There was no point early on in my career that it affected me, but as the years passed it got harder," she says:

> The constant pressure of being someone you are not was starting to wear thin. Not only did I have a major responsibility at a young age, but in my spare time I was trying to be a rock star. Now *three* different lives or masks I wore. Holy cow, talk about a major mind fuck. You can only be someone else for so long until something has to give and my brain just couldn't take it anymore. Depression was my new friend. Anger turned inward; anger at myself, my life, and not being who I truly was. One day I was out on the shooting range, the depression was sinking into every waking moment of my life. I locked and loaded my rifle, and stood there ready to just blow my head off. I am not sure why I didn't do it. I think someone snapped me out of it. It was the first of many suicide thoughts and later actual attempts. I think of it as a pressure cooker, with no release, something has to give.[74]

Martucci reflects on her journey, which symbolized that of so many others, concluding: "The respect you get from your fellow soldiers is earned; you earn it not by the color of your skin or your sexuality. A soldiers' respect comes from character and bravery, and goodness to himself/herself and his unit. You earn respect by your actions not by who you sleep with. A soldier can be as gay as he wants. His sexuality is not in play when there is a fire fight, when lives are on the line. Because, quite frankly, the last thing you are thinking about in a fire fight is if the person next to you is gay. You just are hoping they got your back. That is respect, that is duty, that is honor."[75]

Firework

Jann Wenner credits Madonna for using music and art to generate better understanding of gays and lesbians:

> I mean, she's not overtly political in the sense of partisan politics or big issues, but that stance of social and sexual liberation and empowerment for women was really critical. I mean, all these girls like Katy Perry and all that, they all derive straight from that. Well before Lady Gaga was running around all doing her stuff—and talking about 'it's O.K. to be gay,' or whatever—'be yourself, was born that way.' Madonna was doing all that. Less explicitly, but that was her thing.[76]

By 2011, songs like Lady Gaga's hit "Born this Way" challenged society to think harder. Lady Gaga says: "I want it to be an attack, an assault on the issue because I think, especially in today's music, everything gets kind of washy sometimes and the message gets hidden in the lyrical play."[77] "Born this Way" was the first number one hit to reference transgendered issues. Other artists were also pushing the envelop—with Katy Perry hitting big in 2010 with the song "Firework" (one of the highest-grossing singles in music history) as an anthem of empowerment, self-confidence—and a video including men romantically kissing.

Katy Perry was earlier caught in controversy with her 2008 song "Ur So Gay." It was remarkable for using negative gay stereotypes to make fun of a heterosexual person. Yet, singing about these things was a big step for Perry who was raised by evangelical Christian parents. She explains: "I came from a very strict household, where any of that taboo stuff was wrong. I don't say I hate where I came from, I love my parents and was happy to…have that opportunity to grow, but I came from a strict, suppressed household where that was wrong."[78] "Ur So Gay" appeared on Katy Perry's 2008 breakthrough record *One of the Boys*, which also included the hit "I Kissed a Girl." The song inserted bisexual feelings into mainstream culture. Perry says: "It was a bit radical to sing about bisexuality, but it was a topic that was on the tip of everybody's tongue…And even though it was 'I kissed a girl, and I liked it, and that's what I like to do sometimes'…saying it with a wink. It may be a fun little pop song, but sometimes fun little pop songs most clearly express the zeitgeist."[79] The song was not universally acclaimed. Jane Czyzelska, of the magazine *Diva*, said: "Perhaps she doesn't know any gay people who have suffered verbal or physical abuse."[80] Peter Tatchell, an advocate for gay and lesbian equality, said:

> They're not serious homophobic (lyrics) but they can be read as implicitly demeaning gay people. I am sure Katy would get a critical reception if she expressed comparable sentiments in a song called 'Ur so black, Jewish or disabled.' Should there be different standards for lyrics about gay issues, as opposed to race and disability issues? I don't think so. Having said this, the homophobia of some reggae, rap and ragga music is far worse. Some of these songs explicitly include the murder of lesbians and gays.[81]

The song featured a scantily clad Katy Perry and, at least for some critics, objectified women. Kathleen Hanna was critical, saying: "I mean, is it really that different when it's a skinny white woman in a bathing suit singing these songs?" Hanna added: "'I Kissed a Girl' was just straight up offensive. The whole thing is like, I kissed a girl so my boyfriend could masturbate about it later. It's disgusting. It's exactly every male fantasy of fake lesbian porn."[82]

Katy Perry's transition from a child of conservative Christian believers to an advocate of equality for gays and lesbians nevertheless reflected major cultural change in America. "Really, generally, I was never allowed to associate with anybody that wasn't Christian," she says: "So I was kind of trapped in a bubble and then it finally burst years later, and now I think 90 percent of everyone I work with, from my assistant to two out of three of my managers, is either gay or lesbian. It's been an incredible journey of acceptance and tolerance." She adds, "I think you can be in love without walking down the aisle, or you can walk down the aisle and be in love, but everybody deserves that choice and I think that equality is very important."[83] Glen Ballard, who discovered Perry, says: " 'I Kissed a Girl'—Go Katy! I love what Katy does. I mean, she's so smart. She is so smart, believe me. She knows what she's doing and it's all coming from a place of love with her. She's just a very modern person with an old-fashioned heart. I can tell you that. So I couldn't be more proud of her. When I signed Katy to my label in 2001-2002, it was talent man. She came in and played acoustic guitar, sang a song, I went, 'Yeah! OK!' She had done her homework. She'd been out on the Christian music circuit, she'd done hundreds of gigs. This is what it really means to be an artist, and a committed artist."[84]

High-profile artistic advocacy has helped advance the gay, lesbian, and transgender community by amplifying the movement's issues. Kate Pierson recalls:

> When we became involved in AIDS activism, we gave so many interviews, we did benefits. We talked about it in every interview. So it can't help but have an effect. I mean, I can't really gauge the effect, but it had to have an effect. All these bands and all these people who people admire and look up to are talking and speaking about this.[85]

David Crosby explains how those who take such risks remain transformational. Hip-hop artist Macklemore, Crosby says, is a "game changer":

> I dismissed all rap and hip-hop as being junk—posers out there. Nothing. What I'm saying is, there's a full paradigm shift in Macklemore. My son brought that to me and said, 'You know, when you dismiss all that rap and hip hop, have you ever listened to Macklemore?' I said, 'No.' He said, 'Oh—try this.' He put on 'Same Love.' I said, 'Wait a sec'…'Same Love …Macklemore. Holy fuck, he did say that. Motherfucker.' And I grabbed the lyrics. I have to re-think my whole thing.[86]

Crosby reflects: 'This is evidence. This isn't conjecture. This is meat on the table. This guy is thinking. And he's thinking about stuff that matters. I cannot and will not deny that. I have to take that seriously.' He's not the only one, but he's the one that everybody noticed. And, they gave him a Grammy. That's a fucking miracle. The Grammys usually go to posers."[87]

"No freedom 'til we're equal. Damned right I support it!" sang Macklemore in "Same Love." Macklemore (Ben Haggerty) says: "I knew I wanted to write a song about gay rights, about marriage equality, and about homophobia in hip-hop, but I didn't know how to do it…I tried, at first, writing from the perspective of a gay, bullied kid. That's what sparked the song in the first place: reading the story of a 13-year-old who committed suicide."[88] The song became a reflection on his identity experiences and on the life of his gay uncle. "Same Love" links gay rights to human rights and notes that all lose their freedom when some are not equal. A certificate of marriage, Macklemore noted, is not going to solve it all—"but it's a good way to start." Charlie Joughlin of the Human Rights Campaign observed: "The fact that a song solely dedicated to the message of marriage equality is climbing the charts and quickly becoming a popular song across the country is a big deal… It's indicative of a changing attitude."[89]

"I Don't Think Most People Are Haters"

America settled the question of marriage equality in June 2015 when the U.S. Supreme Court ended marriage discrimination by guaranteeing equal access. The American conversation also moved forward to transgender rights. Concurrently, Kate Pierson launched her first solo record with a single "Mister/ Sister" in support of transgender people. Surprisingly, Pierson was criticized within the transgender community for advancing misconceptions.[90] This was surprising as Pierson is a long-standing ally of the transgender movement—with the B-52s including iconic transgender television personality Ru Paul in their path-breaking video to "Love Shack" from 1989. Pierson says: "Yes, a non-trans person can't be or feel what a trans person feels. But who can feel what another person can feel? I don't think beyond what any individual can know of another individual, it's just important that everyone—the more voices that come in, and the more they're heard. What I heard of the criticism of 'Mister/Sister' was more that people latched onto that as a way to give voice to their frustration." Pierson says: "There could be a lot of infighting and that infighting is what can really hurt the voice. The more force you can get behind it, obviously the better, and people kept saying about this dialogue with 'Mister/Sister': 'Oh, why are you criticizing someone who's for you, trying to help.' So focus on people who don't understand." The news is good, says Pierson: "I think the trans-movement is sort of 'out.' So people are beginning to understand more. I think that the younger generation, and people in general, want to understand. They want to be educated. They're sympathetic. I don't think most people are haters."[91]

LEGALIZE IT

Rock and roll has a complicated history with drugs. It is impossible to ignore the creative impact that mind-altering substances have had on rock and roll.

At the same time, drug and alcohol abuse took the lives of many great artists and wrecked many more. Drugs were also seen by right-wing political and religious leaders as moral failings, and a "war on drugs"—targeting the American people—was launched under President Ronald Reagan in the 1980s. Little thought, however, was given at the time to the relative harmless nature of marijuana compared to legal drugs like alcohol, prescription pain killers, and the ravages of cocaine, heroin, and other seriously dangerous products. By 2016, however, twenty-five states had some form of legalized marijuana—a drug with medicinal benefits and whose recreational use is considerably less dangerous or addictive than alcohol. Colorado, Washington State, Oregon, Alaska and the District of Columbia—legalized its recreational use and more were coming. As with marriage equality, a sea change among the American public was moving faster than politicians could handle—but which rock and rollers have long understood.

Everybody Must Get Stoned

Elvis Presley was apparently an abuser of legal prescription drugs. The Beatles famously used "uppers" to stay awake during all-night gigs in their early years. Bob Dylan scored a major hit in 1966 with "Rainy Day Women" with its chorus that "everybody must get stoned." Dylan introduced the Beatles to marijuana, which they consumed heavily and with major effect on their musical evolution. Meanwhile, LSD revolutionized artistic and social morays. Bob Weir of the Grateful Dead, however, also notes the perils: "…if you're reasonably well-informed that heroin's a very risky proposition, that cocaine is a very risky proposition. Marijuana, for instance, is not quite so risky—but I know guys who are thoroughly addicted to marijuana. Alcohol, of course tobacco, are very risky propositions." Weir survived losing close friends—not only Jerry Garcia—to drugs: "It's a lot of faces. I was close to a lot of folks. I was good friends with Jimi Hendrix, I was good friends with Janis Joplin. Jerry and I were tighter than that. And you know, they're not here anymore." Bob Weir also notes: "…if you just look at the cold, hard facts, we can't afford to be spending our money having our law enforcement chase people who are arbitrarily criminals because the law states that they are criminals—where are the victims? None. But O.K., well, '…let's bust 'em and put 'em in jail anyway 'cause the law clearly states that that's what we're supposed to do.' It costs us a lot of money. It costs us a lot of money to pursue them. It costs us a lot of money to incarcerate them. If you, on the other hand, legalize it and tax it—you bring money in. It can be spent on teaching kids, for instance, the perils of drugs."[92]

Rock and rollers long associated, fair or unfair, with drug use could not push this issue on their own—other popular responses helped consolidate what many artists had long known—that marijuana should be legalized. In calling for ending its prohibition in 2014, the *New York Times* editorialized:

> There were 658,000 arrests for marijuana possession in 2012, according to F.B.I. figures, compared with 256,000 for cocaine, heroin and their derivatives. Even worse, the result is racist, falling disproportionately on young black men, ruining their lives and creating new generations of career criminals. There is honest debate among scientists about the health effects of marijuana, but we believe that the evidence is overwhelming that addiction and dependence are relatively minor problems, especially compared with alcohol and tobacco. Moderate use of marijuana does not appear to pose a risk for otherwise healthy adults.[93]

David Crosby, meanwhile, knows as much about the dangers and ravages of drugs as anyone can and survive. He and his loved ones suffered from his over-a-decade-long addiction to hard drugs. Crosby eventually spent time in prison on a weapons charge. He says this limits his influence: "Who are you to stand in judgement? I'm certainly not in a place where I can. I've made more mistakes than five of you. So I can't. I can't stand there and [go] like: 'Furthermore!' I was a junkie for God's sake. I did a year in prison in Texas. I've got a record as long as your arm."[94] Even before his deep dive into addiction, David Crosby noted the limits of what drugs could offer. LSD, for example, could open minds to a wide range of thinking and perspectives. However, Crosby says of Jimi Hendrix's ability to perform while on acid, "I couldn't do that. I tried it once in the Byrds and the guitar was three feet thick and made out of rubber. I was playing a really great song. The band was playing another, different, really great song." He takes a clear-eyed view on the heroin crisis in the United States: "Here's my idea: Go in and wipe it out. Tell them to grow coffee. That's my idea for cocaine too. We know where it's all grown, we know what soil, and what altitude, and what countries—we know exactly where it is." He argues for a crop substitution plan—offer to buy coffee from cocaine growers at the same rate of price they would have gotten for growing the drug. "You'll make as much money as you make now," Crosby says regarding the growers, "and we won't have cocaine. And the cocaine cartels will not have cocaine." He adds that there would be an implication: "…if you grow it again next year, we're going to come in and people are going to get hurt because we're going to napalm it."[95]

David Crosby is adamant there is no equating these drugs with marijuana. "That's one of the biggest mistakes they ever made was trying to lump them all together," he says. When presented with the idea of legalizing marijuana and diverting the profits away from violent criminals into education and treatment, Crosby responds, "You're singing my song." The problem with some of the legalization efforts, he adds, is that it's: "…because they've seen that there's money and that's the only reason they're doing the right thing. The voters made it happen. But the voters made it happen because it was allowed to happen because there was money there so that you could get it on the ballot. What would get it on the ballot? Let me think—if somebody was going to make money from it." Crosby adds: "Better people be smoking pot than drinking—drinking's poison. The poison that really pisses me off is the cigarette people. They know they're killing you. They know perfectly well that it gives you cancer—that the chemicals that they're putting in the cigarette are giving you cancer. They know all the numbers as well as we do. And they're doing it anyway and they should be charged with murder—first degree, premeditated." Crosby says: "Follow the money. The people who've been paying to keep pot illegal—the tobacco companies don't want it. Seagram's, Anheuser-Bush, Jack Daniel's—they want—the booze people, there's hardly anybody in this country that's got that much money—Coors? We're talking serious bucks."[96]

In 1969, only 12 percent of the American public supported marijuana legalization, while 84 percent were opposed. In 2013, that had inverted with 58 percent favoring legalization and 39 percent opposing.[97] In fact, the only age group of Americans opposed to legalization was those over age 65. By 2015, marijuana was legal in several states and medical marijuana legal in a majority of states. But for the rest of the country, that level of freedom did not exist—and thus a broad coalition of activists, including rock and rollers, kept the pressure on. Some artists like Snoop Dog campaigned for legalization. Melissa Etheridge said: "As a cancer survivor, I know the ravages of a serious illness, and patients who are suffering deserve access to a medication that can provide them relief."[98] Carlos Santana appealed directly to Barack Obama to: "…legalize marijuana, and take all that money and invest it in teachers and education…and you will see a transformation of America."[99] John Legend said: "I think we need to legalize marijuana…There's no good reason to continue prohibition, and we need to consider ending prohibition in general. I don't know if prohibition has ever been an effective way of getting people not to use banned substances…They find a way to use them, criminals find a way to sell them, and a lot of people get killed."[100] Sting went further, writing the drug war offered: "…pretext to lock people in prison for exorbitant lengths of time—people whose 'crimes' never hurt another human being, people who already lived at the margins of society, whose voices were the faintest and whose power was the least. Civil liberties have been trampled. Law enforcement has been militarized. Literally hundreds of billions of dollars—dollars denied to urgent problems ranging from poverty to pollution—have been spent. People who do need help with drugs have been treated as criminals instead."[101]

The Joint

Few artists can top the impact of country music legend Willy Nelson—who is frequently photographed with large amounts of marijuana and campaigns nationally for its benefits. Nelson said (after performing at the White House) in November 2014 about legalization: "I think [it will happen] once people have realized...how much money there is in it...Colorado and some of those other states have shown the people already that it's a very lucrative business. So I think it won't take long before the rest of the states come around." He added: "Well, I really think stress is the cause of a lot of our problems, and I really believe that the best medicine for stress is pot. Yeah, I think it would make us get along better all over the world."[102] Willie Nelson also has a famous son. Lukas Nelson emerged as a rollicking guitar player and a top-line songwriter with his band Promise of the Real in 2008. His fans include Neil Young who recorded and toured with Lukas and his brother Micah in 2015. Lukas Nelson's 2012 song "The Joint" includes the lyric: "I'm gonna smoke my joint all night—and feel alive." His song connected millions of people who have long wanted to say the same thing but perhaps could not because of their job or social position. "I remember reading some reviews," Lukas Nelson says, "and got a lot of flack for it: 'Oh, Lukas is a better artist that that,' you know?; 'He doesn't have to use weed to promote his career'; and all this bullshit. I'm just like, 'You know what? That in itself implies that weed is a negative.'" He adds: "No. This is something that I do every single day, or on most days, I'm proud that I do. I'm happy that I smoke weed. It's a healthy thing for me and I just want to be left alone to do it." He notes it was coincidental, but, "After I wrote that song, I know it became number one on a couple of local stations in some states...and very soon after that, weed was legalized in Colorado and Washington. I'm not saying that song made that. Maybe the national consciousness is all feeling that way and that's why I wrote that song."[103]

DEAR MR. PRESIDENT

In 2006, Pink! recorded "Dear Mr. President"—accompanied by the Indigo Girls. She asked President George W. Bush: "What kind of father would take his own daughter's rights away? And what kind of father might hate his own daughter if she were gay?" The embrace of human rights by rock and roll and associated musical artists—from the global dynamics of Amnesty International to the streets of Northern Ireland and now Russia; from the margins of social acceptance for gays and lesbians to the national embrace of marriage equality; and from the war on drugs to the legalization of marijuana, progress on human rights has been advanced. At the 2013 Grammy Awards, a rocking country star, Kasey Musgraves, won the award for best country album, including the song "Follow Your Arrow" with the lyric: "When the straight and narrow gets a little too straight—roll up a joint, I would." At the 2013 Country Music Awards, Musgraves was censored for "roll up a joint"— but at the Grammys, just months later, Musgraves sang away.

Chapter Five

Peace—Give Peace a Chance

WHEN WILL THEY EVER LEARN?

In troubadour form, Pete Seeger asked in 1955: "Where have all the soldiers gone? They've gone to graveyards, everyone. When will they ever learn?" Bob Dylan challenged military influence in America with "Masters of War" in 1963 protesting how powerful elites fasten the triggers, for others to fire—and then watch "when the death count gets higher." Joan Baez was arrested in 1967 in Oakland, California, for protesting at an induction center for soldiers heading to Vietnam. County Joe McDonald, in 1969, got the Woodstock audience to protest the Vietnam War with the "Feel Like I'm Fixin' to Die Rag." In 1970, Crosby, Stills, Nash and Young bolted to the studio not long after the shooting of college students at Kent State University to record "Ohio." In 1982, Billy Joel released "Goodnight Saigon"—paying tribute to veterans from Vietnam and exposing feelings of guilt among those who did not serve. Bruce Springsteen hit big with "Born in the USA" in 1984 telling of the difficulties soldiers experienced in Vietnam—and on return home. During the Iraq and Afghanistan wars, some artists found that there can be career risks in protesting war. Yet, those who did speak in opposition were proven correct. Rock and roll artists have sustained the spirit of John Lennon who sang: "Give Peace a Chance."

WAR SONGS

Rock and roll has often amplified patriotism—even militarism. For example, the 1986 movie *Top Gun* offered Reagan-era romance with hits like Kenny Logins's "Danger Zone," accompanied by crowd-pleasing images of military power. In 1989, the United States used rock and roll as a tactic in war when it invaded Panama to remove Gen. Manuel Noriega from power. He took refuge in the Vatican Embassy, but the U.S. forces smoked him out with rock music. Initially, the music was blasted to protect sensitive American military communications. When they realized that Noriega, an opera lover, was growing irritated with the rock and roll, they pumped up the volume—bringing to bear Led Zepplin and Martha Reeves and the Vandellas. The Americans eventually escalated to the heavy guns: AC/DC, Motley Crew, and Metallica.[1] After the September 11th, 2001 terrorist attacks on New York City and Washington, D.C., country artist Toby Keith scored a powerful hit with "Courtesy of the Red, White, and Blue (The Angry American)" singing: "…you'll be sorry you messed with the U.S. of A, 'cause we'll put a boot in your ass, it's the American way."

The Weaponization of Music

By 2013, a new arsenal was opened against Somali pirates off the African coast by British naval personnel. According to one officer: "These guys can't stand western culture or music, making Britney's hits perfect. As soon as the pirates get a blast of Britney, they move on as quickly as they can."[2] These dynamics turned more serious as American interrogators applied rock and roll in the war on terrorism after September 2001 as blasting loud music was intended to produce sleep deprivation, disorientation, and to drown out screams of detainees. A leaked playlist ironically included Neil Diamond's immigration-celebrating "America" and material by Rage Against the Machine.[3] The Blues Brothers rendition of "Rawhide" (which ends with shouts and the sound of horsewhips) was used while interrogating Ramzi bin al-Shib as part of conditioning him so the detainee "…knows when he heard the music where he is going and what is going to happen."[4] Detainees: "… were kept in complete darkness and constantly shackled in isolated cells with loud noise or music and only a bucket to use for human waste."[5] Kelsey McKinney, a journalist, wrote in 2014: "Being kept in a pitch black room with rap and metal music blaring for weeks on end can have definite effects on the psychology of any formerly stable person. It is the weaponization of music."[6]

Music artist Kid Rock performs during the Tour for the Troops 2009 concert in Hangar 7 at RAF Lakenheath, England, December 11, 2009. Photo Courtesy of the US Department of Defense; photo by Tech. Sgt. Chris Stagner.

Some artists, meanwhile, use their craft to question the root causes of conflict. For example, in his song "Colony," Damien Dempsey reflects on the costs of empire, singing: "Greed is the knife and the scars run deep. How many races with much reason to weep? And your children cry. And you ask God, 'Why?'" He explains the damage of colonial empire—aligning that experience with native American Indians, aboriginal Australians, African—and, in some performances after the US invasion in 2003, the Iraqi people. Damien Dempsey says: "At the height of the British Empire, when England was the richest country in the world, the people there were hungry and dirty and poor—the ordinary people of England. And they'd been sent to Australia as slaves…and a lot of kids were starving and in the slums around England and the land of Ireland and places ravaged by diseases. So where was all this money going? Where was all the money from colonialism going? It wasn't trickling down, because colonialism favors the few." Billy Bragg campaigned in 2014 for Scottish independence. While some cartoonish versions of Scotland's movement were linked to battle images of Mel Gibson in the movie *Braveheart*, to Billy Bragg, the underlying sources of conflict are often socioeconomic. Bragg thinks to alleviate conflict, it is important to address a constituency directly, which might not be comfortable—"like white nationalism." He says he was criticized for "… supporting Scottish nationalism." Yet, he continues: "Fifteen years ago I wrote a song called 'Take Down the Union Jack.' Now, what do you think that was about? What did you think I was saying there?" To Bragg, conflict in a variety of settings is best addressed via democracy: "It's all about self-determination. It's not about the Scottish Nationalist Party (or their leader) or hating the English. It's purely about self-determination. If I want to talk about the politics of accountability, that is the first step. So of course I'm going to support it."[7]

Rock and roll has also been associated with some of the most dangerous forms of nationalist conflict. Jonathan Landay, one of America's most distinguished war correspondents, is also an accomplished guitar player. Landay says in the early 1990s, rock and roll was used for nationalist mobilization for war in the Balkans:

I remember, for instance, the leading Serbian paramilitary commander, Arkan, ran for president of Serbia. He ran for president, and I covered the campaign. They'd do these campaign tours and he'd take these turbofolk musicians with him. They'd stage this kind of cross between a fundamentalist Christian tent crusade of the old days, and this political rabble rousing—using this music. I remember this one rally I went to, he had this sort of turbofolk going. The lights went out and then they came up with the music going on—and there's Arkan standing on the stage in a traditional Chetnik uniform, holding the Serbian flag. So that music definitely played a role. And it played a role on the other side. I remember in Bosnia, where sort of to try to maintain this idea of ethnic amity and the old 'Bosnia' idea, they had musicians singing those kinds of thematic scenes as well.[8]

Jonathan Landay spent a lot of time in Sarajevo with an artist named Kemo Monteno, who he says, "…was famous for a song called 'Sarajevo My Love'—a huge song at the beginning of the war. I spent a month in a basement with him, up and down. I was living in the same guest house that he was living in. At night, when the bombs were raining down from the Bosnian Serb forces on the mountains around Sarajevo, we sat in the basement exchanging songs. I remember when he sang 'Sarajevo My Love' everybody was reduced to tears, in this basement. And so music did play a fairly important role there. Even now, turbofolk is still pretty big." But, on the Serb side, "It was popular music, so it was sort of seized upon as a motivator of nationalism." [9]

Jonathan Landay says that rock and roll is an important part of his personal experiences as a war correspondent. He recalls:

> I remember one night, I was trying to get into Sarajevo. I was driving down from the north. I was trying to get to Sarajevo and it was the middle of winter. The only way in was over a totally icebound road that the Bosnian Army had dug over Mt. Igman. I had only one chain for the tires on my car. To make the journey more tolerable I blasted Creedence the entire way over Mt. Igman, including—especially—when we were in range of Serbian machine guns. There was this one part of the road that was exposed to Serbian machine guns. In order to keep our minds off that, I just had the Creedence going—big time. [10]

Landay also recalls, while waiting in Kurdistan for the American invasion of Afghanistan in late 2001: "I crossed the border from Iran. The Iranians were kind enough to accommodate me. I crossed the border into Kurdistan to wait for the American invasion. I was there for four months and I started really missing my guitar." He says he found a music store and got a "... bashed up Yamaha, six string—I paid $100.00 for it—but it was serviceable." Landay recalls: "When I went to Kabul, *NPR* and McClatchy shared a compound. We would have musical evenings when people would come by and we'd play music for hours. It was a way of breaking from the routine and the danger and the pressure." Reflecting on Afghanistan, Jonathan Landay says it "...is a place where there's constant music. I mean, they absolutely love music in Afghanistan. It's part of the Afghan soul." And the Taliban banned it: "I got to Kabul a week or so after it fell [in 2001]. One of the first things they did was start playing music and getting Pakistani videos and making satellite dishes. They'd bang Coke cans flat and they'd make these satellite receivers. It was forbidden. So that's a case where a military liberation actually helped liberate people's ability to listen to music. I don't know of another case in history where that's the case." [11]

Many rock and roll stars have served in the military—from Elvis Presley to Billy Bragg. Jason Everman was effectively kicked out of both Nirvana and Soundgarden and his response was to volunteer for the U.S. Army Special Forces. He finished his training around September 11, 2001, and eventually deployed to Afghanistan and Iraq—where: "Iraqi tanks were exploding all around, turrets shooting off into the desert. I saw stuff I never thought I'd see. Buildings blew up in front of me, dude."[12] For some musicians being a soldier precipitated music. Bruce Schmidt and his group, the Ruben Lee Dalton Band, blend a range of traditions into a unique southwest American sound, working out of Santa Barbara, California—and Schmidt is a combat veteran who volunteered for the U.S. Marine Corps in Vietnam. Schmidt remembers: "I didn't really pick up an instrument until I was in Vietnam, with a bunch of southern boys who played every night. We bought a couple of Vietnamese guitars—we had to string them with com wire when the strings were broken. So you could imagine the sound. And that's where I learned." Schmidt says: "I was in combat. I was wounded twice when I was there and I received a Bronze Star. I saw way more action than I ever wanted to see."[13]

"It Comes Out in Music"

Each generation of soldiers since Vietnam has a rock and roll soundtrack. Paul Rieckhoff is the founder and Chief Executive Officer of the Iraq and Afghanistan Veterans of America (IAVA), which advocates for veterans issues. Rieckhoff served as a platoon leader in Iraq as a U.S. Army First Lieutenant doing 1,000 patrols. Rieckhoff says: "I'll never forget about the time I was at a checkpoint and an Iraqi kid came up and started citing Eminem lyrics. I mean, that was how we knew Saddam was gone—because a 14 year old kid just spittin' Eminem lyrics at a checkpoint, that's a whole new world."[14] He adds: "I don't think our soundtrack's been clearly defined yet. Films that have yet to come are still going to do that. If you look at *Generation Kill* or even *American Sniper* you don't have the period captured in the same way. Take *Forest Gump* as an example, all the songs, you know—Hendrix, and the Doors, and these bands and songs that kind of were iconic around the Vietnam experience. I don't think it's yet been interwoven with Jay-Z and Eminem, or Linkin Park, and Korn—and whoever else it was depending on when you went there. You know, that evolution is constant. For some people, they're sitting on a checkpoint right now listening to Taylor Swift." He recalls: "There's a pretty robust heavy metal scene going on. I got tapes passed and CDs passed and we'd hear about guys, but it's not like we could go out and see a show." In Iraq his interpreter was also a painter. Because he could not get the materials he needed, he "… used Beatles [album] covers and melted down Crayola crayons." Rieckhoff adds, "You feel that creative urge, and you also feel that longing to share your experience—and sometimes you can't put it into words and it comes out in music."[15]

LIVES IN THE BALANCE

Questioning war is a patriotic calling, but it comes with risk. Jann Wenner recalls the 1991 Rock and Roll Hall of Fame induction ceremony, held on the night George H.W. Bush announced the bombing of Bagdad:

> Jackson Browne was my guest at dinner. In my prelude to the dinner I quoted from his song, 'Lives in the Balance', which is a beautiful song about, you know, 'Who are these men that send kids to war?' They don't even know their names. And they sell us their wars in the same way they sell us our cars and T.V. That—a very powerful thing to say and articulate on the night that he's announced that we're bombing—you know? Who are these old men sending the children to die? What Jackson asked in that song - it didn't meet with a great response. It wasn't quite an antiwar room, even though it was all musicians and music business people.[16]

Joe McDonald of Country Joe and the Fish, says: "It's box office is all it is. It's just the cash register ringing. It's bad business to do controversial things, and war is controversial. Talking about people in the military is controversial. It's not something that is a smart move in the entertainment business." He adds: "No one of my peers has ever said anything to me about 'Fixing to Die Rag' and my work with veterans. No one has ever. I've been around people,

Country Joe McDonald at Woodstock. Photo by Jim Marshall.

they've never talked to me about it, and said, 'Wow, that was great that you sang that song and what about your work with veterans?' Nobody's said anything to me. It's weird; I think it's weird."[17] He understands that his role is appreciated, but: "What I'm saying is, like Bill Graham; I know that he had a lot of respect for me, but didn't hire me at a certain point. The people that are doing it—and there are people who are writing about war, are not granted access in the music business to the audience. Maybe the audience would like it. I don't know. But it's not good box office. It's just not. And it's known it's not good box office. What is good box office is sentimental songs about patriotism and brave heroes."[18]

"A Real Chill Came Down"

Jann Wenner recalls that after September 2001: "...a real chill came down, I mean—the country was so whipped up into such a state of gung-hoism and the media was so cowed by the war. And *Fox News*—it put a chill on the climate. It was hard for anybody to express it. There is such an impulse to rally around the flag and come together in a time of war [and] crisis. It becomes a question, like a 'time of no questioning' for most people and a 'time of censorship and self-censorship.'"[19] While it did not explicitly "ban" the playing of songs on over 1,000 of their affiliate stations, Clear Channel network released a list of 165 songs that stations might wish to consider before playing on the radio for fear of upsetting listeners after the September 2001 attacks. These songs included John Lennon's "Imagine"—a song of idealism and peace, as potentially upsetting.

In the run-up to the 2003 invasion of Iraq, few artists spoke out against the war. The Dixie Chicks were a standout—making disparaging remarks against President George W. Bush at a concert in London shortly before the attack. Natalie Maines said: "Just so you know, we're on the good side with y'all. We do not want this war, this violence. And we're ashamed that the President of the United States is from Texas (their home state)." Boycotts of the Dixie Chicks were organized, and even George W. Bush interjected: "The Dixie Chicks are free to speak their mind. They can say what they want to say...They shouldn't have their feelings hurt because some people don't want to buy their records when they speak out. Freedom is a two-way street." Country and Western legend Merle Haggard, however, came to their defense: "I don't even know the Dixie Chicks but I find it an insult for all the men and women who fought and died in past wars when almost the majority of America jumped down their throats for voicing an opinion."[20] Natalie Maines was not deterred. On the twelfth anniversary of her comments, in March 2015, she tweeted: "Just so you know,12 years ago today, over half of this country had lost their minds and some questioned my knowitallness. #dummies."[21]

Another group speaking out forcefully was System of Down. In 2005, their Grammy winning song "B.Y.O.B." (Bring Your Own Bombs) asked, "Why do they always send the poor?" Serj Tankian says: "My first thing was growing up in the Armenian community in Los Angeles and kind of being aware of the hypocrisy of the denial of the Armenian genocide [in which between 1915 and 1917 Ottoman Turks systematically killed about 1.5 million Armenians]." Serj Tankain believes security is found by: "Good relationships with your neighbors. Best way to feel secure when you leave your house, is to know that your neighbors like you and that they're going to have an eye on your house even when you're not there. There's a certain trust. That's your best security. That is your best foreign policy."[22] Tankian adds: "...when Bush and Cheney were on a roll with Iraq and everything that was going on, at first there was huge public support—because people were not aware of the truthfulness of the WMD claims. There was a lot of public opinion supporting the war. It was really difficult fighting that. I mean, we did a video with Michael Moore called 'Boom!'—for one of our songs—I remember how much flack we were getting." He says, "As we were about to go on tour, a week after 9/11, we had our song basically taken off radio."[23] "It's very easy to support public opinion, and speak against injustice when public opinion is on your side," Serj Tankian says: "Try doing it when it's not."[24]

Serj Tankian believes artists are often reluctant to speak out: "It's the same kind of common denominator that elected officials worry about. We're not that far off, because we make a living selling our wares - our music and our performances. And if we have a large part or a segment of society that are pissed off and are not going to come and see us because of our statements within our songs, or during press times and stuff, that will alienate." Still, Tankian observes: "We are the most benevolent nation in terms of our non-profits, in terms of things that we have accomplished around the world. Yet we're still an empire. Yet we still do things that are immoral, foreign policy-wise." Tankian identifies the crisis in Syria, which spilled over into Iraq in 2014, with the emergence of the Islamic State—as examples of "ludicrous-ness that we're facing in terms of foreign policy."[25] He points out that the United States had been combating Sunni radical movements in the region while, at the same time, making the Shiites (including in Iran) an enemy: "Since when did the Shiites do anything to the U.S.? Al Qaeda came from Sunni extremism. And the experience in Iraq and the fear of the Shiites gain-ing control—and our allied country of Saudi Arabia and Qatar has, I don't want to say 'confused us', but put us on a road of some elements of our avowed enemies. Against a nation whose government we overthrew [Iran] in the 1950s—a democratically elected government—because the British were afraid they were going to take over the oil company that they co-owned with the Persians." America, he says: "…brought in a king [the Shah] into a democracy. Then what happened? The king got brutal. We sold him a lot of weapons. He had his own intelligence services. He got brutal—and the reaction to that was an Islamic Republic."[26]

Serj Tankian also takes assurance from the public saying "no" to another war that Barack Obama intended to launch against Syria in late summer 2013. Syria was in clear violation of international conventions against the use of chemical weapons—which had been used to kill over a thousand people including hundreds of children. Yet the military plan was to launch a barrage of cruise missiles with no real impact on weapons stockpiles, but rather to send a message of credibility. At the last minute, a negotiated settlement allowed United Nations weapons inspectors to oversee the successful elimination of all of Syria's declared chemical weapons stockpiles. Diplomacy created a better outcome than war would have. Serj Tankian gives credit to the popular pressures, now aligned against war: "People were just, so opposed to it. It's also the Iraq experience and being lied to by Bush about the WMD situation. You know, going into another country, committing troops—who are we fighting for? Of course, Assad [the leader of Syria] is a dictator. His dad was a dictator. A minority government ruling over a majority, there's no question about what that means to any of us. But at the same time, what is just? Who are we supporting against him? And what's going to happen? It's great that, at least, there's weights to these decisions now, whereas eight years ago, there wasn't."[27]

"This Is a World Issue"

In spring 2015, System of a Down performed in Yerevan, Armenia, to commemorate the 100th anniversary of the Armenian genocide by the Turks. Drummer John Dolmayan proclaimed: "This is something that's far-reaching and it's actually bigger than the Armenian genocide itself. This is a world issue."[28] Guitarist Daren Malakian told the audience: "This is not a rock concert. To our murderers—this is revenge!"[29] Serj Tankian understands the geopolitics that have affected political calculations regarding Turkey and the labeling of the Armenian genocide. Tankian says: "There's times where geopolitics rules and times where it's going to reverse. What's really shameful is using something like that as political capital…Genocide or history or truth—Obama knows. He's mentioned the word genocide. He's a smart guy. He'd done it many times as Senator. And when he became president he had to kind of tow the NATO [North Atlantic Treaty Organization, which includes Turkey] line, if you will."[30]

FEAR IS THE ANTITHESIS OF PEACE

The meaning of peace is open to interpretation. Graham Nash defines peace: "I think that on a human, individual level, and as a society, I think what we all want is to be left alone—to have our families, to have our children be well-fed, and well-educated, and have our children have a better life than we had. That's what peace is. Peace is being able to talk to other people, whether it's one human being or an entire country, and make compromises to get the best life for everybody."[31] "Peace," David Crosby says, means: "I don't want to get shot this morning. I don't want my children to worry about a car bomb going off while they're on their way to school. So peace sounds pretty good to me. I value it highly." "I like peace," Crosby says: "I like peace as a lack of war. There's been almost no time, in the history of the United States when we weren't at war with somebody. And it's a really stupid way to solve problems." Joe McDonald says: "Peace is inclusive, not exclusive. If we persist on having an atmosphere of no peace, we will destroy ourselves."[32] Sinéad O'Connor frames the question introspectively: "Peace is about silence. Silence is something that is achievable and thus so is peace. Ultimately, when we're peaceful, there is a silence perhaps about the Earth. If there was peace in the world, there wouldn't be a whole lot to make noise about other than music and having a laugh."[33]

Ohio

David Crosby and Graham Nash have long used music to advance peace. Crosby focuses on how war harms civilians. "That's very disturbing to me," he says: "innocent people who haven't done anything to anybody. That's my criticism of drones. That's my criticism of carpet bombing. That's my criticism of being able to kill people with a nuclear weapon from thousands of miles away. You don't know who they are. If you have to face somebody and say, 'No, you're not getting over this threshold. If you want into my family, then I'll lay my life down right here to stop you.' But it's a different kind of conflict."[34] Nash sees fear as driving "security" over "peace":

> You never heard a fucking word or saw one photograph from Grenada. You never saw one photograph or one bit about Panama. Don't forget, it was illegal to photograph a fucking coffin with a flag over it. That's how much control the media has on the American public. How would you feel if it was your son or your daughter or your uncle or your brother? Lying there in a fucking coffin and people not being able to honor them in a way that they should for their sacrifice?[35]

"Fear," David Crosby sings in his 2014 song "Time I Have," is "the antithesis of peace." Crosby says, "People whose main thing in life is manipulating other people have found out that fear is a great way to do it." Crosby says: "National security is a way to justify the militarization of the country and the surveillance level that they want and the degree of funding that they want. They want you to be afraid. They want you to think those bearded terrorists are going to come over the wall tomorrow. And, 'You need to be afraid.' And, we need to be able to look in your computer to make sure." "Fear now," Crosby adds, "is a tool for the people who are running things."[36]

Graham Nash and David Crosby (with Stephen Stills) contributed to Neil Young's song "Ohio," which tells how the government of Ohio killed college students on May 4, 1970 for exercising their rights of assembly and speech protesting America's illegal bombing of Cambodia. After several days of protests and overnight disorder in Kent, Ohio, Governor James Rhodes ordered in the National Guard. A unit opened fire, killing Allison Krause, Jeff Miller, Sandy Scheuer, and Bill Schroeder while wounding nine others. In the days following, David Crosby handed Neil Young a copy of *LIFE* magazine, which included iconic photographs of the shooting. This prompted Young to pen "Ohio"—with its imagery of tin soldiers, Nixon coming, and Americans finally being on their own. Crosby, Stills, Nash and Young recorded the song and released it within weeks. Not everyone was impressed. Gerald Casale, who later went on to form DEVO, was at Kent State University and knew two of the shooting victims. He said: "...we just thought rich hippies were making money off of something horrible and political that they didn't get."[37]

For artists who were there or experienced the national pain that followed, the memory persists. One of Ohio's leading guitar instructors and performers, George Gecik was a student at Kent State University at the time. He recalls: "I got arrested on Friday night May 1, 1970 for doing nothing when they closed down the Townhouse Bar and pushed us into the street at Depyster and Main. That's when the police decided to rush the crowd and I refused to run because I was not doing anything. So I got busted. They took us to Kent City Jail and never officially booked us."[38] Gecik says: "James Rhodes was running for re-election on Tuesday May 5, and never let anything get in the way of politics. In my opinion he inflamed the students and bears the responsibility for the death of those four students. They would be alive today had he closed the school."[39] Kate Pierson of the B-52s recalls her reaction:

> I never thought it would come to that, that students were actually shot. I realized, suddenly, that this is what really pushing for change in America meant. People that have done that have been killed. And so it just seemed to me—I lost that sense of optimism about America. To me it was just sort of the end of optimism, or naïve optimism, anyway, and the beginning of maybe more 'realistic optimism.'[40]

Michael Stanley, who was a student at Hiram College just up the road, says of "Ohio": "Think how quick that came out. That's the folk tradition." Stanley today is now an afternoon D.J. on 98.5 WNCX in Cleveland, Ohio. He observes: "That's a staple on our station. When it comes on it's still like, 'That's a good one.' You hear that opening guitar riff and it takes you right back to that. That's the power of rock and roll. It's that it can transcend a generation, it morphs. It gets amoeba-like. It spreads out and comes back."[41]

David Crosby acknowledges that the group exercised power via that song. Today, he worries that new generations:

> ...have no idea what happened there. The American people got shot—students. They have no idea. They don't know about the governor. They don't know what really went down there—and, that's a horror show. There's a thing I'm fond of saying, 'When a country starts killing its young children, you know there's something wrong.' That was—that moment—in the United States. It was very bad. And that was us, probably at our best as the town crier. That was probably the best job we did.[42]

"We looked at it as shining a light on them, which if you do that on cockroaches, they scurry off under the floorboard," Crosby says. He recalls: "Every campus in America was a hotbed of antiwar activity because they were all staring it in the face. Let's be real. That's what was pushing them to do it. God Bless them for seeing it, and then looking at it and saying, 'Not only am I afraid that they're going to draft me, but this is all wrong.' That's how it went. So they got rid of the draft."[43] Chrissie Hynde of the Pretenders was a student at Kent State University at the time and was friends with two of the victims. "Jeff Miller," Hynde says, "one of the fellows that was killed, he was such a big fan of Crosby, Stills, Nash and Young, you know, and I knew that, so you know that made me happy."[44]

"I Do It Because That's Who I Am"

David Crosby says about today's wars, "The only sane thing we can do about the Middle East is get the fuck out."[45] Of Afghanistan:

> That's a tribal area. We don't really understand that now—our roots are in Western Europe. Tribalism has disappeared from Western Europe a thousand years ago...It's been language difference and countries and politics, but it hasn't been tribal, it hasn't been family oriented, tribal kind of thinking the way there is in the Hundu-Kush. And those people have been fighting invaders forever. When there's no invader, they fight each other just to stay in practice. They're ruthless and they do know where every rock and tree is. They know every cave. They know every path in those mountains. You can't beat them on their own turf.

His 2014 song "Morning Falling" tells a story about drone aircraft in Afghanistan. "I had a vision," he says, "of a family waking up. I saw it through the son's eyes: He sees his mom feeding his little sister, father scraping the fire together—putting water in the teapot. And all during this sort of vision of these people, this thing is falling. It's like a dark presence, falling. It's slow. It's very slow in my vision. It's falling. And eventually, of course, it hits. And, the reason is that the Taliban had come the night before and he wouldn't join them. For once, they didn't just kill him outright." Crosby whispers: "Very surprising—they usually would. The father, he relays, said: 'I've got twenty-two goats and a baby and my son and my wife. I can't come to your war.' They left, but they were seen leaving." "Of course," Crosby says: "the people watching screens never heard the desperate pleas of 'I can't come to your war.' And now they were hitting, dropping a fucking bomb on him the next morning, because those guys had been there." He says, "It's not a fantasy. It's happened many times. Not just accidental—targeted." David Crosby concludes: "I like doing that. I don't care if it pisses people off. I don't care if they don't understand it," adding: "I don't do it because I think I'm going to win. I do it because it's the only way I can be proud of myself. I do it because that's who I am."[46]

WHAT ARE WE FIGHTING FOR?

Bill Payne of Little Feat reflects on the Vietnam period saying: "My parents, you'd think after World War II, after the Depression—they wouldn't say what they did. But they asked, 'Why would the government lie to us?' And not only my parents were saying it but a lot of parents were saying it. It wasn't until Walter Cronkite came in [1968] and said, 'This is a bunch of hooey' that people began to take notice."[47] Payne uses the analogy of the poppy fields' scene from the *Wizard of Oz* in which Dorothy and her companions are lulled into sleep, show to how people can become complacent. "I think we're in the same conundrum, in regards to peace, that we've been in," Bill Payne says.[48] He sees peace as an uneasy truce between future battles being conceived of while the "...dance of war and peace continues amidst the flickering shadows." He invokes the imagery of the bombing of London in World War II, which became "normal" for people as they went about their lives: "War seems to be part of peace. You try to establish a peace as long as you can—based on keeping people apart from one another. Giving people a breathing spell—let them re-organize. Unfortunately, what we seem to reorganize is our ability to formulate new ways of conducting other warfare."[49] Still, Bill Payne says, "When you look at Vietnam, the people shut that war down—the government didn't."

"It Was Dark, and They Were Frightened"

Liberty Devitto explains how the Vietnam experience shaped the Billy Joel Band's song "Goodnight Saigon." The song was one of the first major hits (released in 1982) to address Vietnam veterans and their experience. Liberty Devitto says the song had personal meaning:

> Four days before my nineteenth birthday I got my draft—it was still a draft, it wasn't the lottery yet. It was still a draft. I got my notice—'You are hereby ordered to report for your physical.' And I remember going to the beach and my father was there. He was in World War II. He was in the invasion of Normandy, the Battle of the Bulge, all that kind of stuff. I'm named after his brother; five sons went in, my father [and his] brothers, and then only four came back. I'm named after the one that was killed in France. So I walk up to my father and I said to him, I said, 'Look, you fought the war to end all wars and now they want me to go for this physical!' And I crumbled up the paper and I threw it at him at the beach. He just looked at me and he said, 'Go. I bet they don't even want ya.' I was like, 'Oh my God! This World War II vet just told me I was a wimp?'; 'Go. They probably don't even want people like you.'[50]

Devitto adds, "So I did go for my physical. I did do everything I possibly could to get out. I managed to get out. I was actually 'medically and mentally disqualified from the armed services'—in other words: 'women and children go first, before me.' I think 'Goodnight Saigon' was written more out of—it was written as a tribute to them. But it was also written out of guilt that we didn't go. Why were we so lucky and why did so many die? And why were they treated the way they were treated when they came home? They were just doing their duty." Devitto says:

> The song—the way it's played, the drums: I chose to build tension when it was supposed to build tension—'And it was dark!'—and, it *was* dark—and they *were* frightened, you know? There was nothing about like 'we're big heroes.' World War II guys, who my father talks about; everybody says they're the heroes. [But] my father says, 'We were so scared at one point,' when bullets are flying over his head he was digging his nails into the ground to try to get lower, and he thought he would 'never see Brooklyn again or eat a ham sandwich.' And so that part about them being scared is really like this—like 'They're the greatest and they just walk into battle.' No man. They're scared. They're scared. You know? These guys now today have taken on this job to do this. Maybe because they couldn't get an education or the right way to get an education, to get a job, whatever. Whatever it is, they're scared."[51]

So, "'Goodnight Saigon'," Liberty Devitto concludes, "was written in that way. Like—it was not easy. It was not nice."[52]

Some artists have sought to understand these dynamics by going to war zones to make music. Michael Franti, for example, went to Iraq in 2004, meeting with Iraqis and American soldiers, playing music and producing a documentary film. Franti says: "I met so many people who just said: 'We know about how dark war is, and how it affects people for generations. What we really want is music that helps us to get through each day—and to get through life and to give voice to that pain, that sadness, but also finds a place to celebrate and to laugh and dance and sing, despite all the chaos that we see around.'"[53] There was also some significant protest music—including Le Tigre's song "New Kicks" in 2004. The song was built around sounds and speeches from antiwar protests gathered under the guise of "Peace! Now!" Johanna Fateman says, "That wasn't a risk for us, for sure. Well, I mean the risk was just—the risk was that it was on a major label (Universal) and having a song that they actually released as a single without our own vocals on it." "I don't even know if you would call it a risk," Fateman recalls: "I remember reading a bad review, or a couple of bad reviews of that song, that it was just kind of like 'us doing our schtick' you know what I mean?" Le Tigre, Fateman adds, wanted to get the choir ramped up: "This was like, we wanted to get Bush out office—we felt very personally affected by [the] post-9/11climate and, like, distorted use of New York City. It was an emotional time. I think that we really felt, it's not like I don't think things are really bad now, but we felt like things were *really* bad and, you know, there was nothing like Obama, or even like a Democratic victory on the horizon. We just thought it was going to get worse and worse."[54] In 2010, Willie Nelson and his sister Amy used their song "Peaceful Solution" to spread a message of peace: "There is a peaceful solution, called a peace revolution." Lukas Nelson, who performs the song in concert, says: "My dad wrote that song. He wrote that song, and then he sent it out for a free download, and he invited all of his fans to write their own versions of that song; Kind of a cool thing. People resonate with that." Nelson adds: "Instead of going out and waving signs and protesting, it's like, 'Well, you now what? We like peace, so we're going to go out and be peaceful. We're going to go out and sit on the grass and listen to music and, you know—have joy in our hearts. And, that's just going to spread on its own."[55]

Among rock and roll war songs, few artists have made as significant a contribution as Joe McDonald. A veteran, McDonald and his band Country Joe and the Fish became a staple of the mid- and late-1960s San Francisco scene. Joe McDonald says, "It's a metaphor but it's also a truth—we turned the volume up to ten. We turned it up to ten and it was shocking. It was powerful, the volume was powerful." He says: "The Woodstock music festival was so important because it was like a potluck dinner. All the groups were different, but it reached an audience. The Woodstock moment, 1969, was eclectic."

McDonald says, "By using Woodstock, I'm saying that it mainstreamed. It mainstreamed then and reached out to the whole middle class world, because of the movie and because of the music. And in a way that was remarkable, really in a global way because it was accessible and it validated something in the audience."[56]

Woodstock, according to Joe McDonald, affirmed, "…the alienation that young people felt from mainstream society and created their own mainstream—which became the mainstream." He says of his song "I Feel Like I'm Fixing to Die Rag":

> War songs before that time were patriotic, in other words 'my country right or wrong.' Or, they were anti-soldier in that they said, 'It's your fault for blaming war, universal soldier.' My song didn't say anything about being bad being a soldier. It just expressed the opinion of a soldier having to do a job that he or she did not want to do. And it did it in a teenage way, in a sarcastic G.I. way. And it validated what they were feeling—and liberated them in that case. Many people told me that when they were flying into Vietnam in a plane full of soldiers, the whole plane would start singing 'Fixing to Die Rag' which really upset the older leadership of the military.[57]

Joe McDonald stresses Woodstock was: "…very empowering because you thought that they were out to get you—they were going to arrest you for this or that, or scold you because of your hair. Your parents were scolding you. The government wanted to send you to Vietnam. Your parents or society told you not to have sex or to wear a bra. But when you've got 100,000-plus people gathered together enjoying what was happening—rock and roll. And no one telling you, 'Put your bra back on'; 'Don't smoke that weed'; 'Be patriotic and go to Vietnam.' You could do your own thing."[58]

Joe McDonald recalls: "I've been interested in war since I was young as a victim of war because being Jewish I was aware that war could ruin your life or kill you. Also, I'm a military veteran. I served in the Navy and I knew that I never felt comfortable with civilians. It's something that a military veteran can understand—the definition of a civilian and the definition of a veteran. I feel comfortable with veterans, and I particularly felt comfortable with anti-war veterans and Vietnam War veterans and was aware of their music." "Oddly enough," Joe McDonald says: "I think that war music has not mainstreamed and the public is generally not aware of it. And I think that the problem with that is that civilians feel ambivalent about war and military service. They're plagued with guilt and their own definitions of patriotism. I mean, if you're a military veteran, your patriot box is checked off."[59] McDonald believes:

> For a large segment of the population, rock and roll validated what they were experiencing. Liberated them, right? But for the military community this has

not happened. That has not happened. It's extremely sad because the way that the industry and the way that the civilian population relates to the military community doesn't validate their feelings. It doesn't address their perspective. It's skewered by the guilty, nervous attitude of, 'We admire and respect so much.' What drives me crazy is the attitude of, 'Our brave men and women.' Because most people in the military are not brave. They're not brave. So what about the non-brave men and women? What about the cowards? It creates an ambivalence and a confusion in the mind of the military family."[60]

Key for his role as an artist and as a veteran, Joe McDonald says, was the act of singing with the audience rather than at the audience. "This phenomenon, for me," he says, "launches itself in an explosion at Woodstock, circled the globe."[61]

Feel Like I'm Fixin' To Die

Joe McDonald is interested in war, he says: "…from a working class point of view. That's how I see it, you're a worker. You're a worker in a system doing a job and I find that very interesting. In that particular time of turbulence and the Vietnam War, I found Vietnam Veterans Against the War, I liked hanging around with them. It was fun. We had good times together." Yet outside that community, understanding could be difficult to find. In late 1969, Country Joe and the Fish performed "Feel Like I'm Fixing To Die Rag" on the *David Frost Show*. A letter sent in response read: "It has taken me a week to compose myself after seeing your show with 'Country Joe and the Fish.' Did you stop to think that in your home audience there might have been mothers that lost sons in Viet Nam? 'Be the first one on your block to have your boy come home in a box.'" Another read: "The unbathed folk group who sang about Vietnam this morning should be shipped to any country of their choice. They are cowards of the worst degree. I'm proud to say my son fought and met the commies standing for freedom. He was shot 3 times. *CBS* should pay the folk singers to leave the country."[62] It was ironic as these writers protested a veteran.

BRING THE BOYS BACK HOME

When Roger Waters reproduced *The Wall* in 1990, the song "Bring the Boys Back Home" was backlit with imagery of war. Names from the Vietnam Veterans Memorial in Washington, D.C. bring the song forward. It then morphs into images of military crosses as seen in Arlington Cemetery. In other productions, the song "Vera" led-in with imagery of soldiers returning home to families from recent wars. One image showed the face of a young girl surprised at school by her father returning from deployment. The joy and the pain all in one, she embraces her father dressed in his desert fatigues. The segue into "Bring the Boys Back Home" featured images from the recent war campaigns, juxtaposed with script letters from a 1953 speech given by Dwight D. Eisenhower: "Every gun that's made, every warship launched, every rocket fired, signifies in the final sense, a theft from those who hunger and are not fed, from those who are cold and are not clothed." Today, rock and roll artists devote much time and effort to advancing veteran's causes.

Fortunate Son

Bruce Schmidt reflects on his experiences as a Vietnam combat veteran. He remembers that:

> I came home with feelings that I'm proud of and feelings that I'm ashamed of because of the welcome I got coming home. Basically as I got off the plane, I got pelted with fruit from a fence line that was about fifty yards away. I mean, that was getting off the plane from Vietnam. So I knew—I had a pretty good idea that it wasn't going to be a warm and cozy welcome, just from what I read in the papers. Actually you had to have security come and get me off the plane and into a safe place. This was like, 'O.K., this is not something I'm going to be telling lots of people about.' And so for a couple of years I basically was sort of ashamed of the fact that I was over there. Even going to college, these young kids would come in and ask me questions like, you know 'Did you kill women and children?', and 'Were you involved in things like the Mai Lai Massacre?' and all this. How do I answer that? I was. I mean, if not directly, I was there. I was indirectly involved.[63]

> Schmidt recalls eventually:

> I ended up on the front lines of a lot of demonstrations [up against] tactical squads. They were full-on military organizations that would face us. You can imagine a body of students, headed up by a bunch of Vietnam vets—disgruntled Vietnam veterans—trying to stop the war. And then on the other side, tactical squads standing there with bayonets on their weapons approaching us. We got to the line where I'm literally three or four feet away from a guy, who I'm looking at, and I see a Vietnam veteran ribbon on his tactical pocket. And I'm wearing fatigues. The whole point of us was to 'be' veterans. We gave credibility to that march being people who had been there and come home and were now marching against the war.[64]

The tactical officer relayed to Schmidt: "'You're a traitor. How can you do this when we are over there still fighting?' Schmidt responded: "'You know every bit as well as I do what a waste that war is, that we are over there dying for *no good reason*—your friends and my friends.' We went back and forth for about three or four minutes until some provocateur in the crowd, from our side, threw a bottle through a window, and then everything broke loose." Schmidt took off running: "I hear these footsteps behind me and here this guy's chasing me. I finally just stopped and turned around, and I said, 'You know why I'm here and I know why you're here, and it's a sad situation.' And he just sort of dropped his weapon. He was really bummed and just turned around and walked away."

Christine Martucci says: "Veterans are not treated well enough, there is not enough medical attention, there is not enough housing assistance or family support. Once you are damaged goods, you are tossed aside and replaced."[65] For veterans of the Iraq and Afghanistan wars, job opportunities for veterans were especially scarce. About 30 percent of veterans who had some degree of employment or other disability related to service came from service after 2001. By 2015, unemployment among veterans aged 18–24 was 16 percent.[66] Estimates suggest that by 2015 there were on average twenty-two suicides among veterans per day in the United States.[67] There are 2.7 million veterans from the Iraq and Afghanistan wars and about 8.2 million who served during the Vietnam War. About 20 percent of Iraq and Afghanistan veterans suffered from some form of post-traumatic stress disorder (PTSD). Only about half of those who seek treatment for PTSD got adequate care and about fifty percent of those suffering do not seek treatment at all.[68] Rock and roll has been an effective tool for helping wounded veterans and those suffering from PTSD recover and adjust back to society. For example, a nationally oriented organization, Musicorps: "...integrates regular visits by accomplished musicians who serve as mentors, the use of traditional instruments along with computer workstations and custom equipment, and projects tailored to individual circumstances, interests, and goals. Working in a variety of styles, and overcoming any obstacles, wounded warriors are able to learn, play, write, record, and perform music as a core part of their rehabilitation."[69] Founded in 2007 by musician Arthur Bloom, the group has worked with hundreds of wounded veterans using music to rehabilitate themselves. Bloom says of working at Walter Reed hospital: "I've seen guys come in here, and they're going through such a tough time with their injuries that they are very withdrawn...The music becomes their new way of communicating. It can be just as powerful as the spoken word."[70] Another organization, "Guitars for Vets," based in Milwaukee, Wisconsin, has thirty chapters in fifteen states. The group provides free guitar instruction, a new acoustic guitar, and a guitar accessory kit to Veterans enrolled in its program. They have given over 2,000 guitars with support from Gibson and from artists like Lynyrd Skynard, who performed at a fundraiser in Nashville in 2013.[71] Meanwhile, the band KISS held a contest called "Hiring Our Heroes" in 2012 to employ a veteran as a roadie with full-time pay and benefits for a national tour. Army veteran Paul Jordan (who had done three tours in Iraq and Afghanistan) was selected out of 1,000 applicants.[72]

Paul Rieckhoff and his organization IAVA emerged as a lead advocacy group for the new generation of American veterans. They have integrated rock and roll to publicize and advocate for veteran's issues. Rieckhoff notes: "We've tried to quantify it—we've probably done close to a dozen music partnerships that have reached well over a million people." In summer 2014, Rieckhoff recalls:

> We did something called a 'Convoy to Combat Suicide'—it was the Mayhem Music Fest: It was O.A.R., it was Linkin Park, and we even did some shows with Lady Gaga. Park is probably the best full integration. We did a video with them. We launched it on the *Real Time* show with Bill Maher and we did a full integration across every show they did on the Carnivores Tour. So Chester (Bennington) would get up and stop the entire show, wearing an IAVA shirt, and talk to the entire crowd about our programs. He and Mike Shinoda and Joe Hahn and the whole crew were all in. O.A.R. is another band that's really been great. We did a music video and a song with them, 'War Song'…you can see how the whole campaign was woven together.[73]

Rieckhoff adds: "We've got, essentially, a music program that involves artists and veterans in local events that helps us connect with people that probably wouldn't be tuned onto our issues otherwise." At concerts, he says: "We're tabling, we're doing texts to donate, we're selling merch." The Linkin Park tour was especially interesting, he says because: "We actually put a guy on the road with them named Quan Nguyen. Quan was at every single stop and was basically a part of the crew. At every stop we'd bring wounded vets backstage to meet the band, to get the IAVA access to tell their stories—and he (Nguyen) was just like a roadie, man, like the entire tour he was with them."[74] Rieckhoff says: "We deal with some tough issues. I can get a guy to go to an O.A.R. show or a Linkin Park show, or a Brantley Gilbert show, and connect with other veterans—and that's a bank shot into PTSD treatment or employment help—all the tough stuff." "The key for us is community and music gives us a rally point for our community," Rieckhoff adds: "A lot of guys will not go to a crowded event, but they will go to a music event with their fellow veterans. So that's really, I think, a key outcome that we see over and over again."[75]

A seminal event for IAVA came in 2012 when they gave an "Artistic Leadership Award" to Roger Waters. In his writing for Pink Floyd, Waters extended a motif of feelings about war—especially in *The Wall*. Waters says: "We invite 20 vets to every show we do, wherever we are in the world.

For instance, on the last leg of the tour we were playing in Sao Paulo (Brazil), and the vets were coming out, and these men seemed like they were in their Nineties. They were Brazillians that volunteered to fight for the Allies against the Axis powers in the Second War, because Brazil had no official involvement." Paul Rieckhoff recalls:

> I actually went to *The Wall* show with my nephew and I was sitting there going, 'My God, this guy's telling our story.' There's nobody who's more virulently antiwar than Waters is. But, what they also show is that you can hate the war but love the warriors. That's really key for us…I think the real key too is that it helps us reach people who are Roger Waters fans. We've got to find ways to break out of the echo chamber. There's only a little over 2 million post-9/11 vets. We have got to talk to the general population—we need storytellers.[76]

Rieckhoff notes that when he first sat down with Mike Shinoda (of Linkin Park), "I said 'Mike, you know, we need you to tell our story.' I don't even know if they realized how much their music was the soundtrack to our existence. But now they're getting it, and they're telling our stories, and they're writing music about our experiences."[77]

Paul Rieckhoff feels IAVA has made great strides in alliance with rock and roll artists to advance veteran's causes. "I still think," he says, "we're a step away from a tipping point. There's still an opportunity for artists to really move the needle." He notes there are political challenges to a honest discussion of veteran's difficulties—as in November 2014 when *HBO* and Starbucks put on a "Concert for Valor" on the Mall in Washington, D.C. for Veterans Day. At the concert, Bruce Springsteen was criticized by some conservative media outlets for performing Creedence Clearwater Revival's song "Fortunate Son." The song, written by veteran John Fogerty, protests how wealthy people avoided war while less fortunate do the fighting. Fogerty responded:

> 'Fortunate Son' is a song I wrote during the Vietnam War over 45 years ago… As an American and a songwriter, I am proud that the song still has resonance. I do believe that its meaning gets misinterpreted and even usurped by various factions wishing to make their own case. What a great country we have that a song like this can be performed in a setting like Concert for Valor…Years ago, an ultraconservative administration tried to paint anyone who questioned its policies as 'un-American'…That same administration shamefully ignored and mistreated the soldiers returning from Vietnam. As a man who was drafted and served his country during those times, I have ultimate respect for the men and women who protect us today and demand that they receive the respect that they deserve.[78]

Nevertheless, Ethan Epstein at *The Weekly Standard* wrote: "The song, not to put too fine a point on it, is an antiwar screed, taking shots at the red

Bruce Springsteen plays harmonica and guitar during his performance at the Concert for Valor in Washington, D.C., November 11, 2014. Photo courtesy of the US Department of Defense, November 11, 2014.

white and blue...It was a particularly terrible choice given that 'Fortunate Son' is, moreover, an anti-draft song, and this concert was largely organized to honor those who volunteered to fight in Afghanistan and Iraq."[79] Rieckhoff addresses this reaction saying: "There's nothing more American than writing a rock song and criticizing the government."[80]

"Every Day Is Veteran's Day"

Bruce Springsteen sang "Fortunate Son" against the backdrop of Capitol Hill. At that time, Congress had failed to even debate war powers while Americans were in harm's way again in Iraq. Paul Rieckhoff says: "There's no shortage of ignorance out there, and there are people who don't know their history. Music has been a great form of satire, it's been a great form of political criticism and it's been the voice of the people. I think for us, as veterans, we're so small in number, and so much has been asked of us, that music can amplify what we can't say for ourselves."[81] Joe McDonald, reflecting on the Concert for Valor, suggests a deeper problem: "The important thing, I think, to think about is that there was only one song that was controversial about the subject. The rest of the stuff that went on was done by civilians who are very very rich, who didn't know anything about the military experience. John Fogerty *was* in the military, so he's entitled. Of the 100 percent of that performance, shown to millions and millions of people, people making money off of it, only like what—1–2 percent of it was about a military experience for real and only 2 percent of it was by military veterans…So you've got people that don't know shit talking about something they don't know shit about."[82] McDonald also points out that this was a "…special, not normal event. It was a special, not normal, thing that happened, in that special, not normal event. It was not an everyday occurrence."[83] Joe McDonald adds that for people in the military and veterans too, "every day is Veteran's Day."[84]

WAR—WHAT IS IT GOOD FOR?

If the continuity of war is a measure, then rock and roll artists have not been a success at stopping it. However, many have advanced steady critiques of mistaken wars and advanced peace. Bruce Springsteen has long sung against war—from his 1973 "Lost in the Flood" (which detailed the visions of a soldier returning from Vietnam and finding a changed America) to his 1984 hit "Born in the U.S.A.," which told an all-American story of a young man who gets into a "hometown jam" and gets "sent off to a foreign land to go and kill the yellow man." Introducing his 1984 cover of the Edwin Starr classic "War," Springsteen said about Vietnam: "If you grew up in the '60s, you grew up with war on T.V. every night. A war that your friends were involved in" adding: "I remember, a lot of my friends, when we were 17 or 18, we didn't have much of a chance to think about how we felt about a lot of things—and, uh, next time—they're going to be looking at you. And you're going to need a lot of information to know what you're going to want to do. Because, in 1985, blind faith in your leaders—or in anything—will get you killed." Joe McDonald cautions that today: "We are taking energy away from solving the problem of ozone layer and global warming, and the act of war itself is a determent to the environment—not just to our feelings of being unsafe. There's a physical reality that if we continue to explode things in a profound, enormous way, we will chew up the very air that we breathe. We need to be globalcentric—we still are infantile in our ability to love our neighbor."[85]

Part III

CHANGE

Chapter Six

Education—Teach Your Children Well

THE SUPREME ART OF THE TEACHER

Education secures and extends the values that rock and roll advances in America and the world. Today, many rock and rollers provide educational opportunities as a lifeline for children in America and the underdeveloped world—advancing freedom, equality, human rights, and peace. As Serj Tankian says: "Extremism dissipates when you bring in education. You can fight the issues, argue the issues either way, on any political level, domestic or foreign policy. But who are you arguing with if you can't actually reference the same things—facts."[1] Music education, in particular, fosters creativity by spreading innovation and progress for individuals and nations alike. As Professor Albert Einstein said: "It is the supreme art of the teacher to awaken joy in creative expression and knowledge."[2]

DON'T KNOW MUCH ABOUT HISTORY

"Don't know much about history, don't know much biology," sang Sam Cooke in his 1960 recording "Wonderful World." Cooke was well educated— but he showed that important lessons can come from living life, not always in school. At the same time, many rock and roll artists are products of their education. The Beatles got a boost out of the Liverpool College of Art where John Lennon and Stuart Sutcliffe were students. Keith Richards was enrolled at Sidcup Art College in London when he encountered his childhood friend

Mick Jagger, who was on a train bound for a course at the London School of Economics. Before becoming a rocker, Sting was a teacher at St. Paul's First School in Cramlington, UK. O.A.R,'s founders met in high school in Maryland and performed while students at the Ohio State University. Jerry Dipizzo, who joined O.A.R. there, says: "It was the goal—to get there and to go to school and be able to get an opportunity to get into school there. Not only people from Ohio, but people from all over the world. So we knew that if we were able to get something going at Ohio State, it would work other places."[3] Dipizzo got his degree in information systems while thriving as a musician in an environment where gigs could be had and creativity rewarded. O.A.R. now raises money for education projects at their concerts.

"Never Judge a Book by Its Cover"

Liberty Devitto says, "Anybody who tries to crush your dreams is a bad teacher." Furthermore: "A band is only as good as its drummer because, the drummer is the center of the band. The drummer keeps everybody in time. Everybody looks to the drummer at the beginning and at the end of the song. And, when people get up off the chair it's the drumbeat that's getting them up—the driving beat of the music. The drummer pushes the other musicians to play harder." He adds, "...to have that kind of control, and to really hold that control in your hand and not let it get out of your hand, and get away from you? It's something that everybody can take in life no matter what they do." As to bad teaching, Devitto recalls: "When I was in sixth grade, I went to join the sixth grade orchestra. I couldn't play the buzz roll from the Star Spangled Banner all the way through. The teacher said, 'Put down the sticks, you'll never do anything with the drums.'"[4]

Bill Payne's experience shows, conversely, the positive effect of music education. Payne recalls his first teacher, Ruth Newman: "What made her a good teacher was her ability to, at least with me, suss out who I was as a person, even at that age, and tailor what we were doing to a curriculum that was already in place, but gauge it to where I was in terms of what I could perform and what I could absorb."[5] Detailing a discussion he once had with a teacher, Payne recalls she was saying about a student: "'Poor thing, she can't draw, or make any kind of art.' And I thought, 'Well, what steps have you taken to find out where she is? Does she have any interest in it?' She said, 'Oh, yes, she does, she just doesn't have any talent.' And I thought, 'Well, I think that's incumbent on the teacher to dig a little deeper with the student, to find out where they live. That's where you draw things out of the child.'" "I often ask people at my concerts," Payne observes: 'How many of you took piano lessons? How many of you were hit on the hand with a ruler?' Which a lot of them were, and I'm like, 'Great way to teach kids how to learn piano, right?'"

Reflecting on the experience that Liberty Devitto had with the "Star Spangled Banner," Payne says: "I was relegated to percussion in the orchestra. They take the fun out of it. When I was trying to play the clarinet, I kind of lifted it up in a Benny Goodman fashion. It was kind of as a goof, but also because music is fun. The guy [the orchestra director] reprimanded me severely for it. I didn't want to play the instrument anymore—which doesn't show a lot of depth from my standpoint either." "I'll tell you," he says, "these people have a way of talking you out of things, which doesn't meet their view of what the world should look like."[6]

For many artists, exposure to music at a young age was central to their education. As Michael Stanley, the Cleveland-based rocker, came of age: "It was a great time for rock and roll. The early influences, when I was like seven, or eight. That's when Buddy Holly hit—Buddy Holly, Little Richard, and Jerry Lee Lewis, the Everly Brothers. It was like, 'Damn! This is so cool!'"[7] Stanley adds that his father was a disc jockey: "Every night of my life that I could remember, my dad came home and threw three or four albums and ten singles on my bed. I mean, literally, in the course of one night, he would

Slash of Guns & Roses with Little Kids Rock participants. Photo courtesy of Little Kids Rock.

throw a Miles Davis, Hank Williams, Nina Simone, the Everly Brothers, Screaming Jay Hawkins. I mean, it was like *everything*. And not knowing you were only supposed to limit yourself to one side of the record, I would listen to everything that was there. It was just—it was a wonderful education." He reflects: "I mean, if you're eight or nine years old and you put on Miles Davis, it's kind of like, 'O.K., what are we dealing with here?'" He says: "Nobody in my family played an instrument, I never saw an instrument, none of my friends played instruments. I didn't grow up in that sort of, 'Well, you know my uncle would come over on Saturdays, with his 1934 Martin and sit there and play Blind Lemon Jefferson songs.'"[8]

Some artists, however, have gone through educational programs to prepare for careers as artists. Damien Dempsey attended Ballyfermot College in Dublin, Ireland—a vocational school specializing in music and media: "There was," he recalls, "a songwriting class. There was production where you learned to do amps and sound and mics and all. And, there was a business class where you learned about record contracts [and] publishing deals. They had people like Christy Moore and people from Sony in there."[9] Dempsey stresses there is what you learn in school, and what you learn in life, "Big time." He adds: "Oscar Wilde was great, he had a phrase: 'Education is an admirable thing, but it's worth remembering, from time to time, that nothing worth knowing can be taught.' That's always really worked for me. I read some Patrick Kavanaugh, and he said, 'I have a feeling that through the hole in reason's ceiling, we can fly to knowledge without ever going to college.'" Often, Dempsey says, he would be mixing in different circles than he was used to—with "…a lot of people who had gone on to third level education and they'd be very eloquent speakers. And I'd be made to feel like I didn't have that many words, and I wouldn't be used to having debates and all, the way these people were. I'd feel like, 'I'm a fucking idiot,' you know? So Oscar Wilde said this, Patrick Kavanaugh said that. I could quote those two things when there were people looking down at me." "Always," he concludes, "never judge a book by its cover."[10]

College Radio

Much of the contemporary rock and roll ethic emerged from the college music scene in the 1980s, which witnessed the expansion of "college radio" —a unique and independent sound defined in particular by R.E.M. Eventually, hits like "Losing My Religion" grabbed the hearts of a generation, but their start was around the University of Georgia. They were often seen as a "frat band," yet, R.E.M's longtime adviser Bertis Downs says: "In fact, they never played a single frat party—ever. But, their rise in popularity coincided with the new button-down, Ronald Reagan era in the nation." Downs adds: "We did have plenty of frat kids show up—for their early shows. There were a lot of kids in polo shorts and whatever those shoes are called—duck shoes." More likely their sound reflected the climate of their college town—Athens, Georgia. Bertis Downs says: "I think if you've ever lived in college towns, everybody wishes they could stay. A few people do figure out a way to stay. The charms and love of a college community—it seems bigger than it is in multicultural opportunities, and concerts and the various things that come to the campus."[11] Other artists found their way to Athens including Kate Pierson of the B-52s (who sang on R.E.M.'s "Shiny Happy People"). Pierson says:

> We rented this house for fifteen dollars a month, this little tenant farmer's house, in the middle of a field—like the 'Love Shack'—funky little shack. We had a huge garden. We had goats and chickens. For about a year I didn't have any contact with anyone in town. This person gave me a horse to ride, so we were riding bareback through the fields—it was just great. But we had no money. We used to ride our bicycles if we had to go into Athens—which at the time had two feed stores and a farmer's hardware; and no club, no place to play, no bands.[12]

Pierson adds: "I met the other [B-52s] band members because I eventually had to get a job. I got a job at the Georgia Center for Continuing Education setting up slide projectors and video stuff for conferences. That job was kind of a 'student job.' I met the other band members and we started hanging out and going to parties. And one night we started the band."[13]

Whether it was Bob Dylan performing near the University of Minnesota at the Ten O'Clock Scholar coffeehouse or Green Day at Gilman Street in Berkeley, the college rock scene has been at the forefront of artistic progress. Still, for many, the best education can come from life's adventures and not necessarily a university classroom. Bob Dylan, for example, recalls how hearing songs on the radio opened his imagination: "It made me listen for little things: the slamming of the door, the jingling of car keys. The wind blowing through trees, the songs of birds, footsteps, a hammer hitting a nail. Just random sounds. Cows mooing. I could string all that together and make that a song. It made me listen to life in a different way...I'd think about them even at my school desk."[14] Bob Dylan was awarded an honorary degree from Princeton University in 1970, but was skeptical about attending the ceremony. His friend David Cosby persuaded him to go. Crosby remembers:

> You know, an honorary degree from Princeton didn't really mean that much to him. I thought, 'It's got to be a curious experience, you know? A lot of brains there. Might be somebody interesting, you know—might be.' So we went down and it devolved into an argument between him and them about whether or not he would put on a robe—cap and gown, right? And he said, 'No. Not going to do it.' And they said, 'Well, you have to do it, we're Princeton, and this is...We're giving you an *honorary* deg...', you know. They got all huffy and he was even

less impressed with that. I said, 'Bob, what's the difference?' He said, 'Eh.' So
he reluctantly put a gown around his shoulders—but you could still see he had
a T-Shirt and jeans under. He was singularly unimpressed.[15]

Today, scholars study Bob Dylan intensively and in 2016 he was awarded
the Nobel Prize for Literature.

Meanwhile, many artists also demonstrate that education, of course, comes
in handy. Dar Williams says of a course she took called "Human Prospect"
at Wesleyan University: "That was a class that introduced 'think global, act
local.' Literally it was the first time I heard that expression, and the first time I
heard about global warming. That sort of made its way into my music."[16] Tom
Morello has his degree from Harvard: "I went there with the explicit purpose
of it steeling my resolve to create revolutionary change in the world." "I wrote
my senior thesis," Morello says, "on student uprisings in South Africa, and
was part of the student uprising at Harvard against Harvard's investments."
He adds: "…when the alumni would come a couple of times a year, to see
how beautiful the university was and to write big checks for the university,
we would build shantytowns that looked exactly like the Johannasberg shantytowns, where people were suffering under Apartheid rule. So that when
they would arrive they would see their beautiful lawns covered with debris
and these shanties."[17] David Crosby reflects on his experiences as a student
at Santa Barbara City College where he studied mass media and communications. "I read a book by Hayakawa called *Language in Thought and Action*,
which is sort of where semantics came from. I was fascinated by language—
not just by languages, but by how language worked, and why it did what it did.
Because, to me it was the bridge between human beings. It was the thing that
lessens the distance between us, was the communication. It was our big plus.
Communication got to be sort of, my magic."[18] Today's challenges for education, he says, are the value systems inculcated in society: "The value systems
now in this country are completely haywired. It's all about surface and nothing about substance. It's not— 'Are you a good human being—Ms. Jones?'
It's— 'Do you have big enough tits? Here, we'll put little plastic cupcakes in
there and you can fasten your sense of worth to that.' Instead of: 'What do you
know? Who do you care about? Where have you been? What have you seen?
What kind of human being are you? What do you value? What matters to you?
Who do you help? What's the best idea that you had this week?'" Crosby says,
"It's about surface, not substance, and that's a terrible, terrible set of values."[19]

Wetlands, Rivers, and Schools

Some of America's most influential artists' managers have worked at
unique crossroads of educational and musical experiences. Kathy Kane,

who manages Bonnie Raitt gained her college experience at the University of Michigan—included building a self-designed major in "International Economic Relations of Developing Countries." This allowed her to study in Brazil where her research showed export-processing zones were not solutions to the economic development problems facing Brazil. "When I graduated from Michigan," Kathy Kane says: "I answered an ad in the *New York Times* about 'chasing rainbows.' I went in for this interview at Wetlands nightclub in New York City, with the owner named Larry Bloch. He was hiring Environmental Directors for his nightclub. And his nightclub, since the beginning, had always been about 'a watering hole for activists too'—a place where activists and nonprofit working groups could get together and have meetings and take action." She went to work at Wetlands Preserve, where education about environmental issues was integrated with rock and roll, Kathy Kane says: "We had an Earth Station inside the club that had petitions, literature to take with you and a calendar of activist events going on around the city and at the club; and an old VW camper where I used to sell t-shirts and merchandise like bumper stickers with political slogans on them."[20]

Wetlands Preserve became a form of advanced rock and roll education. Matt Busch, who manages Bob Weir of the Grateful Dead, was also involved in the Wetlands scene. Busch went to SUNY-Albany where he "had no direction whatsoever." At the same time, Matt Busch adds: "I 'grew up' in the Wetlands in New York City…I feel like I grew up in that bar as much as anywhere." Busch remembers, "I saw everyone there—Blues Traveler, Spin Doctors, Phish, all those were bands we grew up with." He found a job nearby that included distributing merchandise for bands playing Wetlands:

> It was our Haight-Ashbury so to speak. It was a club where you could come in and it was unique in that it wasn't just design, stage, and audience. If the club held six or seven hundred people, I believe, you could really only fit two or three hundred of those people right in front of the stage. Then, it had this basement that was, depending on the night, it either had its own entire music entity happening down there—whether it was another live band or D.J. or taped music; or they would pump the upstairs music to the downstairs if it was that popular. But the downstairs was sort of a place where you could go smoke a joint down there. You could bring anything you wanted down there and get away with it, and do almost anything. It was very lounge-oriented. That little free-for-all created a vibe and so it made it a place for people like us to go five nights a week. We didn't even care who played half the time. Now, it's an apartment building.[21]

Busch says: "The amazing thing about the Wetlands, at that time, was that [when bands from outside the region came in] suddenly there were all these college kids with southern accents at the bar. Widespread Panic, first couple of times they would play, same kind of deal. As other regional bands would finally get on tour and come to the Wetlands, it brought kind of like a commu-nity together because none of us knew the others existed." Busch adds: "That was sort of the introduction, at least for us, of shows involving nonprofits and an educational aspect too."[22]

For Cameron Sears, education in and out of the classroom brought him to be the Grateful Dead's manager in the 1980s. Sears grew up in New England where his grandfather was Pete Seeger's high school adviser. "After I graduated from high school," Sears says, "I did a NOLS [National Outdoor Leadership School] course in Wyoming; three and a half months of wilder-ness training. And it was when I got back from that that I became a river guide. I worked in the Grand Canyon, Tuolomne, Rogue River—all over the Western states basically."[23] Sears was also a student at U.C. Santa Cruz majoring in Environmental Studies:

> I wrote my thesis on protecting the Tuolomne. I was working doing grassroots organizing in California. Then I moved into doing all the river trips one summer in the effort to either raise money or introduce influential people to the plight of the Tuolomne. This was '83-'84, I was running two trips a week. I had one day off and we just kept running trips—whoever we could take down; congressional people, actors, people of influence, philanthropists from the city. Ultimately that fall, the bill was passed and the river was protected. It was in that vein that I contacted the Grateful Dead, to try to introduce them to water politics in California.[24]

Sears says: "The one thing about water politics and river politics—the best tool that you have in terms of educating people is actually taking them on the river and experiencing what it is. If people haven't seen it, it doesn't make a lot of sense." Sears recalls: "I wrote the Dead a letter, and I hand-delivered it to the office. My future mother-in-law [Eileen Law] answered the door and took it and put it on the way. I called back a couple of weeks later to follow up on it. It was a, 'Don't call us, we'll call you,' kind of response." But: "A month or so after that, Danny Rifkin who was managing the band at the time called me and said, 'Hey, I've got 20 people who want to go on a river trip with you—can we still do it?.'"

Bertis Downs, longtime adviser to R.E.M., serves on the Board of the Network for Public Education, which opposes privatization of public edu-cation, mass school closures to save money or to facilitate privatization, demonization of teachers, lowering of standards for the education profession, and for-profit management of schools. Downs says: "It seems like it's the issue that matters to me politically because of all the things that Republicans and Democrats don't seem to get together on, they get together really badly on this one."[25] Since 2008, about $330 million has been diverted from public to private schools in Georgia. Nationally, the total amount of money diverted via tax credit scholarships or direct vouchers to private schools approached $1 billion in 2014.[26] Downs says this is happening, "…while we're cutting public schools and we have less librarians, nurses, and teachers year-by-year—drip, drip, drip. We're diverting all that money to tuitions for private schools; some of which teach creationism and virtually none of which have encountered diversity." But, Downs adds the government is: "…padding them with taxpayer dollars and then there's no testing. Then they leave a, by definition, 'failing' public school and then the minute they get to this marvelous private school, they're never tested again. We have no idea if the kids are learning anything or not." He warns: "In testing like crazy—and, what we're starting in Georgia now—even the no-tested subjects. Music, art, PE, will now have multiple-choice tests, multiple weeks, at the beginning of the year and at the end of the year, which takes away from instruction in things like—arts, music, and PE. The idea, Downs says, of evaluating a teacher based on standardized tests is, "Madness, but it's the law. It's fifty percent of their evaluation."[27] In March 2014, Bertis Downs wrote an open letter to Barack Obama in the *Washington Post*: "Surely you must recognize that privatized models of competition conflict with American education's historic commitment to empower each child to reach his or her highest potential, a commitment based on educators working together in collaboration as a team."[28]

"You're Doing It Exactly Right"

Bertis Downs has long taught writing and entertainment law at the University of Georgia. He says: "When the band would come off the road, after being busy and out of town for two years, we would come back (to Athens, Georgia) and have essentially a year off. I'd go and teach my Entertainment Law class."[29] Similarly, Johanna Fatemen of Le Tigre teaches "Art and Protest" at New York University. She says: "What I try to encourage my students to do, what I think is important, it's just so basic; is to find something that you're personally invested in. Aesthetics, of course, are crucial. I just think that what's going to carry you through can dictate the form. The style is something that you actually care about. And whatever skills you learn, they're not going to be meaningful unless they're in service of a vision that has some real meaning to you."[30] Dar Williams has taught a course called "Music Movements in a Capitalist Democracy" at Wesleyan University. She says:

> We did a map of Greenwich Village. I named some things and I told the kids to look up addresses. We found things in Suze's book [Bob Dylan's early girl-friend, Suze Rotolo] and in *Don't Look Back* and in some other things. There were these things that were named and I said, 'Pull out addresses, pull out names.' So we had White Horse Tavern and we had the Café Wha? We had

the whole 9 yards of all those things. I had the bagel shop and I had Allan Block's sandal shop because people used to play old time piano there—and Washington Square Park and an unfinished furniture store there. I said, 'Why do you think I put the bagel shop and this coffee shop and the unfinished furniture in the mix?' And one of the kids said: 'Because they're all cheap?' And I said, 'Because they're cheap!'[31]

Dar Williams showed that people, at a key historical moment, had "…all of this music as part of their lives. They could afford it. They were together. And they listened to each other's music. Out of it you say, 'Dylan, Dylan, Dylan.' But when these kids got to Greenwich Village and started playing music side by side, they had Pete [Seeger] and the Beat poets and old Irish guys. You had a lot of avuncular players coming along and saying, 'People, we've been doing this for decades now—welcome to the party. You're doing everything right.'"[32]

SCHOOLHOUSE ROCK

The rock and roll challenge to institutions of power often begins at school, with teenagers rebelling against authority. When Chuck Berry sang about freedom that came with the ringing of the bell at 3:00 PM every school day, or when Twisted Sister was singing "I Wanna Rock" —they helped define freedom for a new generation. At the same time, rock and roll has been applied as a positive influence empowering children's education. This was true of the *Schoolhouse Rock* series that ran Saturday mornings between 1973 and 1985 on *ABC*. The idea was that children might better learn via rock and roll. Similarly, *Sesame Street* has long had rocking guests and Beatles songs, like "Let It Be" became "Letter B" —learning the alphabet with song. The spinoff *The Muppets* featured rock and rollers as guest hosts and had its own puppet house band—Dr. Mahem and the Electric Teeth. Many children grew up to know Ringo Starr—not as the Beatles's drummer; but as the host of *Thomas the Tank*. Steven Van Zandt, of the E. Street Band, took this rock and roll education a step further, through his Rock and Roll Forever Foundation. "We realized," Van Zandt says, "there is a drop out epidemic that is appalling" —with over 1.2 million students dropping out of high school every year.[33] "Statistics show, if the kid likes one class, or one subject, or one teacher, that's enough to get them to school," Van Zandt observes: "And, we want to be that class."[34]

Little Kids Rock

Little Kids Rock offers rock and roll support for cash-strapped public school music programs. The organization, based in Verona, New Jersey, was created in 2002 by David Wish, an elementary school teacher, with initial support from John Lee Hooker, Bonnie Raitt, and Carlos Santana. Since 2002, this program made up for cuts in music education in 1,750 schools; provided 50,000 instruments; and invested $12 million in twenty-nine cities across thirteen states, serving over 400,000 children.[35] Wish says:

> Music education is delivered best when students are at the center of their own learning—when the motivation to learn is internal as opposed to external. So my vision is that the entire U.S. public school system—not a portion, not a couple of cool schools, but the whole, big, sprawling, overwhelmingly enormous organism - makes music universally available to children. What does that translate to? Rock and roll, reggae, popular music—youth culture being reflected.[36]

To David Wish, "Children who see themselves reflected in their schools feel valued by their schools. Children who see themselves reflected in the curriculum and their culture reflected in the curriculum, feel valued by the curriculum."[37]

"The way I've been trying to set the agenda," David Wish says, "is by defining a new category of music education in U.S. public schools, which I call 'Modern Band'":

> If you look at the landscape of music education, it's divided into: marching band, you know, the music of John Philip Sousa on trombone and tuba, etc.; jazz band, the music of Ellington and Basie on saxophone and rhythm section; orchestra, which is classical music, strings, etc.; then there's general music where you learn about theory; and then what? Modern Band. Modern Band is the category of music education that everybody's been waiting for. Everybody. All the millions of people that you can meet today had music as kids. But it didn't stick because the methods that they were introduced to music by and the actual material that they were introduced to did not connect with them where they were.[38]

Creative activities are not limited, in his view, to the artists and an elite group. "No, that's not true," Wish says, adding: "Anybody who's ever built or done a thing of value at all in their lives is creative. If you've built a family, didn't you create them, quite literally? Didn't you fashion the family bonds that bind them together? Didn't you navigate difficult situations and create solutions? When you build your business, aren't you creating it? When you come up with a new marketing strategy—aren't you creating it? And when you put a child in touch with their creative sides, they're infinitely less attracted to the cheap thrills of destructive behavior, because kids are looking for agency. And they're going to get it wherever they can." Thus, if a child is disempowered they can get some of that "release" through destructive behavior. But, Wish adds: "I think those things are cheap and empty calories whereas being in a band, writing a song, communing with the music that you know and love and creating something of beauty in the world—even if it's only beautiful to you—is, in many ways, the best possible gift we can give to our children—and to ourselves."[39]

Little Kids Rock is not intended as a policy or a frame or a movement. David Wish explains: "I started to realize that the organizational efforts of Little Kids Rock were beginning to convene a movement and define a frame. And I had my epiphany when I was talking to a partner in one of our school districts who said, 'Dave, do you realize that at the schools you're in, in my district, you're reaching about a third of our kids?' and I said, 'Yeah, I guess,' but I couldn't tell why she was so excited. She was like, 'Do you understand that I take my marching band, my jazz band, my orchestra and combine them, we're not reaching thirty percent of the kids. So you've completely built-out the number of kids in my district that are doing music.'"[40] Wish points to Little Kids Rock programs like "Amp Up New York City": "That's where we're going to be launching Modern Band programs in New York City public schools, 600 of them building on the over 200 schools they are already engaged at with New York City."[41] The engagement with New York City began as a partnership with Berklee College of Music and is organized with the New York Department of Education. The goal was, over three years beginning in 2014, to reach 60,000 K-12 children with Modern Band via teacher training, classroom instruction, online technology, and providing instruments. David Wish says:

> If you'd gone into New York City five years ago and asked them about Little Kids Rock, you know what you would have heard from the top leadership?: 'We love Little Kids Rock. Little Kids Rock is great. They support our teachers, they give us instruments. We really like them. They're wonderful.' Now what they say is: 'We have an educational priority in our district to build Modern Band programs and Little Kids Rock helps facilitate that for us. They're helping *us* build *our* Modern Band program—not theirs—because we're paying the teachers. They're just giving them the training that they need, the curriculum that they need, and also instruments to kind of get the ball started. But this is very much *our* program.'[42]

"You can't absolve the public," David Wish says, "because those schools— they are the public. They're funded by the public."[43]

An "epic scale" vision for music education interests David Wish the most and he says the vehicle is not Little Kids Rock:

> The vehicle is the public school system themselves. Working in partnership, I say: 'Guys, this is a priority. Don't drop the ball. It's one of the most important priorities you can have above all of the other things that you've got. If you're

going to churn out a generation of non-creative children, we are in deep trouble.' First of all, we're already in deep trouble. But we have no chance of getting out of the hole unless we can start graduating generations of creative problem solvers. And it's not going to come using the formulas we've used in the past.[44]

"Modern Band," David Wish says, "is just a tactic. The fissile material that we carry—the real stuff—is our method which is really more like Suziki meets Orff meets the Rolling Stones meets your first grade school teacher—all in the blender and nobody gets hurt." In the Modern Band curriculum, students are playing songs in the first five minutes of the first class. Wish asserts: "I can literally prove to any music teacher that before that child even walks in your door, they've already acquired a huge amount of music—and starting your program with reading and writing, it goes against what I think is the natural way that humans acquire music. You don't learn language, not your first one. You acquire it through use. I don't think people really learn music. I think they acquire it. Once they've acquired it, they can learn it."[45]

David Wish believes that music education gets cut in school budgets because of a "crisis of relevancy." He notes sports programs get cut but parents tend to get vocal over sports cuts because they understand the educational value in teamwork and physical fitness—and because they are often sports fans. Wish says: "When music programs get cut, there's less of a hoot and a holler." For music education:

It's death by a thousand cuts—It's actually site by site by site, school by school by school. The decision is made generally by a beleaguered executive who has a reduced budget from the state and has to decide, 'Where am I going to get rid of something?' He looks at his science teacher and says, 'Well, this science teacher is reaching 250 kids a week,' and looks at his math teacher and is reaching 250 kids a week. He looks at the librarian and she's reaching this…whatever. And he gets to the music teacher, who runs a killer program for the band—a great marching band, gets the whole school really excited at the football games and there's thirty eight kids participating. And he's got to figure out who to cut. And he doesn't want to fire that person, but if he's going to fire someone, that's the job to go. Now, what if that teacher was also reaching twenty or thirty percent of the school?[46]

Wish believes, "…it's going to make these programs a lot harder to cut because the kids are going to be more emotionally invested. The community is going to be emotionally invested."

The Little Kids Rock program's first rock and roll support came from Carlos Santana. "When I was a school teacher in Redwood City," Wish says, "they [Santana's charity foundation, Milagro] gave me a grant to buy guitars.

That was, in many ways, the first inkling that I had that, 'Wow, this little thing that I'm doing with my kids has resonance beyond my four walls. I was like, 'Woah, Carlos Santana heard the music that our kids wrote and was moved and decided to invest so that I could serve more kids." Wish says about the rock and rollers engaged with Little Kids Rock:

> There's a deep personal resonance. You know, when Slash [guitarist for Guns & Roses] walks into a school in East L.A., and sits down with 60 middle school kids who fall into playing 'Sweet Child of Mine'…I mean, you know, here's the man who wrote the song. And these children are paying homage to the impact that he's had on their lives, playing his song back to him. What's not to like? And, by the way, they're learning to play in much the same way that Slash learned to play. The difference is that Slash had to learn on the street and in the backs of guitar stores and diving into the back of *Guitar Player* magazine.[47]

Liberty Devitto, a longtime supporter, says: "It's harder to learn how to play an instrument than it is to shoot a gun, or go to the mall. Do you want to do something different? Do something difficult? Try to play the drums. Try to play a guitar." Devitto asserts: "So with Little Kids Rock, the government is taking it out of the schools and we're putting it back in—saying: 'This is *really important*. It's as important as sports. It's as important as learning math."[48]

Little Kids Rock operates on an annual $4 million budget generated from donations, events, and sponsorships. The Little Kids Rock's staff measures their outreach: tracking 2013–2014, sixty-two percent of teachers responding felt capable of teaching new styles of music and fifty-seven percent felt fulfilled as an educator and sixty-two percent greater connection to their students; ninety-eight percent of those responding strongly recommended Little Kids Rock to their peers.[49] Wish explains: "We are working on a sustainability plan for all of our existing markets (about 30) and it sees us at being in more than half of the schools of our partner districts. We estimate that this would cost us approximately $12M to accomplish and that would empower us to build a program that will serve over 600,000 kids annually. That sounds like a lot of $ and it is but…our annual budget now is over 4M and we currently are serving 195,360 kids."[50] Prominent rock stars raise funds and educate about Little Kids Rock. Pearl Jam donated forty drum kits to Nashville Public Schools. Korn guitarist Munky delivered instruments to the McKinley School in Pasadena, California, while celebrating a $1.2 million donation from *Hot Topic*. A 2014 event honoring Joan Jett raised $1.5 million for Little Kids Rock programs.[51] Jett remembered: "… in my music classes, we didn't get those options: you'd play violin or you'd play clarinet or something like that. They certainly didn't have drum sets, they may have had cymbals or a marching snare. But kids hear a lot of music from a young age, and if they have the inclination to want to try playing, they should have the option."[52]

Little Kids Rock supports an innovative international program founded by Sara Wasserman, called "Music Heals International," which focuses on music education in Haiti. The poorest country in the Western Hemisphere, eighty percent of Haitians live below the poverty line and fifty-four percent live in deep poverty.[53] The island is vulnerable to political turmoil and corruption, earthquakes, hurricanes, and poor agricultural conditions. Literacy rates are among the lowest in the world—about fifty-five percent. Only two percent of children pass exams that take them past the fifth grade.[54] In this context, Music Heals International and its leader Sara Wasserman are helping a local district in Haiti build Modern Band. Wasserman, the daughter of Grammy-winning bass player Rob Wasserman, is also an accomplished singer having worked with Lou Reed and Aaron Neville. In 2012, Wasserman was invited by J/P Haiti Relief Organization (HRO) [a relief organization founded by Sean Penn] to teach music in Haiti:

I invited Lukas Nelson, Willie's son, to go with me and that's how it all started. We spent ten days, and nothing like that had really been done at J/P HRO,

Children participating in Music Heals International perform in Port-Au-Prince, Haiti. Liam Storrings for J/P Haitian Relief Organization

immersing the kids in music and songs and performing. I made a promise to the kids and to people I was working with there, that I would come back. Because people are in and out of their lives that they never see. I just wanted to keep my commitment. I came back two months later and I brought instruments every time. I bring guitars, just somehow sneak them on the plane. I brought a keyboard and percussion eggs—these tiny little kids were running out of the community center with their pockets shaking (from the eggs). Those things matter to them. They were just so excited to have access to those instruments, and that's when it hit me.[55]

Wasserman adds: "For kids who are growing up in such poverty, it can inspire them to feel like there is something bigger than where they are. It's a big part of what I'm trying to do with this—to empower them to think outside of their environment and where they are, and what's possible."[56]

The first full program commenced in 2014 at the Port-au-Prince district Delmas 32. With a population of about 90,000, this area is one of Haiti's poorest. The program ran in the "School of Hope" at a local community development campus where there has been scarce access to instruments and instruction. Jean Marc Didis (the community project manager) says of the initial impact: "While children are learning music, they are also learning their mathematics. Music is very helpful in mathematics because when you play music you have to time your notes accurately as you're playing. This is very important—and, it brings social cohesion to the community."[57] The first program reached sixty students and resulted in 11 trained teachers working with the Modern Band curriculum. As they were getting organized, Wasserman recalls a friend suggested she meet David Wish. Wasserman recalls: "We met in New York on my way back from Haiti and in that conversation we decided that I was going to bring that program [Little Kids Rock] to Haiti. We're basically transcribing the Little Kids Rock program to Haitian culture." It is, she says, a lot of work: "I'm doing all the fundraising for it, and then translating all the material and shipping all the instruments. I mean the curriculum book (from Little Kids Rock) is still 325 pages, because I don't want to cut it back. I want them to have everything. It's for the teachers, but for the kids, that's going to be their lessons for the whole year and so I don't want them to not have access to certain things."[58]

Sara Wasserman observes the impact that Music Heals International is having, and what it can do if expanded:

We did a performance on the roof of a building in Delmas 32 at the end of the summer. We had two boys playing 'Redemption Song' [by Bob Marley]. And then I sang with one of the girls. So just being up there on this roof like, you can't even explain what it looks like, the community, but it's amazing. So we're sitting up there on a roof performing for the entire community just standing, lined up in the entire street. And it was powerful because you realize that was really the first experience they've had being able to perform something that they've learned in front of their community.[59]

"I want to start small, and then grow it," Wasserman says: "We really are doing something that's never been done in Haiti. And, Haiti is not an easy country to work in as we all know." The impact, she says, goes beyond the children learning, into the community. "I think what's important is for the community to start it small and for the community to see the kids really doing it. I think everybody's going to really believe in what we are doing when you actually see a kid being able to play like that, able to perform. Then they will see the value in it."[60]

Rock and Roll Camp for Girls

Rock and rollers have taken the educational movement further, advancing equality through music education. In 2000, a Portland State University student majoring in women's studies, Misty McElroy, created a rock camp for girls. It first had no financial backing, and logistics were limited to a 100-space room at Portland State University.[61] The initial camp led to an after-school program, a Girls Rock Institute, Ladies Rock Camp (three-day workshops for adult women, which raise money for the children's programs), an internship program, and a record label. Carrie Brownstein of the band Sleater-Kinney has volunteered at the Portland camp teaching approaches to empowerment, self-defense, and anger management via rock and roll. Likewise, Emily Saliers of the Indigo Girls has led a songwriting class at the Atlanta, Georgia, affiliate camp program. These disparate parts come together in the Girls Rock Camp Alliance, which supports forty-three member camps in eight countries around the world. About 3,000 girls participate each year with 750 new bands formed.[62] Girls rock camps are also moving into the Riot Grrrl legacy, as with the Columbus, Ohio, based Grrrls Rock Columbus. When the first camp ended in summer 2014, the Grrrls Rock Camp in Columbus culminated in a performance of the Bikini Kill song "Rebel Girl." Kathleen Hanna says about the rock camp movement:

> Whether the girls who attend these camps ever become full time musicians or not is beyond the point, the fact that they tried something and were encouraged will hopefully allow them to try all sorts of new things. And I tend to think that a person who tries new things often finds what they truly love to do eventually. And that becomes a reason, to get out of bed, to not give up, to keep on going when things really suck. It makes you feel valuable and important and worth defending. And to me, that's why Rock Camps are so much more important than just creating more girl bands.[63]

Kathleen Hanna has been a volunteer instructor at the Willie May Rock Camp for Girls in New York.

THE GRAMMYS AND THE ROCK HALL

The Grammy Foundation and the Rock and Roll Hall of Fame and Museum offer educational programs built around rock and roll. The Grammy Foundation promotes music preservation, recognizes a music educator of the year, provides grants to "Signature Schools" that are innovating in music education, and sponsors music education summer camps. The Foundation gives an annual Music Educator Award and in 2015, seven of the quarter-finalists were teachers working in the Little Kids Rock curriculum. At the Grammy Museum, in Los Angeles, exhibits and extensive curricular programs use rock and roll to educate. Meanwhile, the Rock and Roll Hall of Fame and Museum based in Cleveland, Ohio, celebrates inductees and educates about rock and roll and society.

"It Starts a Conversation"

The Grammy Museum seeks to: "Use music as a gateway to learning; inspiring and cultivating creativity, critical-thinking and self-expression." It helps to: "Equip K-12 educators with strategies and resources to demonstrate the power of music in the classroom" and uses its resources to "…increase access to music programs in underprivileged communities, empowering youth to reach their full creative potential."[64] The Grammy Museum's education program is run by Kaitlyn Stuebner. She says: "Whether you're talking about toddlers up through a 110-year-old that would come in, it's all about creating a community of people who think that music can make a change, or that view music as a way for people to move different ideas forward or to take a stand for something." Stuebner adds:

> We get so many history teachers coming in, or calling me, asking, 'This is my lesson, I have to teach 8th graders about the Declaration of Independence, or we're teaching about American history, we're doing all of these things. How can you help me? What can we do to incorporate music into this?' And that's true of our exhibits as well. We're opening a 'Star Spangled Banner' exhibit. So the history of the 'Star Spangled Banner' as it relates to pop culture to celebrate the 200 years since the 'Star Spangled Banner.' We'll talk about Jimi Hendrix and Jose Feliciano, and Whitney Houston—and kind, of the best and worst of the 'Star Spangled Banner.'[65]

A young teen today might not know who Jimi Hendrix was, but Stuebner says students are, "…making a connection between maybe what their grandparents listened to, or their parents listened to and what they're listening to."[66]

Kaitlyn Stuebner notes that at the museum: "We really are trying to create sophisticated listeners and use music to get students to think critically about other issues." Stuebner says: "Anytime that they can use music as a gateway to learning or replace some of the music classes that have been cut, by playing a Graham Nash song in their 1960s/1970s curricula, talking about the Vietnam War, talking about the civil rights movement, we encourage them to do that." She adds: "We create curricula here as well, so every exhibit that you see has lessons—middle and high school lessons that are attached to it, that are up for free on our website. I probably have 600 additional lessons on my computer, we just don't have the space to put them on the website, so we're building an archive of curricular." The education program does not shirk difficult issues. Kaitlyn Stuebner notes, for example, they use Serj Tankian: "We always talk about him when we talk about artists using their voice for social change." Referencing Tankian's song and video "Empty Walls" (which addresses the September 2001 terrorist attacks via children's imagery), Stuebner says: "It's little kids on a playground going through the motions, so there's paper airplanes and building blocks. We always show that in our Music of War class and students are blown away by it because it's so much of a political statement told through the innocence of children." Stuebner says that in the Music of War class: "We talk about how music inspires soldiers when they're fighting or how they'll use certain songs to kind of pump themselves up. We talk about the difference between 'The Ballad of the Green Beret'; you know, music being on one side, and then we talk about 'War' by Edwin Starr on the other side. So it's kind of talking about the difference in music as its played out in society." She recalls in one program, they had an iPod from a soldier in the Iraq war: "It was a list of his songs—why he chose different songs and what he listened to before he knew he had to go out and do something that was going to be pretty dangerous."[67] They got inputs from the soldier to explain the thought process behind the music they listened to, for example, what they listened to after combat in order to wind down and attain some sense of normalcy. Steubner notes U.S. soldiers in Iraq often chose strong antiwar themes—that is, music by System of a Down.

The Grammy Museum provides teachers with program guides and activities to use with students in an integrated curriculum for before and after visiting. Between 2009 and 2014, the museum estimates it directly engaged over 130,000 students. The curriculum utilizes music to advance learning in areas like English language, science, math, and politics. Kaitlyn Stuebner notes: "Being in downtown L.A., you have a lot to choose from—East L.A., South L.A., just the actual downtown community. We're offering opportunities for students who maybe have never had a music class in their life, have never sat behind a drum kit, never touched a harmonica or recorder." Power, she says:

> …is, for us, the ability to create change and I think whether that's a teacher cre-
> ating change in the classroom, or a student creating change within themselves,
> it's the ability to do something that you didn't think you could do before and
> using music to help find what that thing might be, whether it's a career in music
> or just the ability to understand a certain subject that you didn't think that you
> were good at or interested in. You have that one thing that creates the change in
> you. We hope its music.[68]

Stuebner says: "Macklemore and Ryan Lewis and Mary Lambert marrying couples, whether they're gay, straight, anyone, on the Grammys—that's tak-ing a stand and its using music for social change." She concludes: "It starts a conversation. It starts a conversation with yourself, or with your parent, or with your community. And that's the way that we view change starts."[69]

Cleveland Rocks!

The Rock and Roll Hall of Fame and Museum opened in Cleveland, Ohio, in 1995 "…to celebrate the musicians that changed the world."[70] The Rock Hall is built on the principle that: "…music has the power to bring genera-tions, nationalities and people together. Now more than ever, it's critical to study and understand how music is changing our world as well as reflecting it."[71] The Rock and Roll Hall of Fame and Museum reaches 40,000 students and teachers annually and their distance learning program has been used in forty-five states and eight countries. Vice President of Education and Public Programs, Lauren Onkey, says: "We believe this music has been, and con-tinues to be, a significant art form and we believe it's important to make that case. It's interesting to me that even in 2015, you can still get a bit of snobbery about popular music, that it's not really art, and 'what are you guys doing in there?' and 'it's not really education.' She adds: "It's not like music departments were any friend to rock and roll particularly."[72]

Lauren Onkey says of their approach to learning: "You're trying to teach the same core idea and you're thinking about different platforms for it. You're not dumbing it down or things like that."[73] For its Pre-K program, the Rock and Roll Hall of Fame and Museum hosts "Toddler Rock" that is run by board-certified music therapists (headed by prominent music thera-pist Dr. Deforia Lane) and serves nearly seven hundred Head Start children each year. The goal is to use rock and roll to develop critical thinking, math and reading ability, and cognitive development for success in school. The approach uses creative methods, such as letter identification built around rock and roll artists—"A is for Aretha; B is for Beach Boys; etc." Lauren Onkey says: "Candidly, that program could happen at a lot of places off-site. But the fact that it's here, what we hope is that it gives the young kids ownership of the Rock Hall. These are kids from the City of Cleveland—this is their place. They get to come into this really fun cool space and they feel special."[74] The K-12 "Rockin' in the Schools" provides for free programming for schools in the northeast Ohio region. These are generally day visits to the Rock and Roll Hall of Fame and Museum and include a targeted lecture, a self-guided museum tour, and teacher materials for use before and after the field trip.

The Rock and Roll Hall of Fame and Museum has built a public access digital learning program featuring specific songs, like Bill Haley and the Comets performing "(We're Gonna) Rock Around the Clock":

> There is no first rock and roll record, one moment or location where the music was born. But for many young listeners, Bill Haley and His Comets recording of 'Rock Around the Clock' was the first rock and roll record they ever heard, both in the US and the United Kingdom, where rock and roll had a big impact. The song was recorded in 1954 but got its biggest exposure when it was featured in the opening credits of *Blackboard Jungle*, a 1955 film set in New York City that dramatized the problems of what was called 'juvenile delinquency.' While the song's mix of country, jazz and rhythm and blues might not have had the abandon of some other rock and roll songs, it came to represent rebellion for the young generation interested in rock and roll.[75]

Three major learning objectives are identified: to explain how the song uses and transforms country music elements; understand how the song became an early symbol for rock and roll rebellion when it was used in the film *Blackboard Jungle*; and to explain how the song became one of rock and roll's first hit songs through exposure on radio, television, and films. Jason Hanley, the museum's education director, explains: "If you listen to the sound of 'Rock Around the Clock' you'll hear a lot of country music elements. One really important one is the upright bass. It has this kind of slapping tone to it. It plays what's called 'Walking Bass', where the bass is moving up and down the scale of each chord that's being played."[76] Context for examining "Rock Around the Clock" is provided in a graphic: between 1946 and 1964, seventy-seven million babies were born in America; by 1956, the total teen-age consumer market was worth $9 billion; in 1955, some eight million cars were sold in the United States; and while between 1939 and 1941, some seven thousand television sets had been sold, between 1949 and 1955 that number was over 39.2 million.[77] Teachers are able to download from the Rock and Roll Hall of Fame and Museum's website detailed lesson plans, classroom tools, a glossary, a resource guide, and suggested Power point presentations. Lauren Onkey says: "We're averaging over the last five years a ninety-five percent rating of excellent by teachers on the key learning objectives."[78]

The Rock and Roll Hall of Fame and Museum thrives, but not without controversy. The location upset some people, especially in Memphis, Tennessee, which also lay claim to rock and roll origins. Cleveland's role, however, was addressed by Ringo Starr in his 2015 solo induction:

> I love that I got lucky that it's actually in Cleveland—and I'll tell you why. You know, we lived in England, we only had the *BBC*, but out of madness there was a small country in Europe called Luxembourg. Very small—population about six. For some reason, they had the biggest radio mast and they bought the Alan Freed rock and roll show which came from here! And so the first time I hear Little Richard, first time ever I hear Jerry Lee Lewis who is here tonight, first time ever I heard rock and roll music because we weren't getting a lot of that stuff in England. So 4:00 every Sunday, turn on the radio, and Alan Freed would introduce us to so many great records and acts.

More controversial for the Rock and Roll Hall of Fame Foundation (which is separate from the museum) are the artists who have been passed over. Artists who have had a record at least twenty-five years prior to consideration are eligible to be on the ballot for induction. The decision on who is selected is taken by a group of 600 artists, industry people, historians, etc., but the vote spread is secret. Eligible candidates are selected by a smaller Induction Nominating Committee, which can make deserving inductees wait a long time, if they get in at all. Some critics assert that the Rock Hall is too subjective. For example, ABBA was inducted in 2010 before a long list of enduring and deserving rockers. ABBA had an important place in popular music, but it was unclear their entry justified coming in before, for example, Joan Baez, the B-52s, or Yes. It might, after 2015, become a higher climb as the Rock and Roll Hall of Fame Foundation cut to sixteen from forty-two the members of the nominating committee.

Frustration over who is, or is not, inducted to the Rock and Roll Hall of Fame exists among fans and scholars. John Covach (Chair of the music department at the University of Rochester) wrote in 2010:

> In considering such issues of historical objectivity, it's only fair to point out that the Rock and Roll Hall of Fame and Museum is not primarily a historical institution; those who nominate and vote on the inductees seem to be mostly music industry people and journalists. To the best of my knowledge, none of the academic rock historians I know has ever been contacted about voting or nominating; I know I never have. The voters are thus very knowledgeable about rock music, but are not necessarily historically oriented or trained. Since induction to the Rock Hall can stimulate back-catalog sales, it's also possible that some of the voters have a deep conflict of interest.[79]

Lauren Onkey addressed this issue in a blog post arguing the exclusion of a progressive rock bands like Yes happened because "Prog Rock" was never fully valued at its peak. The problem, she noted, was that standards for artistic merit cannot be objective, precisely "because they are historically and culturally constructed."[80] Her response seemed to compound the problem because the argument hinged on what the definition of rock and roll is yet the Rock Hall celebrates all tributaries.

Controversy over who is inducted is a dilemma for the education program because they are not involved in the decisions. Lauren Onkey says:

> It's a public debate about who should be in the Hall of Fame, and what people are arguing about is how do you define musical excellence; they're arguing about whether or not popularity plays a role; and, they're arguing about expertise and popular culture. That's really what they're arguing about. They may not say that, but they're saying like, 'Why should a rock critic get more of a voice than a fan.' It's really interesting. So actually what we did was we created a program called 'Voice Your Choice,' because I was like, 'Man, this is a teaching tool!'

She adds: "What you can't say, which is sort of what we all want to say when it comes to our music which is: 'Because it's awesome!'" Onkey continues: "I think we identify with popular music which is why it drives people nuts when their band isn't in because it's almost like you've rejected them and their values in a way. But, when you think about teaching young people, what's really exciting about it is that it helps them articulate what they're hearing, why they value it— '…you can say what you like about that.' It helps them listen. And can they persuade somebody else? So we've had debate teams use it, essay writing use it, music use it. The idea is that, in the end, you don't need to convince me that ELO should be in the Rock Hall. But you need to be sure I understand how you're thinking."[81]

Don't Knock the Rock?

Artists have caused controversy at the Rock and Roll Hall of Fame inductions. Bruce Springsteen took heat for excluding the E. Street Band, which was only inducted in 2014. Some bands, like the Sex Pistols, did not bother show for their induction. Darryl Hall said of Hall and Oates being the only Philadelphia group in the Rock Hall: "What happened to Todd Rundgren, the Stylistics, the Delphonics…Chubby Checker? How about the biggest single in history of the world, Chubby Checker, why isn't he in it? So I'm calling everybody out—there'd better be more Philadelphia artists in this place." Perhaps most problematic is that of 685 Hall of Fame inductees, by 2012 there were fifty-seven women—about 8.3 percent.[82] Approaching her induction in 2015, Joan Jett said: "There should be more women in the Hall of Fame, and more women in rock. They're out there, they just don't get the notice the pop girls do."[83] Lauren Onkey notes that the museum featured a special educational program and major exhibit in 2011 on women that rock but, "Given the history of the music, we wouldn't particularly imagine that it would be 50/50, but it's too low."[84] In his 2016 induction speech, Steve Miller said: "And to the Rock and Roll Hall of Fame, I thank you for your hard work on behalf of all musicians and I encourage you to keep expanding your vision, to be more inclusive of women, and to be more transparent in your dealings with the public, and most importantly, to do much more to provide music in our schools."

WE DON'T NEED NO EDUCATION?

Pink Floyd was right to proclaim in *The Wall* we do not need an education that stifles and indoctrinates people. But by 2016, the United States was in crisis as many of its public schools were failing. Music education has suffered but at the same time seen heroic efforts from rock and rollers to fill gaps. Glen Ballard insists society invest in music education: "I will do anything, go anywhere, [and] speak on behalf of anything that encourages music education."[85] Ballard adds when schools cut music: "It's like: 'What?' Who made that decision?' I mean, how could that possibly be? And, what comes next? I mean they're not going to teach Shakespeare anymore?" Meanwhile, Michael Stanley is reflective about his diverse education: "To me it's that whole thing of—going back to my dad throwing all the records on my bed. 'What's here? Oh my God! He's just given me nineteen different worlds that I can go play in!'"[86]

Chapter Seven

Activism—We Are the World

ROCK AND ROLL ACTIVISM

The 1971 Concert for Bangladesh was the first major benefit rock concert. Organized by George Harrison, it raised money for Bangladesh following civil war and floods. Harrison's efforts raised an immediate $240,000. However, the record and movie rights were assigned to Apple Records and millions of dollars were frozen over a tax dispute. Eventually, in 1985, about $12 million was released via the United Nations.[1] Today, the record and movie rights are managed by the "George Harrison Fund for UNICEF," which continues to aid Bangladesh. In 1979, the No Nukes concerts were held at Madison Square Garden in New York City. Coordinated by John Hall of the band Orleans, these concerts included Jackson Browne, David Crosby, Graham Nash, Bonnie Raitt, James Taylor, and others performing as Musicians United for Safe Energy (M.U.S.E.). Graham Nash writes: "It gave the rock community—meaning all of us—a sense of how powerful our voices could be. And you'll notice that there hasn't been a nuclear power plant built since. I'm not saying the No Nukes concerts pulled that off, but we certainly made things difficult for the Nuclear Regulatory Commission."[2] The M.U.S.E. artists continued advancing No Nukes releasing information videos and staging a reunion concert following the 2011 Fukushima nuclear accident in Japan. Jackson Browne took his activism to a next level when he was arrested along with 2,000 other activists in 1981 for protesting the Diablo Canyon nuclear plant in California. Jackson Browne was, of course, not the first rock and roll star arrested for activism. Joan Baez was arrested in October 1967 in Oakland, California seeking to prevent conscripts from embarking to Vietnam. David Crosby observes: "They'd kick her, they'd spit on her—they, finally, arrest her. She'd go to jail, she'd get bailed. She'd go home, take a shower, have a meal, go right back."[3]

THE LIVE AID LEGACY

Following No Nukes, artists continued advancing important policy issues. Just in 1979 a group of rockers raised funds in concert for the United Nations Fund for Children (UNICEF), the Amnesty International Secret Policeman's Ball was held, and the year closed with a concert for Kampuchea advancing human rights in Cambodia. Graham Nash and others put on "Peace Sunday" at the Rose Bowl in Pasadena, California in June 1982. Over 85,000 people called for a nuclear weapons freeze and advocated for world peace. Graham Nash writes:

> I'd gotten a taste of that power and liked how it went down. Without wasting time, I got involved with another benefit after No Nukes. A man who worked at the United Nations, Irv Sarnoff, showed up at my studio with a proposal to do something to support people less fortunate than we were. He felt it would be more efficient to funnel money to those in need through local churches, and I agreed. I went away from the meeting committed and enthused, and that night, on the edge of sleep, I mapped out the entire event: who to invite to perform, which people to speak, what organizations to include, the staging, the name. We'd hold it at the Rose Bowl, which held one hundred thousand people, and call it Peace Sunday.[4]

The impact of the concert was to consolidate a growing community of likeminded people—and to foreshadow what came next - Live Aid.

The Global Jukebox

In 1984, Irish rocker Bob Geldof was motivated to use music to address hunger and starvation in Africa. That December, Geldof and a team of artists called Band Aid released "Do They Know It's Christmas?" which raised $10 million for famine victims. The song became the largest selling British single at the time. This led Geldof to visit Ethiopia where he conceived of Live Aid - a day of concerts in Britain and the United States (co-produced by Bill Graham), which became a historic event. The effort had already gone global as the U.S.A. for Africa charity followed Band Aid with the hit single "We Are the World" (written by Lionel Ritchie and Michael Jackson) in early 1985 (raising over $63 million for aid to Africa). Live Aid thus was a third pillar of rock and roll assistance to Africa. The *British Broadcasting Corporation* summarizes:

> Billed as 'The Global Jukebox' and hosted by Britain and the USA, Live Aid became the biggest live rock event ever, featuring an amazing line-up of rock stars. Spanning two continents, the concerts were broadcast direct from Wembley Stadium in London and JFK Stadium in Philadelphia. There were also contributions from countries including Japan, Australia, Holland, Yugoslavia, Russia and Germany. The whole event featured 16 hours of live music and was watched by over 1.5 billion people worldwide. The final amount raised exceeded all hopes and totaled over £110m.[5]

The list of participating artists was significant. Classic voices of activism like Joan Baez and Bob Dylan performed. The Beach Boys and Paul McCartney were there; as was Eric Clapton, Crosby, Stills and Nash, Mick Jagger, Led Zepplin, Tom Petty, the Pretenders, Queen, U2, the Who, and Neil Young. Live Aid raised money and expanded global awareness of the 1 million people who had died in Africa due to starvation in 1984 and 1985.

Live Aid is a monument to the communicative power of rock and roll. The legacy regarding aid to Africa, however, is complicated. A humanitarian aid expert, David Rieff wrote in 2005: "...every seasoned aid worker knew then, and knows now, that there is no necessary connection between raising money for a good cause and that money being well spent, just as there is no necessary connection between caring about the suffering of others and understanding the nature or cause of that suffering." David Rieff did not maintain that Live Aid was unhelpful, but it did good and harm:

> Having tried, without great success, to run aid efforts directly, the organisers of Band Aid and Live Aid channelled millions to the NGOs in Ethiopia. The NGOs welcomed the money, not least because it came without the strings imposed by western donor governments. Indeed, Oxfam used some of these funds to run covert supplies to rebel-controlled areas, though officially no major NGO sent food aid to rebel-held territory. A strong case can be made for Live Aid's achievements. According to one Ethiopia expert, Alex de Waal, the relief effort may have cut the death toll by between a quarter and a half. The problem is that it may have contributed to as many deaths. The negative effects of the NGO presence on the government side became more pronounced as the crisis went on. Moreover, the government in Addis Ababa became increasingly adept at manipulating these Live Aid-funded NGOs.[6]

Bob Geldof answered general criticism saying: "I am withering in my scorn for the columnists who say, 'It's not going to work,'" he said: "Even if it doesn't work, what do they propose? Every night forever watching people live on TV dying on our screens?"[7]

A shift followed Live Aid as mega concerts were increasingly used to raise awareness and political pressure. In 1996, the Beastie Boys organized concerts challenging China's oppressive rule over Tibet. The idea was spurred by Adam Yauch of the Beastie Boys and activist Erin Potts, who met while on a trip to Tibet. Erin Potts reflects: "The Beastie Boys are an interesting case…because of who they were when they were 18 years old and hit it big, or 20 years old and hit it big. That Beastie Boys persona, and the misogynist lyrics - on and on and on. It's a beautiful thing to watch a person and a band, or a group of people change."[8] Despite the early Beastie Boys image, in fact, Yauch was a fourteen year old attendee of the No Nukes concerts in 1979, handing out leaflets as a volunteer.[9] Yauch said of his role as an advocate for Tibet: "The more I got involved with the Tibetan cause, I just started realizing that the only way a change is going to come about is through spreading awareness, because our government isn't going to take a stand unless they're forced to."[10]

Erin Potts says of these concerts (held in multiple cities featuring David Crosby, Sean Lennon, the Red Hot Chili Peppers, and U2): "We always called those concerts 'message concerts' not 'benefit concerts'—a benefit concert is to raise money and so a goal of measurement, is: 'How much money did it raise?' and then, hopefully, 'How much money went directly to whatever that cause is?'" Potts says this was a lesson from Live Aid where: "…the money was deployed, but apparently sat on docks, not able to get to actual people." She adds:

> With our concerts, measurements that we were looking at included growth of our partner organizations, for Free Tibet. Before the first concert, there were thirty chapters. Three months later, before school even starts—obviously, it's a school based organization…within just a couple of months, it had tripled. And then it blew up—the last time I counted, which was admittedly five years ago, there was like six hundred and fifty chapters in thirty-something countries around the world. So, that's one of the metrics that we used. We also were advocating for political prisoners—Tibetans who had been arrested inside Tibet and were inside Chinese prisons, trying to get them freed. There were a dozen political prisoners who were freed during the times of the concerts.[11]

Bob Geldof furthered this approach to the 2005 follow up to Live Aid— dubbed Live 8. An estimated 3 billion people watched or heard parts of ten concerts featuring 1,000 artists. They asked people, "Not for their money, but for their voice" - publicizing a "Call To Action against Poverty" which resulted in 30 million signatures presented to then British Prime Minister Tony Blair. Blair took this to the global leaders he hosted in Scotland simultaneous to the concerts. They made promises to: spend $50 billion more aid per year by 2010; provide AIDS drugs to all those who need them and care for all AIDS orphans; debt cancellation for thirty-eight countries, with eighteen benefiting immediately; guarantee of free, quality primary education and basic healthcare for all children; treatment and bed nets to halve deaths from malaria; and vaccinations to eradicate polio.[12]

The legacy of these efforts continued in 2014 when Bob Geldof coordinated a new effort for Band Aid's thirtieth anniversary. This charity record focused on an Ebola outbreak which spread in West Africa. Over 200,000 copies were sold in the first twenty-four hours following its *X-Factor* debut. One artist's critique, however, was difficult to refute. Fuse ODG wrote a considered response to the Band Aid invitation explaining his absence: "Saying no to Bob Geldof is one of the hardest decisions I have had to make this year." Fuse ODG continued:

> I pointed out to Geldof the lyrics I did not agree with, such as the lines, 'Where a kiss of love can kill you and there's death in every tear,' and, 'There is no peace and joy in west Africa this Christmas.' For the past four years I have gone to Ghana at Christmas for the sole purpose of peace and joy. So for me to sing these lyrics would simply be a lie. In truth, my objection to the project goes beyond the offensive lyrics. I, like many others, am sick of the whole concept of Africa—a resource-rich continent with unbridled potential—always being seen as diseased, infested and poverty-stricken.[13]

He wrote: "That image of poverty and famine is extremely powerful psychologically. With decades of such imagery being pumped out, the average westerner is likely to donate £2 a month or buy a charity single that gives them a nice warm fuzzy feeling; but they are much less likely to want to go on holiday to, or invest in, Africa. If you are reading this and haven't been to Africa, ask yourself why." Nonetheless, a lot of money was raised for an important humanitarian priority.[14]

"Our Job is to Give the Power Back to the People"

Graham Nash embodies this activist tradition still. Since 2013, he has offered the song "Burning for the Buddha." Nash recalls: "…when I was introducing that song [during a Columbus, Ohio concert in 2014] I said that one of the images from the Vietnam War that really turned me around was the 'Burning Monk.' It was on the front page of every fucking newspaper in the world. But what the audience did not know is that in the last year and half, over one-hundred and thirty monks have burned themselves to death—you never heard one fucking word about it." Graham Nash says:

> That's our job. Our job is to give the power back to the people. Our job was to go from town-to-town saying, 'Hey, you know that fucking Emperor you thought had a beautiful fur coat on? He's totally naked!' It's our job. And I don't know why we think it's our job. But I think it's our job to communicate. It's our job to let people think about stuff they may never have thought

about and may never know—specifically like the one-hundred and twenty-eight Tibetan monks. It's our job to bring this information to people. But, the art about it all is to be able to write something serious like that. Do you know how difficult it is to write about a hundred and twenty-eight people burning themselves to death? It's not easy. But, you've got to do it as an artist, 'How do I get this information and how do I enable people to actually absorb the information and not get put off by the dreadful aspects of the truth about what was going on?' You have to put it with a melody that is incredibly enticing to people, a melody that they may not be able to forget once they've heard it a couple of times. That's our job.[15]

Regarding Tibet, Erin Potts notes: "I share [Adam] Yauch's focus on non-violence and universality, there's also a side of me that is like - 'Yes, Tibet is a model for all of us. But Tibetans deserve the right to self-determination now. It's not just about them being a model for the rest of us. It's also about the Universal Declaration of Human Rights. It's also about self-determination and the fact that Tibet was an independent nation and should be again. It's not just this sort of bigger thing. It's also very specific and very much like 'Tibet should be free.'"[16]

ROCK AND ROLL NONPROFIT

The most visible action that rock and roll artists engage in has been performing at benefits. This can, however, be more difficult than it seems. Matt Busch, manager of Bob Weir from the Grateful Dead, says: "The last thing I ever want to do is do a benefit and they lose money. And it has happened. It's just the worst. It's having the charity understand that when the artist—a Warren Haynes, the Bob Weir, the Phil Lesh says, 'Sure, they'll do the benefit,' they can't jump to that assumption that everyone else is just as enthusiastic about the cause."[17]

Kathy Kane, who manages Bonnie Raitt, adds to the challenges of benefits:

It's not easy to be selective, you'll get a call with an organizer saying 'Oh, come do this benefit—everybody's doing the benefit' but, did anybody ask to see the event's financials? The organization's past few tax returns? Did anybody vet the groups? After we do a benefit, we always follow up and ask not just how much was raised, but what was the net profit from the event. I think being an informed activist is really important and can definitely be challenging if it's not your main gig. Management isn't just telling people what to do, it's making sure it's getting done. So if an artist is going to go tell everybody we have to save the rainforest and you can work with XYZ group to save the rainforest, then I think it's really important to make sure that that group you are turning people onto is efficiently and effectively working to save the rainforest.[18]

Many artists of course use publicity tools, like their webpage, to advertise causes. Lukas Nelson, for example, has a "Giving Back" page on his website linking to eleven nonprofit organizations. Nelson says, "Everything helps, you know?"[19]

"The Fifth Member of My Band is My Nonprofit Work"

Bonnie Raitt set out as a freshman at Harvard/Radcliff to major in Social Relations and African Studies but instead became a prominent rock and roll activist. Bonnie Raitt has operated on a vision: "The fifth member of my band is my nonprofit work."[20] Raitt's web page lists about 100 nonprofit organizations she has worked with or supported throughout her career and a history of performances at benefit concerts—starting in 1971 with an "End the Vietnam War" concert in Boston, Massachusetts. Just since 2000, Bonnie Raitt has performed at over 300 events that raised money for nonprofit causes. David Crosby says: "Bonnie is a *fiercely* principled human being. Fiercely. Principled. Human being." Crosby adds: "She is the best singer in America. The best. Period. Of anybody. She's the best singer, probably in the world. I don't think anybody comes close. Bonnie is a hero of mine. If you want to talk about somebody that is an inspiringly brave human being, let's start with Bonnie Raitt."[21]

David Wish and Bonnie Raitt. Raitt is highly regarded as one of the world's most important nonprofit rock and roll activists. She was one of the first to support Little Kids Rock. Photo courtesy of Little Kids Rock, October 26, 2009.

Kathy Kane blends activism with her work as manager for Bonnie Raitt. Beginning at Wetlands in New York City, she came to understand the economic and artistic side of nonprofit work. Kane says she was "…hocking bumper stickers and pins and Wetlands T-Shirts—and sometimes the merch for the bands. We were all pitching in because it's not easy for a nightclub to afford to pay people to just work on 'environmental issues'!"[22] Kathy Kane continues:

> I was working at Wetlands in the early '90s and a couple bands that were hanging out in that scene in those days—like Blues Traveler, Spin Doctors, Phish, and Dave Matthews, Widespread Panic all got together to form a music festival. Guys with Blues Traveler and Spin Doctors came to me and said, 'Oh, we're going to do this touring music festival. Do you want to come do it with us?' You can green it, you know, get nonprofits at the shows and get the venues to recycle.' So, we all went out and started the H.O.R.D.E. tour and it was a blast. They called me a couple months after the first one ended and asked if I would come on board for the next summer and not just to do the nonprofits but help with the entire 'front of the house' festival stuff which was coordinating the tents with vendors and other activities, in addition to the nonprofits and whatever else we could dream up that was going on out front in the concourse area.[23]

This level of coordination and management was hard, Kane says: "Health Departments were shutting down our traveling food vendors, getting real specific about where we were allowed to set up our traveling festival." She describes being at one event where they consulted with the American Civil Liberties Union because the venue would not allow Planned Parenthood to do information tabling at the show. "So," Kane says, "we made a big stink about it. The bands all talked about it from stage."[24]

When the second year of H.O.R.D.E. ended, Kathy Kane accepted a job with Greenpeace, to coordinate information booths on tours including the Grateful Dead, Phish, R.E.M., and U2. "I really enjoyed my work merging the worlds of music and activism," Kane says, "because I always believed the common space created at a concert is a place where people can talk about topics that might be a little bit uncomfortable for them on their own turf. So instead of knocking on one's front door and asking if they want to learn about toxic pollution going on in their community, a concert is a place where you can break down some of those barriers to approach sensitive topics." Kane adds:

> I always thought that a concert provided a location - a space - where no one was forcing political or environmental issues on you but if interested, and groups were there tabling, you could find out more information—and be in a place you felt comfortable because for instance you might not feel comfortable asking those questions at school, or maybe your family wasn't an environment where

you could question social justice or political issues. But because you were in this free spirit, free space, of a concert and music and celebration, it was up to the person to decide if they want to take it to that next level. And if they did, we were there.[25]

"I think it was a really good opportunity," Kathy Kane says, "to help people learn more about these issues going on in their own community." Kathy Kane also coordinated political and social action causes at the 25th anniversary of Woodstock concert in 1994. "People showed up," she says, "in the middle of the night, barely clothed, crying—high as a kite, can't find their friends. They'd come to the Greenpeace booth which at some concerts had a reputation for being the meeting spot. We would shut down at night, but we'd keep taking in these strays and we would assess their condition and send them on their way—'First Aid's that way, the Rainbow Tent is that way.'" They also innovated an off the grid zone at the festival, for example, getting a solar generator to power the nonprofits.

Reflecting on working for Greenpeace, Kathy Kane recalls: "You'd be sitting around at the backstage catering having dinner chatting with band and crew, and then you might get a chance to say to a member of U2 or R.E.M.: 'Wow, it'd be really great if attention could be drawn to a campaign, but we're having XYZ trouble with it."[26] Kane recalls: "Natalie Merchant used to challenge the audience to give a dollar—and for everybody who gave a dollar, she would match it." She adds: "I remember in the mid-90s, Bryan Adams had a big indoor arena tour. He was really upset with the way the whales were being treated. He came to Greenpeace and said, 'What can we do to get people involved and stop the slaughter of whales?' And we said, 'We can get voices heard' - and so we actually did a whole postcard campaign." The volunteers had to slip postcards into the metal frame of every seat on the arena tour so they wouldn't blow away by the indoor air circulation systems and Bryan Adams would talk about the postcard from the stage. She reflects on another important moment: "I got to go to U2's studio in Dublin and sit down and talk politics for a couple of hours with Bono about whether or not Greenpeace should be boycotting the French due to the French nuclear testing." So, really wonderful, exciting, dynamic experiences integrating activism into the music industry. And watching these bands say something from the stage—like if R.E.M. said something about visiting the Greenpeace booth to learn more about environmental issues the response was huge. You were seeing how artists could impact change first-hand and it was amazing."[27]

In the late 1990s, Kathy Kane moved to California, where she set up a nonprofit organization called the ARIA Foundation (Artistic Resources in Action). ARIA provides an opportunity for musicians and people in the music industry to make charitable contributions and raise funds for work on environmental protection, clean energy, arts, education, social justice, and assistance in the event of natural disasters. Kane says: "ARIA was an extension of the Greenpeace work and then when I started working with Bonnie Raitt, we were able to work with her and her longtime nonprofit activist partner, the Guacamole Fund run by Tom Campbell, to assist with her on-tour fundraising efforts as well. That's where we do the tour ticket fundraising and other special benefit tickets." Via ARIA, Kane says: "We did do a campaign in 2009 with Bonnie and Taj Mahal - the BonTaj Tour - and we tried to get every 'player' involved with the shows - promoter, venue, ticketing agency and artist - to give twenty-five cents; so the artists, the promoter, the ticketing agency, and the venue. And so everyone gave a quarter to collectively become a dollar per ticket and we directed people to a website where they could vote on the cause area they wanted to support."[28] Kane adds that the idea of "scalping for charity"—i.e. offering V.I.P. access to good concert seats in turn for charitable donations can be difficult when competing with scalpers trying to resell premium seats for profit: "The problem that we've found, what it really comes down to, I think—is that people wanting to get great seats, they just go to their ticket broker that gets them great seats. Or, they have their scalping website and they go there. The challenge is how to find these folks and redirect them to go buy premium seats at inflated prices but for charity instead! Kane says, "We've come up with solutions, we've talked to promoters. We did a lot of trials over the last couple of years experimenting with different ways to try scalping for charity, not third party profit. We try to capture the people that are buying the up-charged tickets from scalpers. We definitely try to advertise and go through our campaigns with information on how to buy our Special Benefit Seats that are premium seats but the upcharge goes directly to charity."[29]

Together Bonnie Raitt and Kathy Kane worked hard on environmentally sustainable touring. "Especially with Bonnie," Kane says: "We had a touring arm called "Green Highway" we started in the early 2000's when hybrid cars were just being introduced mainstream so we had them at our shows and we would put them on display in the concourse area for people to check out so folks could see that the hybrid car looks just like a normal car."[30] As well, they were: "Really working to 'green' the backstage. Doing what we can. Always in the contract, always in the rider - asking for no plastic utensils, reusable cutlery and dishware, cloth napkins, using cups to refill drinks instead of plastic water bottles." It is not always easy as progress means venues and promoters have to change. Kane says: "One solution is to show the economics of it. If I can show a venue that if they could just, 'Get rid of disposable products backstage, put in halogen light bulbs, use water saving toilets, they'll save money in the long run.' For years we tried to do auditing of venues, and help with ideas on how to green a venue." Kane also notes that, "When we did Green Highway [their 2002 environmental sustainability nonprofit and educational program on tour], that really felt like the first time an artist brought strictly an 'eco-fair' on tour with them. It felt pretty fresh, especially working with alternative power. We were making sure that we were offsetting everything we did with 'green power.'"[31]

A prominent example of Bonnie Raitt's and Kathy Kane's impact is the nonprofit REVERB, founded by Lauren Sullivan and her husband Adam Gardner of Guster. Sullivan says in 2004: "Adam's sister had attended a Bonnie Raitt show in Berkeley at the Greek Theater and sent us a pamphlet about Bonnie Raitt's 'Green Highway.' That was Bonnie's green touring program, which incorporated an eco-village, biodiesel use, and carbon offsets. It was the best version of what I had thought about and could ever have imagined." Sullivan explains:

REVERB EcoVillage on a Dave Matthews Band tour (which featured the nonprofit's Farm to Family Program). Photo courtesy of REVERB, www.reverb.org

I finally called Bonnie Raitt's manager and said, 'Hi, this is who I am and where I come from, and who my husband is and where he comes from. This is what we're interested in creating, and we want to talk to you about all the work you've been doing.' Kathy Kane, Bonnie's manager, immediately said, 'Are you guys going to be in L.A.? Can we meet? Let's talk.' So when we were in L.A. shortly thereafter, we sat down and talked some more. She said, 'Well, I manage a foundation. We can act as your fiscal sponsor. We also have all of these tents and banners and flags in storage. You're welcome to use them and take the 'Green Highway' idea and run with it.[32]

Sullivan recalls, "…we used all the Green Highway supplies from Bonnie Raitt's tour and Kathy kind of mentored me through the logistics of some of it; and obviously working with Adam and his wealth of knowledge about how the music industry works and how to navigate it." "Kathy, she is just a dynamo, she's just an incredible person and we feel so, so grateful to kind of been 'launched' really by Bonnie and Kathy and all of their energy and expertise and passion. They're the reason we are here, honestly," Sullivan concludes.[33]

When they formed REVERB, Guster had just finished touring with Barenaked Ladies who were going out again on the road with Alanis Morissette. Sullivan and Gardner approached them about joining the tour. The artists were amenable - only wanting to vet the nonprofits and coordinate on messaging. Sullivan says: "We proceeded to borrow the Guster van and I, along with some volunteers and friends at the time, chased the tour back and forth across the country: setting up the tents and banners and flags and coordinating groups of volunteers—all that fun stuff." Sullivan recalls: "We were talking about biodiesel at that time and the idea of biodiesel and alternative fuel sources was very strange. But we connected with all these interesting people who were retrofitting our cars, using grease, and had some demos and solar panels." Now, Sullivan says, "…every element of it—the texture—the feel—everything about it is so different now." "Today," she adds: "I think the thing that we are always wary of is the 'environmental eye-rolling' that's happening now—because people are over-saturated, I think, with the political 'green' terms and all of it."[34]

REVERB now participates in major national tours incorporating ecological education and environmental programming - particularly advancing the "green contract rider," advising artists how to guarantee environmentally friendly contracts with venues. Lauren Sullivan says:

We've been doing the green contract rider pretty much since we started. Just giving advice to the artist and kind of redlining:—'tweek this, let's change this, request this—let's make this mandatory. It's always a dance again, and depends on (i.e.), 'Is the artist selling out the venue?' If they're selling out the venue and they're guaranteed then they're going to have a lot more power than somebody that has only sold half of the tickets. Like most things that we've been doing, the conversation with the venues has evolved tremendously from, 'Oh My God, you guys are a total pain in the ass—asking me for dozens of recycling bins to be out front when we don't normally do that.' But now were talking about, 'O.K., let's try and do some pilot projects with biocompostables being used at concessions.'[35]

Now, Sullivan says: "I actually still coordinate the biodiesel for the Dave Matthews Band and I adore all the drivers that I've worked with for years and years. We started doing that back in '06, maybe even '05—it's been many years. We have a giant database with all the suppliers that we've worked with. If somebody's shut down or been bought out, we just kind of follow the scent and try to figure out how to make it happen."[36] They also try to find the best locally produced sources of biodiesel as possible. Sullivan notes Adam Gardner testified before Congress about biofuel and touring.

REVERB also helps artists present "Eco-Villages" at concerts. Lauren Sullivan describes the 2014 Dave Matthews Band summer tour: "The issue that was near-and-dear to them is 'anti-GMO campaign.'" They would, "... find farmers in the area, each stop of the tour, and work with them to find out what they've got, what they can source for meat, vegetables, fruit, whatever it is. And then that goes to catering so they're using as much local produce and meat as they can." They also:

...raise farms on site, where folks will donate a couple bucks and we might take that money and then purchase CSAs [community-shared agriculture] from local farms that then will be donated to a local food pantry to help families dealing with food insecurity. This sort of 'daisy chain of goodness' to my mind - is connecting food, which is one of those kind of visceral things that we all feel very strongly about. Especially when you don't have it? You know - critical. And connecting it to local farming and making sure that, ideally, your food's not totally 'bathed in petroleum' as I've heard people say, because it's not traveling from New Zealand or Chile or wherever.[37]

Sullivan says the: "...tour coordinator on the road has a giant spreadsheet that they work with [measuring] general attendance at the show and that can be connected to offsets that are happening. We'll look at the biodiesel that we're using; talk about the number of groups that came out, volunteers that we had at the show that night. Often times collecting folks' e-mails, doing photo booths, pictures and posts, social media posts, a passport program (where one can get a stamp at multiple booths and enter a contest to win, i.e. a Dave Matthews Band autographed guitar)."[38] REVERB created a database to assess how fans are donating, how much money caterers are spending on local farmed food, and how many bags of recycling are collected. They also look at the bands' demographic because, for example, a thirteen-year-old Maroon 5 fan might have a different set of environmental assumptions than a fan of a different group. One of the trickiest aspects, Lauren Sullivan says, is to keep the momentum going locally after a concert has moved on. REVERB thus looks at how many people signed up at the concert and adds them to their e-mail list. They also publicize local groups and connect environmental volunteers to them. REVERB had, by 2015 greened 160 tours, reached 20.6 million fans, supported 3,664 local groups, reduced 115,510 tons of CO_2 emissions, and provided $610,328 in support of community programs.[39] In 2015, REVERB again hit the road, with the "Campus Consciousness Tour" designed as half music event and half environmental activism, which since 2006 had reached 1 million students at 150 college campuses around the United States.

"We Are Who We Grant"

Established by the Grateful Dead in 1984, the Rex Foundation (named in honor of the late Rex Jackson, a roadie and road manager for the band) has since provided grants totaling $8.9 million to over 1,200 recipients—mainly with money raised at Grateful Dead concerts and special benefit shows. The foundation prioritizes relatively small grantees, for example those with under a $1 million budget, to achieve maximum impact. Longtime environmental activist and former Grateful Dead manager, Cameron Sears, is the Executive Director of the Rex Foundation. Sears explains:

> The first show they ever did as the Grateful Dead was a benefit [for the San Francisco Mime Troup in 1965]. They did an enormous number of benefits. In fact, my understanding why, one of the reasons why, the Rex Foundation was established was that they were giving away enough money that it caught the scrutiny of the IRS who kind of doubted the legitimacy of that. So the answer was, 'You know what? We're just going to become a *bona fide* foundation. I'm fairly certain that they were, probably, the first rock and roll band to do that.[40]

The Rex Foundation, Sears says, is "...one of the crowning achievements of the Grateful Dead."[41]

There is, Cameron Sears reflects, a motto in the Rex Foundation that: " 'We are who we grant'—so, we're putting our grantees front and center. When you look at the breadth of who these people are, the work they're doing—that speaks to the work that we do. People may think that the Dead left us a huge endowment, but that's not the case. They left us with this incredible legacy and they established a foundation from which this thing can take off."[42]

Cameron Sears sees Jerry Garcia reflected in their ongoing work: "With regard to where the Rex Foundation is today, he would be thrilled. He'd be absolutely thrilled. I mean, his daughter is on the Board with me, Trixie [Garcia], and MG's on (Mountain Girl, Carolyn Garcia). He was all about, 'Letting it fly' and so we're flying!."[43] Sears references an example:

> We funded this thing '88 Bikes.' It's a great example. Two brothers were on a bike ride in southeast Asia and they've got their bikes at the end of the thing. They're in front of an orphanage in Cambodia or something and they want to give their bikes to the two orphans that they see. But then they look and realize that there's eighty-six other kids in there: 'Well, what are they going to do?' So they said: 'You know what? We're going to come back with eighty-eight bikes.' They just did it. So then they cobbled it together and somebody hipped us to what they were doing. Their annual budget is probably $250,000 but what they've now been able to do is: they're doing it in Southeast Asia, they're doing it in Africa, and now they're focusing on young women because if young women have transportation, they're less victim to predators.[44]

"I think the main tenet," Cameron Sears says, "is we're all capable of helping create positive impacts in the communities and locales that we inhabit."[45]

In 2010, the Rex Foundation presented their Ralph J. Gleason Award to Michael Franti—who had global hits with songs like "Say Hey (I Love You)." Michael Franti has made contributions on war and peace, ending the drug war, advocating for fair trade, raising funds for disaster relief in Australia and Japan, supporting St. Jude's Ranch for Children in Nevada, visiting CARE projects in Timor Leste, performing with inner-city school children, and for inmates at San Quentin and Folsom prisons. Michael Franti promotes environmentally friendly touring using biodiesel and does not have plastic bottles at his concerts. Building on that experience, in 2013 Michael Franti and Sara Agah [his partner and an emergency room nurse] founded the Do It For the Love foundation: "…a global nonprofit wish granting foundation that brings people living with life-threatening illnesses, children with severe challenges, and wounded veterans to live concerts."[46]

Michael Franti says the idea for Do It For the Love came from a uniquely personal inspiration:

> We started Do It For the Love Foundation when we had one of our fans [named Hope] Tweeting me, saying that her husband was dying of ALS—Steve Dezember—and that he wanted to come to a show. It was perhaps going to be the last concert he ever attended, so he wanted to meet me. We invited him to the show and then me and my wife-to-be, Sara, we met with them before the show. Actually, the night before we saw a video of them, it was their wedding. Just this really beautiful wedding. You could see that Steve was beginning to have the

early symptoms of ALS. The next day when we met them, he was completely wheelchair-bound, could hardly move at all. I invited them out on to the stage on a song—this song 'Life is Better with You.' He whispered into his wife's ear and said he wanted to dance. So with all her strength, she lifted him up out of the chair and they danced in front of this festival crowd of 20,000 people. Everyone cheered and cried."[47]

Franti recalls: "Hope told me later that before, they were just like, 'the guy in the wheelchair'—going around, and people kind of ignoring them and looking at them kind of funny and after that, everyone went up to him and said, 'Oh, you're Steve!' They felt like this new sense of community." Michael Franti says: "I think there's something that's really powerful that takes place through music. There's a healing power that allows emotions that we never knew existed to find a voice and be able to come out. And there's also this sense of community that we develop when we're in this place together with other people that we've never met before, and all sharing in these emotions. That's where the empathy is—that deep sense of community that is spoken through that universal language of music."[48]

"I've learned over time," Michael Franti says, "that unconditional love is really the most powerful gift that you can share with anybody." He shares that his son (who in 2014 was fifteen years old) had been recently diagnosed with a rare kidney disease called FSGS, and Sara's mother was being given chemotherapy for breast cancer. He says: "Having the experience of having that—all the different families that we have on tour, has really been a big gift to both of us in learning how families really come together and bond around when you have a sick family member. So, the gift of giving to others through the foundation has really changed us and touched us in a way that we never imagined."[49] Franti observes:

> You know, fans come to our shows all the time and they're inspired by the music and the lyrics and they think, 'What can I do to give back,' which leads to, 'A big network of volunteers all over the country who are working to be what we call 'Fanbassadors.' They're the ones who are actually bringing the families to the show, making sure that they get to their seats O.K., get food and drinks at the concert, and help to link up with the artists after the show—and also do fundraising for it. That's been really amazing, the sense of community that's been built up around people who put on their own 'Home Party' as a Do It for the Love fundraiser.[50]

Franti says: "I remember there was one guy in Columbus, Ohio, who was battling lung cancer and he came to one of the shows. He heard the song 'I'm Alive' on the radio. It was the day after he was coming back from knowing that he had cancer. He heard the song and he said, '…this is going to be my mantra for my whole battle.' The night that we met him for the show, he brought eighteen family members. They all danced and laughed, cried—and he came up on stage and sang 'I'm Alive' with me. A few months later he passed away. It was really just amazing to share that moment and have all the family members come up to me and say, 'This is really one of the only times we've all been together at the same place and same time. We'll always remember this night.'"[51]

"Our aim," Michael Franti says, "is to create a make-a-wish foundation for music." The goal is, "To provide live concerts to anyone who needs it. We're starting small—we don't send people to Disneyland to see a show, or whatever. But we get people out to local concerts and any artist, at any level—stadium shows down to small clubs, the opera or symphony—whatever it is."[52] Franti says: "All of us have this unlimited capacity to love and to give," Franti says. "Sometimes," he adds, "we wear out. Our mind becomes taxed and our body becomes tired and we feel like, 'Man, I don't know if I can do this anymore.' In those moments, when our soul kicks in and says: 'You know what? You can love a little more. You can go a little a little further.' I think that really is the most powerful part of music—that it accesses the windows to the soul. And when we need it, music is there for us—that medicine that says: 'You can go a little bit further than you've ever imagined."[53] Steve Dezember's wife Hope says: "It's such a moving moment to have Michael care about us so much, and to have so many people receive us and care about us so much. It literally changed our lives."[54]

Like the Grateful Dead and Rex, Carlos Santana advances progress locally and globally via his nonprofit Milagro Foundation. The Santana website proclaims: "Today we invite all the soldiers of all nations to utilize the ultimate weapons of compassion, mercy, and forgiveness." Santana created Milagro (which means "miracle") in 1998 to benefit "underserved and vulnerable children around the world by making grants to community-based, tax-exempt organizations that work with children in the areas of education, health, and the arts."[55] The foundation generates income from ticket donations and licensed Santana products in addition to individual donors and brand partners. Between October 1998 and August 2014 the Milagro Foundation provided grants to low-income and under-represented children in thirty-six states and thirty-five countries granting $5,881,213 to 355 agencies.[56]

Ruthie Moutafian, Associate Director of Milagro, says one of Carlos Santana's particular passions is in his hometown of Autlán, Mexico where they fund a medical clinic that serves the indigenous people of this mountain region. The Milagro Foundation also partnered with the Kellogg Foundation which provided Milagro with a three-year $720,000 grant to "...support low-income communities around the United States in their development of healthy alternatives for children in the areas of food, nutrition and health."[57] Ruthie Moutafian says:

That was really exciting for us because we were kind of sought after by Kellogg. We had a similar mission as Kellogg. So what they were looking to do was to grant to a foundation who could support their own grantees that fell into the food movement. So what we were looking for was children who had no food access and nutrition and health issues. Kellogg noticed that we were already connected to some of those organizations and so they basically gave us a big chunk of money and asked us to go out and find some grantees to fund.[58]

With this partnership, Milagro funded the Edible Schoolyard in New Orleans; the Johns Hopkins Center for American Indian Health; the Historic 9th Ward Council for Arts & Sustainability; and for Sausalito-Marin County Schools. Kellogg continued funding these programs after the initial grant cycle. The only exception was Marin City, a farmers market and food program that Milagro sustained—reaching a pocket of poverty in one of America's wealthiest counties.

Just as Rex invested in an artist like Michael Franti, Ruthie Moutafian celebrates Little Kids Rock as one of Milagro's earliest grantees: "In all the years that we've known Little Kids Rock and his [David Wish] work, you know, we've done a lot of connecting with him. We've hooked him up with schools, we found Hermes Music who has given him a ton of guitars to distribute across the country. We haven't had to give him a grant in a long time because David, he finds his way. Now he meets the big guys, and he's well supported."[59] Little Kids Rock held an event at Mission High School [Carlos Santana's alma mater] in Oakland, California, in 2011. The initial recipients of guitars (now into their twenties) stood with Carlos Santana to hand out instruments. David Wish says: "The Milagro Foundation was the first funder to believe in our vision for transforming and restoring music education across the country, and they have been with us as supporters ever since. I love them more than words can say."[60] Moutafian points to Milagro's support for music education: "For Carlos, that's really what helped him make it in life. He's met some kids along the way from his own experience and from the organizations that we fund who have told him that if they didn't play a guitar or violin, [they] wouldn't be in school and even, 'I wouldn't probably be alive.'"[61]

"Weapons of Mass Compassion"

Ruthie Moutafian reflects: "I think what Carlos really focuses in on is: 'a child is a peaceful soul.' A child is innocent and when you have a chance to help a child, to make that child become a whole and a peaceful person, to spread that sentiment, that value around the world - that's a good investment.

That's the best investment you can make. I think that's why our focus has always been children, because the child is—not to sound cliché - but that child is the future."[62] Carlos Santana says: "To me, making music wasn't good enough...It doesn't mean that much to win eight or nine Grammys in the same night and then the next day I am like, 'So what?' I am so grateful to play my music and share my music, but I started realizing that I get more joy helping children than I do being number one on the radio."[63] "Carlos talks a lot about fear," Moutafian says, "and how fear is destructive. He has this quote that he says over and over at his shows, whenever he can; he wants 'weapons of mass compassion.' And those weapons are love and respect and goodness and light."[64]

ROCK THE VOTE!

Traditionally, rock and roll artists avoided partisan politics although James Taylor and Carole King performed at a benefit for the presidential campaign of Sen. George McGovern in 1972, the Allman Brothers performed for Jimmy Carter in 1976, and in 1980 Linda Ronstadt brought a number of artists together, including the Eagles, to support California Governor Jerry Brown's campaign for the Democratic presidential nomination, and Stephen Stills performed for Walter Mondale's presidential campaign in 1984. Some artists including Bono, Adam Gardner, Dee Snider, Lars Ulrich, and Frank Zappa— have provided expert testimony on issues before congressional committees. Sony Bono [of Sonny and Cher] and Rob Hall were both elected to Congress. Bono and Bob Geldof regularly meet with world leaders. Bruce Springsteen resisted political endorsements until 2004, when he supported John Kerry for President, repeating that in 2008 for Barack Obama. Jann Wenner explains:

> Before it was viewed as a very tainted thing to do. There was no purity of out-come. It's always going to be a compromised outcome. Because running for office, becoming president, means you have to compromise; bring all sorts of people together, and compromises and coalitions. There wasn't that clear moral purity to it and so people walked away from it. Didn't want anything to do with it. And Bruce [Springsteen] for years—as political as he is - as educated, smart—wanted to step back; stay away from the political arena. Really it's only in times of war—as we had in Iraq that finally you sort of wake and say, 'I've got to do something about this.'[65]

In 2004, Bruce Springsteen performed on the eve of the election to rally for Sen. John Kerry in Cleveland, Ohio. Jann Wenner recalls of Springsteen: "We flew out there together. He was in Cleveland the night before—the eve of the election. It looked like we were going to win. We were all high-fiving each other. It was a good moment. I think people have realized the complexities of all these issues and the need to speak out for them."[66]

"You Were Just Miracled by Obama"

Rock and rollers and political figures have often found themselves in conflict. Political campaigns, for example, are not necessarily required to get specific permission to use a song if a campaign paid licensing fees for prior approved material. This, nevertheless, became an issue in 1984 when Ronald Reagan referenced Bruce Springsteen's "Born in the U.S.A". Springsteen objected:

> I think people got a need to feel good about the country they live in. But what's happening, I think, is that, that need—which is a good thing—is getting manipulated and exploited. And you see the Reagan reelection ads on TV—you know: 'It's morning in America.' And you say, well, it's not morning in Pittsburgh. It's not morning above 125th Street in New York. It's midnight, and, like, there's a bad moon risin.' And that's why when Reagan mentioned my name in New Jersey, I felt it was another manipulation, and I had to disassociate myself from the president's kind words.[67]

In 2008, Heart filed a "cease and desist letter" to Sarah Palin whose Vice-Presidential campaign used their song "Barracuda". Nancy Wilson said at the time: "I feel completely fucked over - Sarah Palin's views and values in no way represent us as American women."[68] Heart's request was not honored. In 2015, Neil Young objected to Donald Trump using "Rocking in the Free World" at a Republican Party presidential nomination campaign event. Young explained: "I do not trust self-serving misinformation coming from corporations and their media trolls. I do not trust politicians who are taking millions from those corporations either. I trust people."[69] Some artists' material has been appropriated by radio personalities as with Rush Limbaugh's use of the Pretender's "My City Was Gone." Limbaugh used it without licensing permission (and with the lyrics removed). Limbaugh boasted: "It is anti-development, anti-capitalist, and here I am going to take a liberal song and make fun of [liberals] at the same time."[70] Chrissie Hynde allowed its use but insisted that license fees be donated to P.E.T.A. David Crosby says he had to threaten to sue Bill O'Reilly of *Fox News* over use of his song "Long Time Gone": "I said, 'Hey, I need to talk to you. You've got to stop using my song.' He said, 'Why?' And I said, 'Bill, 'cause you've got no right to use it and I don't want my song associated.' He said, 'Why don't you come on the program—we'll talk about it.' Crosby declined, saying: "'You're just a punk and I'm not going to let you use my song.' And he said, 'Hmmmph,' and I said, 'Do it or talk to my lawyers—it's your choice.' He took it off."[71]

Politicians have not always done well with rock and roll. In 1983 Ronald Reagan's Secretary of the Interior James Watt sought a ban on the

Beach Boys performing on the 4th of July at the Mall in Washington, D.C., because, as he put it, they attracted "the wrong element." In 2010, former Florida Governor Charlie Crist got in trouble for using the Talking Head's song "Road to Nowhere" during a Senate campaign. David Byrne filed suit for $1 million against Crist because the song had not been authorized for advertising. Crist settled the suit and was required to make a video apology. In January 2010, lawyers for rocker Joe Walsh discovered that a Republican candidate for Congress, also named Joe Walsh, was rewriting the lyrics to his song "Walk Away". They warned: "As a candidate for Congress, you probably have a passing familiarity with many of the laws of this great country of ours. It's possible, though, that laws governing intellectual property are a little too arcane and insufficiently populist for you to really have spent much time on."[72] During the 2012 election, Republican Vice-Presidential candidate Paul Ryan said that Rage Against the Machine was one of his favorite bands. To this Tom Morello said: "Paul Ryan's love of Rage Against the Machine is amusing, because he is the embodiment of the machine that our music has been raging against for two decades...I wonder what Ryan's favorite Rage song is? Is it the one where we condemn the genocide of Native Americans? The one lambasting American imperialism? Our cover of 'Fuck the Police'? Or is it the one where we call on the people to seize the means of production? So many excellent choices to jam out to at Young Republican meetings!"[73]

Rock and rollers have also found that when common interests align, they can be effective in supporting political campaigns. In 2008, Matt Busch noted that Barack Obama was surrounded by a number of advisers who were long-time fans of bands like the Grateful Dead, eventually leading the band to reunite in concert to support Obama. Busch recalls the origins were in a chance meeting after Bob Weir sang the national anthem at a Baltimore Orioles game:

> That evening Bobby and Jay [Lane] were doing a HeadCount benefit, I forget whose backyard, but it was a posh D.C. mansion, it was kind of a, 'Sing-along with Bobby night.' It was a van ride out of Camden Yards—it was me, Bobby, Jay Lane, Dennis McNally, and maybe a HeadCount rep. Earlier that day, is when Pete Rouse's [Obama's Senate Chief of Staff] name came on our radar. We had a couple of hours to kill before the benefit, 'Did we want to sit down and meet Pete Rouse?' We figured out who he was pretty quick and said, 'Absolutely, we'd love to.' We left that meeting an inspired group of people. Bob left that meeting and was like: 'I know what I got to do, and it's get the Dead back together and do this, we need to do an event for them.'[74]

Matt Busch subsequently volunteered for the campaign during downtime from Bob Weir's tour schedule.

When Obama campaign officials asked Matt Busch what he would like to do, he said: "'I've never been to an Obama rally, but I imagine as your crowds are growing, producing an Obama event is a lot like producing a big rock show."[75] Busch recalls an hour later he got a call from the national director of advance work—how soon could he be in Philadelphia to help produce a rally at Independence Hall?" Busch remembers:

> This was one of the first-ever [Obama] events that was going to have a musician perform. Maybe three days before was when I heard: 'Will I. Am coming in.' That was completely handed off to me. They didn't know what they were doing. They knew I wasn't going to be a permanent fixture on the campaign [so] essentially at everything I would do, one of their full timers would be with me, if only to learn how I was getting it done. I said, 'You've got a musician coming in, you need—knowing that we're not doing an arena show with the Dead, there's some simple basics that'—they can pull it off. Just for Obama to speak you need a monitor, you need a microphone, you need a PA system. Well, if you're bringing in another guy to play, you probably want another microphone and then another channel for him to put in a guitar, and maybe a third channel just in case—an input list, and how that would work.

Matt Busch was left to 'press play' for the rocking soundtrack as Barack Obama took the stage. "That," Matt Busch says, "was an unbelievable moment. I don't have the words for that. I got the ear piece in and—'milk it, milk it' - he's ready to start speaking but, 'Nope, milk the crowd, keep the song going, milk the crowd - and then: Stop!' Then when I hit stop, he'd start speaking."[76]

At the Philadelphia event there was a reserved VIP area for a thousand people including staff and volunteers. So, Busch went to the Obama organizers and said:

> 'Can you guys give me ten tickets for that pit? Because what I'm going to do is, as this field starts filling in, I'm going to go three blocks down the street—to the people sitting the furthest away, and I'm going to give 'em out.' And I'm going to say, 'You were just miracled by Obama, you can watch the speech from up front', and I guarantee those ten people will vote for you come this fall because they will be so thrilled that they got a miracle.' Basically took the miracle philosophy and put it onto the campaign. They'd never heard anything like that idea. They were stunned by it. And I went and did it. I found a family of four and I found a couple of college kids sitting on a blanket, and I went and miracled people.[77]

Busch recalls it was, "That type of, whatever you want to call it, 'way to live your life'—if we do something like that for people, we only hope they go back to their homes and schools and that—and feel like they can do that for others."[78]

Vote for Change

Rock artists have had measurable success when focused on broad-based principles and R.E.M. set a high standard for successful political engagement with lead singer Michael Stipe becoming an activist for the environment, HIV/AIDS, and voter registration. Stipe reflects: "In the 1980s, I was made to be something that I wasn't—and I came dangerously close to being the poster boy of a generation for various social and political ideologies."[79] Bertis Downs says: "Being the lead singer and being charismatic and having that edge factor, or quality or whatever, that anybody would say Michael had. The same thing that Bono had and Sting had. He certainly got a lot more focus and attention and so, I guess that came with the territory."[80] R.E.M. had a critical impact spurring voter registration in the United States. Bertis Downs explains how a problem of compact disc packaging helped to pass the 1992 "Motor Voter" bill in Congress (meaning people could easily register to vote when they registered their automobiles or got their driver's license). Downs credits industry executive Jeff Gold with the idea, but R.E.M. made it happen: using compact disc packaging to advance voter rights. The band was upset about the existing long box format (which was used because store shelves were built for vinyl records thus the small compact disc was otherwise unseen) as it wasted cardboard. Bertis Downs recalls: "Jeff said: 'Let's take this negative of this long box instead of having people throw it away into a landfill, which is wasteful and dumb.'" The solution was to use the long box to print a postcard the purchaser could mail to their senator supporting the Motor Voter Bill. Bertis Downs says: "When you bundle up 100,000 postcards it takes lots of wheelbarrows or even trucks and so it made a really good visual—and it worked."[81] Between 1995 (when the "National Voter Registration Act," went into effect) and 2012 the percentage of registered voters in the United States grew from 69.5 to 79.5 and 150 million people were registered to vote this way.[82]

R.E.M.'s commitment to voting rights complemented the "Rock the Vote" campaign. This movement began in 1990 registering voters opposed to music censorship. Eventually it became a rock and roll voter registration drive: "Fusing pop culture, politics, and technology, Rock the Vote works to mobilize the millennial voting bloc and the youth vote, protect voting rights, and advocate for an electoral process and voting system that works for the 21st century electorate."[83] The organization helps people learn how to register to vote, provides information on voting rights and procedures, advances international voting rights, and educates about democracy. Rock the Vote's online voter registration guidelines have been translated into thirteen languages. In the 2008 election, Rock the Vote registered 2.6 million young voters—a demographic that proved pivotal to Barack Obama's election as president.[84]

Bertis Downs assesses this rock and roll voting rights activism: "It's an ongoing work in progress. It was a chapter, I guess, in democracy and political power and dynamics of parties, and the extremes and the mainstreams. There was no particular 'winning the game.' It was another chapter that moved the needle toward more participation, more enfranchisement, more inclusivity, making it more convenient, making it easier to vote." Downs says there are: "Lots of people in power who want to figure out the best way to game it so they can stay in power. If that means getting rid of precincts and making it harder to vote, and making it harder on people who don't have a schedule of their own, to vote, then so be it. That's why we have such a low turnout."[85]

Complementing Rock the Vote, HeadCount organizes volunteers to: "... stage voter registration drives at concerts and run programs that translate the power of music into real action. By reaching young people and music fans where they already are—at concerts and online—we make civic participation easy and fun."[86] The organization was co-founded by Marc Brownstein [of the Disco Biscuits] and writer Andy Bernstein in 2004. Between 2004 and 2014, HeadCount registered over 300,000 new voters at over 1,000 concerts a year. Just registering voters, however, is often not enough as (especially) young voters are historically least likely to vote. Andy Bernstein says in 2008, "We had the third highest voter turnout percentage" among groups that are annually surveyed for voter registration work. In 2012, he says, "It dipped, and a lot of it has to do with just data, and how data's crunched. You can take both with a grain of salt. At least with 2008, we were able to see very strong correlation in terms of people we registered and [their] going out to vote." "Very cynically," Bernstein says there is a limitation on the work: "...it's that we're registering a lot of white people, and not traditionally disenfranchised groups." Bernstein adds: "I always try to be deferential to groups that register populations that have been traditionally disenfranchised—that they do have a harder job than we do.[87]

Andy Bernstein says HeadCount's volunteer network makes the organization a unique community: "If they buy into the system and become leaders within HeadCount and become part of what we do, they'll come out of it with a very strong sense of efficacy and the ability to lead. And still probably, usually in that case, not particularly 'politically oriented'—not reading *The Hill* and *Politico* - but more so in touch with their own leadership skills. It's very powerful, very motivating, and it's the 'secret sauce' behind HeadCount and it's our emotional core, leadership development." Bernstein says, "Our stat that I'm very proud of is that fifteen of our volunteers have gotten full-time jobs because of HeadCount—directly because of HeadCount. That's fifteen lives that were changed and that's fifteen people who are bringing the values of HeadCount into the position they are in." One volunteer became a talent buyer for a top regional concert promoter. Now, that person, Bernstein notes, "...is going to be in a position of a lot of influence...and he'll never say 'no' to a nonprofit. He will always think about the message behind the music—that's where he got his start."[88]

Andy Bernstein makes a broader point about the culture of rock and roll nonprofit activism and saying:

> We've excelled at just taking a little bit off the top or the bottom and fund a significant part of our operations by doing that. We try to be very crafty and try to use tactics that are kind of pain-free for the musicians and the music industry—but very advantageous to us. So, some examples of things we do—the classic is the .50 cent surcharge. That's how a lot of bands do that. It just builds-in the ability to fund causes in a fairly passive way—and, I think the Grateful Dead were the first to do that through Rex. Now it's pretty common, and we benefit from that sometimes. Or, we'll often create meet-and-greets and packages and things like that and create value; we'll get every artist at an event to sign a poster and make a really unique item and auction it. So we're taking these things that have no 'hard cost' and turning them into funding. This is being done up and down in the music industry and we've gotten pretty good at it. We're taking in maybe $200,000 a year from that stuff—not huge money, but half our budget in some years.[89]

Andy Bernstein notes: "Nobody was doing an online auction for a meet-and-greet backstage at Woodstock."[90] Now, they can rally over 200 artists on a single day to post photos holding signs saying "Register to Vote" with a link to HeadCount's voter registration page. Bernstein adds: "It's visual. It's something people can connect to right away and it's very action-oriented." Bernstein notes with that campaign, they registered 35,000 people in one day - about half of what they did digitally in that same year.[91] This approach is, Bernstein says, "painless"—adding: "in a perfect world, the artist and the musicians and all would be willing to take on some pain because real change happens with sacrifice."[92]

"The Guitar Went for $526,000"

HeadCount assumed a key role at the final Grateful Dead concerts in Chicago in July 2015, coordinating "Participation Row"—where the nonprofits clustered. Bernstein recalls:

> We created limited edition postcards the nonprofits could give away for people who take action. The action could be signing a petition, it could be joining a photo campaign—the nonprofits decided, 'What is the most valuable thing I could get somebody to do while I interact with them?'—and for that they get a postcard. We printed 10,000 of these really beautiful limited edition postcards for Fare Thee Well. At Fare Thee Well, where everything cost forty bucks or more, people were really excited to get something for free. The nonprofits were just slammed. We gave out all 10,000 postcards. In addition to that we did a silent auction of a signed guitar and posters. The guitar went for $526,000.[93]

The guitar sold for $526,000 to raise money for HeadCount at the Grateful Dead's Fare Thee Well concerts in Chicago in 2015. HeadCount registers people to vote at rock concerts. Photo courtesy of Headcount.

"We really ramped up the notion of creating incentives for people," Bernstein says, adding: "We had the guitar customized in Fare Thee Well graphics, we had it played on stage, we had it signed by everybody; we only did one." He adds: "One of the nicest things I ever heard is Matt Busch told me backstage people kept coming to him and saying, 'Have you seen Participation Row? It's great!' Of all the things that would be on someone's mind to say to Bob Weir's manager at a Grateful Dead show, to talk about the nonprofit activiation? I was like, 'Are you shitting me?'"[94]

"ARTISTS ARE THE ARCHITECTS OF CHANGE"

Erin Potts now heads Revolutions Per Minute (RPM), a nonprofit organization based in San Francisco advising activist artists. RPM has over 1,300 artists in its network focusing on forty-three issues. Artists working with the organization have, combined, raised over $463,000 for environmental, climate change, and climate disaster relief organizations. They have helped to raise and re-grant $2 million. In the 2012 election they helped artists reach 620 million fans via social media, registered to vote 11,442 music fans, and made 3,000 voter protection impressions.[95] Potts references William S. Burroughs who wrote, "Artists to my mind are the real architects of change, and not the political legislators who implement change after the fact."[96] She says: "I think that there's an imagination process that happens in art for social change, meaning that we can envision a future. I think we often times get too stuck in reacting to the present and being negative. But, I think that also helps energize and articulate frustrations that people are feeling."[97] Potts also says: "I would love to be seeing the way in which artists and movements work together [to] be more about envisioning that future and bringing about that future, and more about leading along the lines of that William S. Burroughs quote rather than reacting to current situations."[98]

Chapter Eight

Money—Welcome to the Machine

"HOW DO YOU COMPETE WITH FREE?"

Billy Bragg says: "The most important break, step you can take, in your career is when you give up your shitty day job and make a living from music."[1] Increasingly that can be a difficult consideration. Speaking at the Rock and Roll Hall of Fame and Museum in 2013, Alan Kreuger, economist and Chair of the president's Council of Economic Advisors, said:

> The music industry is a microcosm of what is happening in the U.S. economy at large. We are increasingly becoming a 'winner-take-all economy', a phenomenon that the music industry has long experienced. Over recent decades, technological change, globalization, and an erosion of the institutions and practices that support shared prosperity in the U.S. have put the middle class under increasing stress. The lucky and the talented—and it is often hard to tell the difference—have been doing better and better, while the majority has struggled to keep up.[2]

Technology and the consolidation of corporate power in the music business have created a dual challenge for artistic expression. There is now more access to recorded music available free via Internet streaming. But, as Bertis Downs asks: "How Do You Compete with Free?"[3]

RADIO

In 2012, the Future of Music Coalition (a Washington, D.C.-based advocacy group) conducted an artist survey showing: "While there are a handful of musicians who are wealthy, the vast majority of working musicians in the U.S. are working or middle class earners."[4] They found that if including other jobs, pensions, or other income, the gross annual salary for a musician in America was $55,561 (i.e., pretax earnings)—and when aggregated for just music income, the gross annual salary was $34,455.[5] While consumers benefit from free downloading of music, productive technology has collapsed revenue from physical recordings—vinyl, cassettes, or compact discs. Dar Williams explains:

> If you talk to people in the industry, they're just going to say, 'It's just so different now, it's a different model.' No, it's not a different model. There's less money; because, well there's less democracy because it's not a million people buying an album. People don't buy albums. It's streaming entities deciding how to distribute their streaming royalties—which aren't very great to begin with, I'll give 'em that. It really freaks me out when people say, 'It's just different now.' It's not different. There's less money for music now. I think that's why there's a lot of really horrible music out there, because people write their songs to be in car commercials, then they can afford their tour car. Or, 'I sang for a pharma commercial so I could get SAG insurance'—I mean it's all very 'funny.'[6]

In 1999, the total revenue in the United States from record sales was $14.6 billion. By 2009, the advent of digital downloading and Internet streaming services caused sales to fall to $6.3 billion.[7] Bertis Downs observes that: "A hit song used to—one song—think of an example in the '90s—Alanis Morissette, Hootie and the Blowfish, they sold 10, 15, 17 million records based on one song. It doesn't happen anymore. Now, the best you're going to do—if somebody really likes your song and doesn't go download it for free, maybe they'll buy it for .99 cents."[8]

Working for a Living

In 1981, there were fifty different large-scale media companies in the United States, which owned 90 percent of the outlets that people got information from (print, television, or radio). A consequence of deregulation of the telecommunications industry, by 2012 only six national corporations owned 90 percent of media outlets.[9] The Future of Music Coalition found in 2006 that the top four radio station owners had almost half of the listeners and the top ten almost two-thirds of listeners in the United States. Local or regional ownership had declined by one-third between 1975 and 2005. Meanwhile, just fifteen format styles (i.e., "classic rock") constituted three-quarters of all commercial programming and radio formats with overlap of up to 80 percent of songs played on them. Niche music (classical, jazz, Americana, bluegrass, new rock, and folk) was provided almost exclusively by local stations if at all. Listenership also declined by 22 percent between 1989 and 2006. The Future of Music Coalition concluded that: "...radio consolidation has no demonstrated benefits for the public. Nor does it have any demonstrated benefits for the working people of the music and media industries, including DJs, programmers, and musicians."[10]

This consolidation trend results from President Bill Clinton signing the bipartisan supported Telecommunications Act of 1996. According to the Federal Communications Commission, the purpose of the law was, "to let any communications business compete in any market against any other."[11] Instead, large companies—many with direct interest in controlling what programming aired—bought out regional and smaller market stations. This trend led to an upward movement of profits generated by advertising sales that increasingly drove programming. The Future of Music Coalition shows advertising revenue increased from 12 percent market share for the top four companies in 1993 to 50 percent market share for the top four companies in 2004 while playlists from commonly owned stations in the same format overlapped up to 97 percent."[12] For example, Clear Channel (now iHeart Radio), the Future of Music Coalition showed: "...multiplied its station holdings by a factor of 30, going from 40 stations to 1,200 within five years of the Telecom Act."[13] If, as an artist, you were already "in" with a major label and you fit preferred formats, then you were likely to get played and be compensated. If you were independent and creating innovative or provocative music, it was an increasingly closed shop.

Michael Bracy, who cofounded and advises the Future of Music Coalition, says the radio consolidation movement was: "...absolutely devastating for the art and culture side of commercial radio. It fundamentally led to the commercial radio industry, in a very comprehensive and systematic way, abdicating its traditional responsibility as being a carrier." Now, an artist like Bruce Springsteen has hits from decades ago on classic rock radio but not their newest material. The way Springsteen achieved success also may no longer be available. Michael Bracy says in the 1970s: "Springsteen would go market to market. It would be a local D.J. who would take a chance, and their intent, pride and competition would be the pacemakers. But what happened post-96 with massive consolidation, it just flipped to a market-based research model. Basically, they had very finely-defined audience demographics and then take all that research to find out what that demographic wanted to hear according to focus groups and their polling results, and that's what they program."[14]

Glen Ballard says now a lot of music just is not heard: "Let me go back to Mississippi [where he grew up in the 1960s]: I could turn on the radio and hear any number of things. Even pop radio in the '70s, it hadn't gotten so segregated into segments and age groups, and race, color, creed, demographics, narrow-casting. I mean, it was just music man. You could hear an R&B song and you could hear, sort of a cheesy pop song, a Beatles song, Rolling Stones. I mean, about half of it was probably interesting and stuff you wouldn't hear in your own little world, but you would go 'God!' I'd hear an Al Green song next to a Beatles song. Those two things don't live together anymore unless it's an oldies station because one of them is an R&B song, one's a classic rock song—they used to be on the same station." Ballard adds:

> Radio hadn't become nationalized and sort of homogenized—just on the radio alone you could hear interesting local music. It could be R&B music it could be country music, it could be just anybody. I mean, I got my stuff on the radio. It wasn't a business the way it is now. It kind of, in my view, served the community in a different way. Local artists could get their songs on the radio. I mean, literally, it was pretty good. It wasn't corporations saying this is what this time slot needs and this is the demographics—all that information wasn't available.[15]

Ballard describes how he benefited as a youngster hearing AM radio out of Chicago—and all the live music one could hear in a place like Mississippi. But, he adds: "We're talking about ancient history. The time of which I speak? Young people can't even relate to it."[16]

The public watchdog Common Cause concluded in 2003 that the 1996 Telecommunications Act negatively impacted free market competition. They found that: "...while corporate special interests all had a seat at the table when this bill was being negotiated, the public did not. Nor were average citizens even aware of this legislation's great impact on how they got their entertainment and information, and whether it would foster or discourage diversity of viewpoints and a marketplace of ideas, crucial to democratic discourse." Common Cause found that between 1997 and 2003, eight of the nation's largest telecommunications companies and three of their trade groups had spent more than $400 million on political contributions and lobbying in Washington.[17] Michael Bracy says: "It's very sad what's happened to commercial radio. We've spent fifteen years finding a whole host of strategies, trying to make it better. Our hope would be that the marketplace would kind of respond to what is happening and understand that the only advantage, the only commercial advantage to those platforms is when they're local."[18]

"That Is Such a Sad, Sad Thing"

Michael Stanley is also an afternoon disc jockey on one of Cleveland Ohio's biggest radio stations, 98.5, *WNCX*. The station is (with Alan Freed's *WJW* and *WMMS*) one of Cleveland's major rock and roll stations. Its Cleveland-based ownership transferred to Clear Channel in 1994 and eventually to *CBS Radio*. Michael Stanley says:

> We have four radio stations there—four different formats. This is the *CBS* conglomerate. But, there's no guys coming around pitching records. There's like three guys that come to the radio station, and play us Katy Perry and stuff, that sort of thing. It used to be another world. Every major label had a branch here in Cleveland. There were twenty branches with ten to fifty people that worked at them. That was the thing—there was regional promoters. The Belkins were the Midwest, and they did it the way it was supposed to be done, as many of the successful ones did. They would take acts and decide—sometimes right, sometimes wrong, and [say]: 'I believe in this guy. We'll play him here. We'll lose a little money, let him grow, come back and break even, you know, hopefully we'll get up to the point where we're all making money at the Coliseum,' that type of thing.[19]

Stanley says, "The thing is—and it's been proven time and time again, it scares me especially in a market like Cleveland, which is always a good, open, relatively knowledgeable music audience—the more restrictive you make your playlist, the higher your ratings go. And that is such a sad, sad thing." The D.J. does maintain room to be creative. Stanley says while the classic rock format is often seen in Cleveland as "not adventuresome enough" he has friends in Los Angeles who listen to his program on the Internet and call him: "'My God, you played Alex Harvey today!.'" "In Los Angeles," Stanley says: "they'll say 'Nobody's played Alex Harvey in this town in thirty-five years.' I go, 'We'll play it a couple of times a month or we'll play this, or that.' I'm thinking: 'Wow, if they're that impressed with this, what does it sound like in L.A.?'" Stanley is, nevertheless, optimistic: "When satellite came around, it was like '…put your head on the chopping block, because we're all going to be out of a job in six weeks.' It didn't happen."[20]

ON THE ROAD AGAIN

As record sales declined, the price of concert tickets (often channeled through corporations like Live Nation and Ticketmaster) went up. By 2012, the average concert ticket price had increased about 400 percent since 1981. This far outpaced the 150 percent increase in overall consumer price inflation.[21] The

2014 Fleetwood Mac reunion tour had an average ticket price of $282.00.[22] There is thus money to be made via touring if the brand is strong. The Grateful Dead, which got its start playing free concerts in San Francisco's Golden Gate Park in 1966, bid farewell to its fans in two concerts in California and three in Chicago in summer 2015. These concerts grossed over $52 million (before special packaged merchandise, compact discs, and videos) and became the largest ever Pay-Per-View audience.[23] Their concerts also saw fans become victims of scalpers—with some resale ticket prices topping over $13,000. One skeptical fan told the *New York Times*: "This isn't the Grateful Dead... It's just a huge, pathetic money grab."[24]

"The Drummer Had to Borrow Money for Gas to Get to the Coliseum"

Concerts and touring make up some lost revenue from record sales, at least for established artists. Danny Goldberg, who has been a publicist for Led Zepplin, headed Warner Bros. records, and managed Nirvana and Steve Earle says:

> I don't see anything wrong with people charging what the market will bear for concert tickets. I mean everybody else in society is operating based on capitalism, why should artists suddenly have to artificially lower their prices when everybody else is getting paid what they can for what they do? I think it's a good thing that people will pay more money for concert tickets. It has a lot to do with the older artists getting the biggest ticket prices. That generation of artists created music that moved their audiences with a level of intensity that was different from previous generations. Bruce Springsteen is sixty-six, and Eric Clapton just turned seventy, Crosby and Nash are both seventy-two or seventy-three, I mean they're still creating powerful, emotional experiences for people, and it's worth the money to see them.[25]

Goldberg adds: "I think the younger artists don't charge as much because they're building that kind of a relationship with an audience. But we've seen artists have forty-year careers, which just didn't used to exist. I think they've earned that money and are absolutely entitled to it."[26]

The top concert earners in 1982 were 26 percent of the total revenues generated by live music. By 2003 the top five percent of earners accounted for 90 percent of overall live revenues.[27] Yet, even that data point does not explain who is making money from those revenues. The Future of Music Coalition reports:

> As ticket prices climb, so do production costs and audience expectations. Touring costs are never reported publicly. Usually, the only people who know about the cost side are band members and—if they have them—their booking agent, their manager(s) and/or their accountant. Sometimes, even the big named

tours that drive massive Pollstar grosses—actually lose money. Additionally, gross tour revenues tell us nothing about how much of that gross actually ends up in artist's pockets.[28]

Audio engineer and musician Ryan Waniata writes: "Unfortunately, the 1 percent you see sparkling at the very top of those ivory towers don't experience what those down below—including musicians, songwriters, and other music journeyman like audio engineers—experience." He continues: "And what if you're a damned fine songwriter, but don't want to tour 360 days a year because you, say, have a kid or a personal life? The ability of an average artist to make ends meet is getting harder and harder, making the profession a lot less possible to sustain."[29]

Touring and gigging is also the way to pay dues and learn the ropes, build a fan base, and sell records. "That's what musicians have always had to do," Glen Ballard says, adding: "My dear friend Mike Post reminds me, not that he has to worry about anything [as a writer of successful television themes]; we're musicians. We come in through the kitchen. We play for the rich people and we leave out the kitchen—O.K., that's what we are. I'm so happy and I'm so in solidarity with being in the service industry because that's what we do—we try to give something special to people, but we're serving them at some level."[30] Even just doing that, however, can be difficult. At one of the Michael Stanley Band's early sold out arena shows in Richfield, Ohio, Michael Stanley says, "…the drummer needed to borrow money for gas to get to the Coliseum." Today he reflects: "I could play—getting offers from the West Coast, all over the place. I can't do it financially. It would be a money losing proposition."[31] David Crosby says: "Being alone in a hotel room, being away from your family, three meals a day of terrible food…I've been doing it fifty years. The two and a half hours that I spend on stage—most fun you can have with your clothes on. Absolutely wonderful. The rest is what we get paid for. It's very tough. I'm so conflicted about it. I don't want to leave next Tuesday, and I'm gonna. When I leave, I'm going to be gone for almost four months."[32]

The Grateful Dead set high standards for touring as a revenue stream. Their steady commitment to the music and their fans built an expansive community reliably filling large venues. They also allowed anyone to record their shows via cassette tape and exchange them. Cameron Sears says:

A lot of what the Grateful Dead are credited with creating, and there's a lot of it, stemmed from not a need to make more money, but a need to solve a problem. For example, when they set up their own ticketing business, it was because the audience wasn't getting the tickets—the scalpers were and therefore the fans had to pay more. Well, if we took over the ticketing we had a better chance of getting tickets to our fans at a reasonable price and fans didn't have to go pay outrageous service fees to get them.[33]

As the Grateful Dead grew in commercial popularity in the late 1980s, they also found themselves supporting a large staff whose livelihood depended on touring. The scene inside and outside their shows eventually became chaotic. At Deer Creek in Indiana in 1995, a death threat to Jerry Garcia forced the band to play with the house lights on. Then, to make matters worse, gate-crashing fans poured through the back of the venue. Bill Kreutzman (the band's drummer) writes: "In addition to property damage and concerns about crowd safety, thousands of gate crashers just negated all the increased security measures that were put in place to protect Jerry from the death threat. It was disastrous."[34] Meanwhile, members of the band had at times descended into alcohol and cocaine abuse or, in the case of Jerry Garcia, heroin addiction. They needed a break that they could not get and instead culminated in August 1995 with the death of Jerry Garcia in a California rehab clinic.

Now, bands that tour have to lower costs and maximize revenue—meaning they travel light. Matt Busch, who manages Bob Weir, says: "I've had my share of interns. I haven't hired any of them. I'm always happy to give people advice, but I just unfortunately can't give anyone a job." He says: "Touring and merchandizing are really the only place to make money these days, unless you can turn any of it into endorsements. But you can't really count on that. When that starts happening, you're probably making a living anyway."[35] Michael Bracy argues the new economics of touring works against emerging artists. "You have a generation of artists," he says, "that really benefited from the previous structures, and they were the successful people and they were able to get, you know, certain levels of notoriety, fame, and it's easier for them to have a different kind of perspective on what does it mean to come out from nowhere."[36] Bertis Downs observes: "I don't know a single musician around Athens who ever expects to make a nickel off a sale of music. Where do they expect to make money? Touring. O.K., great. That's awesome. But, if you're a starting musician it's not like you can say, 'Hey, I want to come and make a bunch of money in your club.'"[37] A band might have a shot at getting noticed at the "South by Southwest Music and Media Conference" held annually in Austin, Texas. Groups can apply to perform at this event but if accepted are payed almost nothing. An artist or band that is offered a spot at the festival only gets a paid guarantee of $250 cash ($100.00 for solo acts or duos) or they can opt for a free pass for the entire festival worth as much as $895.00.[38]

"The Middle Class Is Completely Gone"

Even for a known national act, attending South by Southwest can be prohibitive. The *New York Times* reported in 2015:

> Weaving down to Austin, Tex., from New York in a minivan will cost the Prettiots about $1,000 in gas, plus $3,000 to rent the vehicle with insurance.

Hiring someone to manage the tour will be $1,500. Cheap hotels along the way: $500. And once the band members arrive at the music marathon on Tuesday, they will stay at an Airbnb accommodation, which will run them another $2,500 for four nights—the going rate, as the city is overrun by thousands of visitors. All told, with incidentals and a $15 per diem for the musicians, the trip will cost the unsigned group nearly $10,000.[39]

The costs were fronted by their manager, Asif Ahmed, who says: "The middle class is completely gone."[40] In 2014, Jack Conte (who with his partner Nataly Dawn) heads the band Pomplamoose published details of their recent 24-show tour, which sold $100,000 in tickets. Conte writes: "In order to plan and execute our fall tour, we had to prepare for months, slowly gathering risk and debt before selling a single ticket. We had to rent lights. And book hotel rooms. And rent a van. And assemble a crew. And buy road cases for our instruments. And rent a trailer." This meant putting $24,000 on personal credit cards. Salaries for four musicians and two crew members totaled $43,974 (including a $20.00 a day meal allotment per person). Other expenses included $17,589 for hotels and food (2 people per room, 4 rooms a night at 'Best Western-style' accommodation); $11,816 on gas, airfare, and parking tolls; $5,445 on insurance; and $16,463 for commissions (i.e., their booking agent). Meanwhile, they took in $97,519 from ticket sales; $29,714 from merchandise sales; and $8,750 from a Lenovo computer sponsorship. In total, the tour had $135,983 in income and $147,802 in expenses—a loss of $11,819.[41]

MAKING RECORDS

In 1995, Glen Ballard and Alanis Morissette hit big with *Jagged Little Pill*, riding the last waves of record sales via compact disc. This recording hit number one for thirteen consecutive weeks in the United States and had six hit singles, winning five Grammy Awards. They sold over 33 million records. The industry was then built, Glen Ballard says: "…on a possession of ownership, of psychically owning and having great artwork; that experience is all gone. It won't be back." Ballard adds:

Everybody's a subscriber now because that's the only way you're really going to get music easily. I mean, you could probably find a million people to listen to your music if it's really good. And they're not going to buy it, they're just going to listen. And if you get paid for their listening, that's what we want, right? So that's the only hope. I mean, we can complain all we want, but that's really our only hope. Because otherwise, trying to get paid for recordings that we make? That was [when] people would pay $10.00 for ten pieces of recorded music. Now for $10.00 you can listen to everything that's ever been recorded, and that's not going to change.[42]

The prior model was also no panacea. Producer Steve Albini (known for his work with Nirvana) says, "The whole industry depended on these sales, and sales depended on exposure. Bands on big labels toured, essentially to promote their recordings. And the labels provided promotional and logistical support to keep the bands on the road. This supported a network of agents and managers and roadies and promotional staff, so the expense was considerable." Albini adds: "Radio stations were enormously influential. Radio was the only place to hear music from any people and record companies paid dearly to influence them. Direct payola had been made illegal but this was a trivial workaround. Record pluggers acting as programming consultants were the middlemen. They paid radio stations for access to their programmers and conducted meetings where new records were promoted."[43] By 2015, still the consolidation was near complete as just three major record labels remained after consolidation: Universal, Sony, and Warner Bros.

Independence

There is also a history in the music community of artists having to fight for control over their music. For example, in 2001, a U.S. District Court in Florida ruled that George Clinton did not own publishing rights to songs that he wrote between 1976 and 1983.[44] His label had defined him as "employee for hire" and his songs were "works made for hire" —which apparently granted ownership to the hiring firm.[45] Clinton asserts:

> …a lot of people still in rock and roll don't know that they made a song that they sold, survived, and then that belonged to their heirs. They have the same— because they've been doing it to us for twenty years. They have learned how to do it so good—made so much money—that now BMI itself is participating. So what we are doing? Trying to expose that. The *New York Times* started to do an expose on it, *WXYZ* in Detroit started too. But these are hard-lobbying people. They do not want people to see what they've done to the ownership, the copyright issue.[46]

Clinton says: "With us, the rest of the record companies, they inherit all of those samples that all those people have done—thousands of them." George Clinton is concerned that: "The people that wrote music have nothing to do with those licensing. They got away with the money back then, but the licensing still belonged to those people." He laments, "You can't even have any say so in how it's [the music] applied, and what's done with it."[47]

Michael Stanley reflects of the period his band rose to major label success, in the late 1970s and early 1980s: "I think I was lucky to be in a band and come of age, and do the things I did, in the time I did. I think it was a great time to do it. Radio was good." There was also, Stanley recalls, "...a lot of excess because there was a lot of money."[48] Now Michael Stanley produces his material, part of the independent label movement, which accounts for one-third of the music business. He was spurred on by an old friend Steve Popovich who founded Cleveland International Records:

> He goes, 'You got this ego thing going on. You want to be on Warner Bros, you want to be on Columbia, you want to be on this because it's Warner Bros., it's Columbia.' He goes 'What are they going to do? You know by now.' And this was after MSB had folded. He goes, 'You're going to sell a half a million records. You're going to sell 100,000 records and what? They're not going to pay you a cent.' He goes, 'You sell 10,000 records on your own, you keep all the money. And I said, 'Steve, you don't reach those other 690,000 people.' He goes, 'That's the trade. Are you going to starve to death? Or are you going to do the thing?[49]

Stanley says: "I'm not worried like it was back in the old days—$300.00 an hour or this and that. It's like if I want to spend all day down here I'm just wasting my time, nobody else's. I have a studio that's like a 10-foot-deep pool and I'm swimming in the top six inches of it. And that's all I need at this point."[50]

Joan Jett went independent as a last resort creating Blackheart Records in 1980 with her manager Kenny Laguna after being turned down by over 20 record labels. Blackheart Records became the means through which Joan Jett and the Blackhearts could record, license, and distribute music. Now, Blackheart Records is managed by Laguna's daughter Carianne Brinkman. It handles Joan Jett's catalogue plus several rising acts. Blackheart Records, Brinkman says, works to: "...honor what Joan and my father had done, X-amount of years ago." That spirit is being built: "not just for economic reasons, but [for] the legacy and moving on what they had done—putting it into a different era."[51] Brinkman says:

> We want the bands that are going to work it and build the fan base and do all that because those are the serious artists. Those are the people that are truly authentic because they're doing what they love. It's not about fame. It's not about any of that. I mean Joan, for instance: she's the most authentic person you'll ever find. They are the people that there's literally nothing else that they should or could be doing in the world, doing what they're doing. I think that's a big part of it, and I think a big part of loving it. I think you need that to survive in the music industry—especially in today's market.[52]

Blackheart Records is able to give their signed acts close attention. "Absolutely," says Brinkman: "And, we do that intentionally and really try to seed our projects so that there isn't too much overlap."[53] Brinkman says: "I am not for just throwing money at radio necessarily. I really think that the industry's changed too far for that, especially with the artists that we're working with." Getting new material on the radio—even for Joan Jett, Carianne Brinkman says, is "very hard." Still, Joan Jett provides an anchor for Blackheart Records. Brinkman observes, "There's not too many artists that go on tour with Green Day, the Foo Fighters, the Who."[54]

Building an independent production facility around a successful artist can advance emerging artists and maintain access for established ones. Bob Weir of the Grateful Dead built the "Tamalpias Research Institute" (TRI) in Marin County, California. The studio uses top-line video streaming technology and Meyer Sound, which emulates sound spaces with precision. Chris McCutcheon served as CEO from 2011 to 2015:

> Bob insists that this is so much more intimate than going and seeing them actually live—the camera's right in the face, so you can see. And the sound is mixed better because you're not dealing with the acoustics of a big hockey hall or auditorium. As a Deadhead and fan, it's not in place—the whole community aspect of it. But what we have found is our audience is kind of [like] the Super Bowl party thing. There are a lot of, probably, one guy looking at his laptop online, but there are just as many people who have a viewing party. So the community aspect has changed. It never will be to replace the 'live' live experience but you can't be everywhere at every time. So, why not offer it in the best format possible and having a live performance in a studio environment for the musicians to be able to hear themselves? And, to be able to use the studio quality mics which are infinitely better than mics you take on the road? I mean, these are $20,000 mics that you would never take out on the road.[55]

In terms of financing, McCutcheon says: "It's about reach if you're selling advertising around it. And that's a huge issue where I am balancing Bob's philosophical and ethical thoughts—and the Grateful Dead. If they could have played for free and given every ticket away for free, they would have, on that side. We don't do 'Pay Per View' here and we don't do subscription here. I have to balance that we want to give the best, the most to the audience and as free as possible. But, it does have to pay for itself (largely done via patron sponsorship)." The crucial thing, McCutcheon says, is: "This was done as an art project."[56]

Independent artist Christine Havrilla says: "Most of us are staying at this indy level and only a small percentage get out there and share in advances and get known. But we're still doing our thing, we're still affecting people."[57] Bruce Schmidt, as with most independent artists, sees the start-up challenges. While carrying the costs of studio time, equipment, and logistics for gigs, the band will also busk in the street in Santa Barbara—not for money, but so their music is heard. Schmidt says: "We were rehearsing in my little studio forever and it got kind of old. So, 'Let's just start busking— We'll play out. It will be really good for us because you have to finish the song, you got to get through it,' and so we still busk." Schmidt concludes that help is needed to provide opportunity for music to be heard: "Some sort of social consciousness has to happen. Maybe the government could step in. I know that in other countries, you go to Scandinavia, Norway, they'll pay for a whole CD. Even Canada has programs evidently. I talk to some Canadian artists who get grants—they'll get 8 or $9,000 dollars specifically to produce a CD."[58]

From this pool of independent talent, hits do break through. Glen Ballard and Alanis Morissette's *Jagged Little Pill* was released and distributed by Maverick Records—at the time a subsidiary of Warner Bros. But when they began recording, Morissette had not been signed. Ballard remembers: "She'd been through that cycle—successful album at fourteen; follow-up at seventeen, not successful—dropped from the label at nineteen saying, 'I guess I'm done'; then thinking: 'Wait a minute—what if I just made a record that I want to make?' That's when I met her and that's what we did.[59]

Bruce Schmidt and his group, the Ruben Lee Dalton Band, often busk in Santa Barbara, California as a way to both practice and expand their audience. Photo courtesy of Bruce Schmidt.

I loved her voice immediately. It quickly became evident that we could say whatever we wanted, because nobody was saying we couldn't."[60] Ballard continues:

> Each song was written in a day. She did the final vocals that night, and I recorded them myself—I know, I was there—in maybe one or two takes. 'You Ought to Know'—it was the second take. And it's not a great recording of the vocals, because I did it and I scorched a couple—I was doing it on ADATs. It didn't really matter about how we were doing it. It was much more about capturing that energy—and that's what was great about that particular moment in time, is because the two of us could make a record like that. We could be in a room, in my studio, and make that sound because I had just enough of the digital tools at that point, so it wasn't all the way. It was very handmade. I was programming everything and playing everything. And that's a lot of fun. It's very intense, but she was like, so real. And she didn't have a record deal. So, we weren't writing for the marketplace. It was all about just 'what we wanted to do.' We were not trying to be popular.[61]

Now, the dilemma for artists is not the ability to produce records—anyone can make a recording with good software. The problem for professional artists is how the music will be distributed and whether that supports a sustainable career.

It is still possible for artistic breakthroughs to happen because audiences are looking for them. "Take an artist like Bon Iver," Danny Goldberg says: "People, I think, look at him as an album artist. I think he does very well. He sells hundreds of thousands of records which is very profitable. Those records don't cost a lot to make. He can tour. He makes a cultural footprint. I think there's a lot of people we're not thinking of like that." But, he agrees: "There's just no question that billions of dollars of wealth has been transferred from music companies and therefore the people that they pay—musicians and songwriters—to tech companies and the backers who back them. I mean that transfer has happened. People hope that will reverse itself when streaming becomes ubiquitous, we don't know if it will. But there's just no question—that pie is half as big as it used to be."[62]

Talented and committed artists can find diverse ways to reach an audience. Pomplamoose, for example, could have saved $50,000 in 2014 if they toured as a duo. However, they saw the full band as an investment in future tours. Also, touring is not their only income. They get some payout from monthly sales via downloads of songs from iTunes and Loudr, which allows the two core members to survive on monthly incomes of about $2,500 a person. Pomplamoose also benefited from its sponsorship agreement with Lenovo while on tour. Matt Busch advocates for sponsorship to supplement revenue, asking: "Why couldn't Bob Dylan take $1 million from Victoria's Secret and charge $10.00 a ticket on the road?" Busch adds:

> It seems like the game is rigged against musicians. They're supposed to have all this credibility and all these ideals, and all these beliefs that they stand by so militantly, and it seems like every one of those keeps them from making money. It keeps them from making money because they can't align with a brand, they can't do a commercial, they can't write a jingle you know. I did a tour with a musician in a jam band whose day job was writing T.V. jingles, and he was so embarrassed by that. I was like, 'What's the difference? I mean you get paid and you could be doing anything else so much worse than that.' Why is that not O.K.? Why is a musician not allowed to take money from certain places that [especially] when you can't even sell a record online because everybody knows they can get it for free? Why is it so wrong for a musician to take a million dollars from a corporation for an advertisement? It only means that this guy can now keep making music that his fans want to hear.[63]

However, Kathy Kane says: "We don't spend too much time entertaining corporate sponsorship. It's not something that we use as a tool to make more money or increase profile by associating with products. Bonnie's more about helping raise the profile of nonprofits. Fortunately, Bonnie can make music, offer it to fans, go out on the road and play concerts for people without having to rely on corporate sponsorships to do what she loves."[64]

"Great Artists Do It Because They Have to Do It"

The community that makes music has little choice but to care about how their art is made and heard if the music is to sustain careers. "It's a commitment that most people aren't really willing to make," Glen Ballard says. He adds: "All the great artists do it because they *have* to do it, and the money comes or it doesn't come, but they're going to do it, no matter what." The problem, Ballard says lies deeper:

> The spirit of what really was pop music, but certainly a lot of music from forty years ago, fifty years ago, was very much about not conforming to the accepted normal suburban lifestyle. It was a counter-reaction to a kind of 'way of life' that was a little bit mindless, if not a lot, and the music expressed that. Fast-forward fifty years, music today, if you want to be popular, your music has to conform – it has to conform to what's already there. It doesn't reward you for being a counter-programming head or provocateur. It's just looked at [in a way] so that the whole Zeitgeist is completely different. Music now is all about conformity, in my opinion. A lot of what I hear on pop radio sounds similar, and a lot of it is Auto-tuned, a lot of it is very little harmonic information. I'm hearing some of the same beats, over and over and over and it's computer driven. I mean people

who are serious about music, they already know they're not going to find serious music there, so they've gone a million other places. They've retreated. There's some artists that I actually love who are in the mainstream. But mainstream music, it's not going to reward you for counter-programming against that. And that's what rock and roll was. It pissed people off. Now, if you piss people off, they're just pissed off. It's like, 'That's not the mission anymore.'[65]

If corporate structures and airwaves are driven by satisfying existing demographic preferences, music and art that is critical of those preferences risks being stifled and progress inhibited.

PLAYING FOR PENNIES

The downloading and streaming of recorded music is a tremendous innovation for consumers but not in terms of sustainable music careers. *Billboard* explained the dilemma in 2012:

> Based on numerous reports from artists and labels, Spotify's per-stream payout from its on-demand service can reach 0.5 cents per stream. Although Spotify's mobile radio service probably constitutes a very small portion of its overall U.S. traffic—and an even smaller portion of its global listening—the statutory license allows it to pay less than half when taking into account both master and publishing rights. Of course, lower royalties means lower payouts to artists for mobile radio streams. That could lead to greater consternation from artists who already feel ripped off from subscription services.[66]

Between 2008 and 2013, Spotify indicates it paid out $1 billion in royalties, but the average pay per song was 0.0007 cents.[67] By 2014, Spotify claimed to have paid out $2 billion in total revenue to artists. The model had grown to include 50 million users worldwide by providing a free access area and an additional 12.5 million users paying monthly subscriptions. Free services allow listeners to hear what is available, mixed with advertising, and with a $10.00 per month premium service, ads are eliminated and additional catalogues available. Kevin Kadish, cowriter of the 2015 hit "All About That Bass" by Meghan Trainor, says: "For a song like 'All About That Bass', that I wrote, which had 178 million streams—I mean, $5,679? That's my share."[68] Rosanne Cash explains: "Some will claim that this is the fault of the major labels. There is a problem there in that the major labels do have equity in Spotify. And there are 'black box' payments that artists don't know where they go."[69] Bill Payne says: "I've got reams of paper when I was getting it. It finally showed up; unending pages on our computers of, 'Here's 248,000 plays and here's .43 cents.'"[70] There are signs of hope. Neil Young's Pono service, for example, uses quality sound over quantity to incentivize paying for music. Some artists, including U2 and Taylor Swift, applied more radical tactics.

"Shake It Off"

Even for a mega group like U2, compensation is now problematic. In 2014, U2 aligned with Apple so that it paid the band and then disseminated the music for free. U2 fans were thrilled to get *Songs of Innocence* at no cost. Many recipients found it—and the difficulty in deleting it—annoying. Bono explained: "We worked really hard on these songs and really believed in them. But we were scared people wouldn't hear them. It's a trick these days, you know, to be heard. We've been around awhile, why would anybody want a new U2 album?"[71] For Apple, paying U2 (an unspecified amount) was an effective advertising investment. The approach was also a success in terms of reach. For example, *The Joshua Tree* took thirty years, since 1987, to reach 30 million people. Within three weeks of the iTunes release of *Songs of Innocence*, 100 million people had listened to a song or two, and 30 million heard the entire album.[72] If, however, a goal was to expand U2's audience for back catalogue downloads, that did not work. Only 6,744 extra sales followed the free release.[73] Meanwhile, not all of the 500 million recipients wanted U2 music. A commentator in the *Washington Post* wrote: "U2's new album was just *there*, waiting for you. Like an Ikea catalogue. Or a jury summons. Or streptococcus. The latest inescapable unpleasantry for anyone who's chosen to participate in our great digital society—more specifically, the 500 million human beings on this planet who use iTunes...Okay, this might be the largest album release in history. It's also rock-and-roll as dystopian junk mail."[74]

Where U2's approach may have fallen flat, Taylor Swift sold a lot of records with her hit *1989*. Moreover, she did it while pulling her entire catalogue from Spotify. Released late in 2014, Swift's record had, by the New Year, sold 1,409,000 paid digital downloads as songs like "Shake It Off" shot to number one. By late summer 2015, the record sold over 5 million in the United States and over 8.6 million worldwide. In July 2014, writing in the *Wall Street Journal*, Swift proclaimed: "Music is art, and art is important and rare. Important, rare things are valuable. Valuable things should be paid for. It's my opinion that music should not be free, and my prediction is that individual artists and their labels will someday decide what an album's price point is."[75] Then, in November 2014, as *1989* dominated the charts, her independent label pulled her entire catalogue from Spotify. The move helped Swift because consumers who wanted the record had to purchase the material product (e.g., getting a $13.99 special edition compact disc, exclusive to Target or via a paid digital download). In fact, after pulling her catalogue from Spotify, her (free) views on YouTube doubled from 12.5 million views on November 3 to almost 24 million daily views a week later. Views of the video for "Shake It Off" increased by 120 percent that same week.[76] Brian Anthony Hernandez, writing for *Mashable*, concludes:

> It's unclear what chunk of that amount actually goes to Swift's team because YouTube doesn't disclose royalty percentages; however, music insiders estimate it's between $0.50 and $2 for every 1,000 views. If that math holds up, Swift's label could make between $10,000 and $40,000 from 20 million views, an amount that would be shared among the label, songwriters and Swift. On Spotify, rights holders (labels, publishers, and distributors) make, on average, 'between $0.006 and $0.0084' per stream, an amount that 'goes to rights holders who then pay out to artists,' Spotify confirmed to *Mashable*. When using the 20 million streams in the YouTube example, above, in this Spotify equation, Swift's team could make between $120,000 and $168,000 from 20 million streams to be shared among rights holders and the artist.[77]

Jon Healy concluded, writing in the *Los Angeles Times*, the Spotify decision showed that people who wanted free music would migrate in search of it—thus benefiting YouTube, which paid next to nothing.[78]

Streaming services had by mid-2014 offset declines in digital downloads—though total revenues were still down in terms of retail sales by $3.2 billion.[79] David Byrne of the Talking Heads notes, the problem is transparency: "About 70 percent of the money a listener pays to Spotify (which, to its credit, has tried to illuminate the opaque payment system) goes to the rights holders, usually the labels, which play the largest role in determining how much artists are paid (A recently leaked 2011 contract between Sony and Spotify showed that the service had agreed to pay the label more than $40 million in advances over three years. But it doesn't say what Sony was to do with the money). The labels then pay artists a percentage (often 15 percent or so) of their share." Byrne adds: "One industry source told me that major labels assigned the income they got from streaming services on a seemingly arbitrary basis to the artists in their catalogue."[80] The case had become clearer in May 2015 when the initial forty-one page contract between Sony and Spotify leaked to media. According to the *New York Times*, it contained: "…up to $42.5 million in advance payments and a $9 million advertising credit for Sony, as well as a complex formula for determining Sony's royalty payments each year. A 'most favored nation' clause, common in digital contracts, obligated Spotify to pay Sony higher rates if other labels struck more favorable deals."[81] Meanwhile, Taylor Swift proved she had struck a chord with her main point that artists should be compensated for their work. In June 2015, she challenged Apple Music in an open letter for its new subscription service, which would pay no royalties to artists during an initial three-month period. Swift wrote: "I find it to be shocking, disappointing, and completely unlike this historically progressive and generous company."[82] Apple capitulated, quickly.

Billy Bragg was initially skeptical of the Taylor Swift move on Spotify, believing she had effectively aligned with YouTube. However, when YouTube subsequently rolled out its subscription service, her work was missing. Bragg apologized and welcomed her as a voice for artistic rights:

> Whenever money is made on music, musicians—artists—should be paid. And, that's both when our music is listened to—but when a record label gives an entire catalogue to a phone company, you know—they're exploiting our catalogue. We should get a square of that. For all music streaming services that are subscription – and this is true of Spotify and of Music Key, the new YouTube service, their biggest competitor, their biggest problem is the world's largest free streaming service, which is YouTube. So, if you believe passionately, as Taylor Swift appears to in her interviews, that music shouldn't be available for free, then you shouldn't just be pulling music off of Spotify and Music Key, you should be pulling it off of YouTube.[83]

Sinéad O'Connor confirms what Billy Bragg says. In 2014 she released *I'm Not Bossy (I'm the Boss)* and within a week it was available for free on YouTube. "The bastards" she says, adding: "It's been fucking leaked all over. I'm kind of pissed off with the record company about it because they send these CDs out to people and all they do is watermark them, which means it can be traced if it came from you. But it's already up on YouTube by the time—it's infuriating."[84] O'Connor observes: "That's the way the industry works. And, that's inculcated in us from teenage, from when we signed—the idea that we should be grateful and in spite of the fact that we're paying them thousands of quid, nobody takes our instructions. In fact, it never occurs to us to issue an instruction—we feel bad if we do. You call up accountants and you want to see particular documents and they'll tell you 'you don't need them.'"[85]

"It's Not Just the Music Industry"

Today, national talent contests like *American Idol* imply that one can skip hard work and go straight to famous—devoid of reality except for a small few. Dave Grohl of Nirvana and Foo Fighters says: "I would never have made it," adding: "Who's to say they're not good or not? Imagine Bob Dylan standing there singing 'Blowin' in the Wind' in front of those judges…'Sorry, it's a little nasally and a little flat. Next.'"[86] Damien Dempsey explains:

> All the kids want to be on the *X-Factor*. But it's all about getting rich and famous. Music was never about that. That's only a very recent thing. Music was

always a spiritual thing, to help us through life. If I went on myself, I'd probably be laughed at, you know? Sometimes I watch it to see what's going on.
You see a kid come out and sing an incredible version of something amazing.
There's some great singers that go onto it. And then these three people sit there
and say, 'You were a bit tuney on the bridge, and I go 'for fuck's sake.' Just get
the computer to sing the fucking song, you know?[87]

David Crosby observes that: "...the counterveilling force is money and
fame, both of which are celebrated way over bravery and intelligence.
It's culture. There are people now who are just famous for being famous.
Kardashian? No talent, no contribution. Nothing. Nope, nothing. *Nothing.*
Except she's famous because she's famous. Paris Hilton—she's famous
because there's a video of her getting fucked? I'm sorry, did I miss something?"[88] Glen Ballard adds: "The idea that celebrity is an end in itself now,
I mean it is an actual goal to just be famous. It doesn't matter why, you could
kill somebody or be a really good singer—just get out there. Of course,
it's possible now because of this connectivity—it's so new to everybody.
Polarizing figures are very valuable in media."[89]

Gedeon Luke explains what it really takes to earn it and stay true to oneself. He says that while on *American Idol*, Simon Cowell said: "'Gedeon
you do this very very brilliantly. If you stay in this lane, the soul music—old
school...I think you'll make it. I think you'll go very far.'" "I'm not doing
this because Simon Cowell told me to," Luke says, adding: "I'm doing this
because this is who I am on the inside, inside out."[90] Luke recalls: "When I
left Memphis, what people don't know is, I caught a Greyhound bus to New
York, with two suitcases. I stayed in a McDonald's for three days so I could
find my way. The McDonald's right there on 42nd Street." He recalls: "A lot
of people would notice me for being on *American Idol*. What they didn't
know was that when you go on a big show like that, your value shoots up,
but your pockets are still the same." Luke adds: "When I was on the show,
we were getting like 62 million viewers—we were getting more viewers than
the winter Olympics in 2006. Whether you like it or not, you're going to have
to go through the struggle, you're going to have to go through the journey."[91]
Danny Goldberg also believes that talent finds a way: "There's young artists
that keep emerging. I think that artist from New Zealand, Lorde, is pretty
interesting. She doesn't sound like anybody else. I do think there are people
now that would have been able to make a few albums in the '70s or '80s
that aren't going to be able to do that today. That is true. There is less money
available for certain kinds of risk-taking. But, I think geniuses find a way of
reaching their audience."[92]

Marc Swersky, who runs independent Monocentric Music and has cowritten or produced hits for artists including Joe Cocker and Hillary Duff, sees

difficulties affecting the music community reflecting broader challenges. "It's not just the music industry," Swersky says:

> It's the same thing in any form of creative industry—the film business is going through the same. The book business and the newspaper business is virtually destroyed. It's virtually destroyed. So you want to be a writer? What, are you out of your mind? Look at being an artist, this day and age, you know, people slave for years learning how to paint, learning how to draw, learning how to do this—now you can just get an iPad and do it on an iPad. They provide you with software, provide you with everything, and all you've got to do is run your finger around and pick some colors. Is that being an artist?[93]

Of his prior work with Gedeon Luke, Mark Swerky says: "When you get voted off *American Idol*, you're part of a contract that's called 19 Entertainment. All that they wanted to do was turn him into a pop/hip-hop star. He hates pop music, he hates hip-hop music. He just wanted nothing to do with it. He ignored their phone calls; ignored their e-mails. We got him out of his deal and he fought because all he wants to do is listen to music that he loves. He's not interested in changing." Swersky explains the dilemma of getting heard:

> Why is it not easy? We're an independent record company—we're out there fighting. Everybody that hears his music loves his music. Every time he performs somewhere, you read all the reviews of the record, they're astounding. But yet if you don't have the budget, you can't get it to major radio. That's what makes a major record company, you know the Warner Bros., Columbias, the Sonys and the EMIs, the Universals. That's what you sign to them for. If you can get lucky enough to get inside their food chain, it's with the hope that they have the buying power to get you to radio.[94]

"If they would open up the gates," Swersky adds, "and the powers to be would stop trying to cash in on every moment and stop being so damned corporate, which they'll never do because they're driven by stockholders, by a board of directors and stockholders, we could get the messages back out there again. We can help fan the flame of a revolution. We can help the Gedeon Lukes get their messages out there—instead of playing the 'color-by-numbers, follow-the-rule-book' that's out there."[95]

There is of course still space for artists to earn a sustainable living in the music business. Danny Goldberg now runs an independent management team for fifteen artists, including Against Me!, Steve Earle, The Hives, Ben Lee, and Peaches. Goldberg says:

> I think there's still a lot of artists that can do that. I think that the overall declines in the record business have definitely reduced the number of people that can do that. But it hasn't eliminated that category. I mean, Steve Earle's in that

category. Steve Earle makes a good living. He doesn't have pop hits. He's never had a pop hit and the only rock hit he ever had was in the '80s. But he tours all the time, his songs are used in movies and television and he's able to make records and he definitely makes a living from it. And, there are hundreds of artists like him that we can name like that.[96]

Goldberg also points to the success of Arcade Fire: "They've done everything independently, everything on their own—they've won Grammys, they sell out arenas—completely authentic, creative, one-of-a-kind artist. Certainly Bon Iver and Arcade Fire and Grizzly Bear, the National, and War on Drugs; these are not cookie-cutter pop acts and they're making a living."[97]

Just as there is consternation about the relationship between new technology and artistic compensation, at the same time, platforms like YouTube can advance progress. In 2002, recording engineer Mark Johnson and film producer Whitney Kroenke conceived of "Playing for Change" —which began as a documentary film project highlighting the role of street musicians in the United States. Since then, they produced (by 2015) 118 videos of street artists from locations around the world. In 2005, Johnson recorded video and audio in Santa Monica, California, of Roger Ridley performing the classic Ben. E. King song "Stand By Me." Other players from around the world were then layered into the recording, including legendary New Orleans street players Grandpa Elliot and Washboard Chaz alongside international street players and the occasional rock star. By June 2016, the video of these street musicians performing "Stand by Me" received 88,735,706 YouTube hits.

Mark Johnson's background as a top-line recording engineer primed him for the nexus of music, Internet reach, and progress. Johnson's professional path took him to becoming a sound engineer at Hit Factory studios in New York City and then to California, working with artists like Paul Simon and Jackson Browne. "In 2004," Mark Johnson says, "I was walking towards Jackson Browne's studio and that's when I heard Roger Ridley singing 'Stand by Me':

> I had just heard the John Lennon version two days earlier. It was on my mind and I just started thinking, 'Man, that's the perfect song for the world to sing together. Why don't I ask Roger, this street musician, if he's into doing it? When I did ask him he said, 'If you come back, I'll play this song.' When I came back I said, 'Man, with a voice like this, why are you singing on the street?' Because, to me he sounded like Otis Redding. And he said, 'Man, I'm in the joy business. I come out to bring joy to the people.'[98]

Mark Johnson says, "I loved that sincerity to just be what they wanted to be and that to me was 'successful.' I just started thinking about—a pop star that can't really sing about anything that matters to them isn't more successful than Roger, really, because Roger's out there doing exactly what he wants."[99]

Issues like publishing rights that are complicated for commercial recording have not been a problem for Playing for Change. Mark Johnson says: "I'm now partners with Chris Blackwell, founder of Island Records. He runs Bob Marley's music publishing. If you can't beat 'em, join 'em! From the beginning, I got a letter from Leiber and Stoller and Ben E. King congratulating Whitney and I and PFC and thanking us. So then they called Sony and said, 'Look, these guys are [O.K.]. And then the Marley estate did the same thing with 'One Love' and 'War/No More Trouble.' Since then it's just been—I really don't think about that first because I knew then I wouldn't make it, it would never get done. So I just go make them. And then every time we make them, the publishers find a way to let us use them." Playing for Change is also taking advantage of YouTube to cultivate global empathy. For example, the U2 song—"Love Rescue Me"—features Bono and the Edge with a children's choir from Omagh in Northern Ireland. Johnson says: "I remember getting to play it for Bono and the Edge—them singing 'Love Rescue Me.' I got to play it for them in the studio, watching their eyes with tears and just, so much, to see a song that they wrote representing. I mean what better to rescue that situation than love right?"[100]

"To Share the News and Not Worry about the Economics"

Playing for Change inverted corporate priorities that define much of the music business by advancing grassroots artists. "My biggest payback ever," Mark Johnson says, "is walking Grandpa Elliott onto the stage, with 15,000 people in Brazil treating him like he's Elvis. And he's squeezing my hand. He can't see them [Elliott is blind], but he can feel it, you know? And that moment to me? That's heaven because I know how much that man has given to so many people for so many years—sixty on the streets of New Orleans." Johnson says:

> If you took the commerce thing out, the great thing about YouTube is that there's no filter between the art and the audience. If you make something, it goes back to the street musician vibe. You're not changing who you are. You're looking at that purity of art and intention. That makes the artist as powerful as can be. It may be good or bad—but still, it's at its maximum potential. As soon as you bring money in, it changes all of that. I don't know how much better—if a musician who doesn't suffer, doesn't feel—are they 'better'? It's really hard to quantify that kind of stuff. Sometimes the guy who feels the most pain, sings with the most soul, is the most beneficial in terms of deep, true, use of music [rather] than a pop star who is just writing about commercial content to make money.[101]

"Eventually," Johnson concludes, "they commercialize everything. That's the only thing. I mean, we have to realize we can't live in a society that thinks about money first and then wonder why we lose things like soul, redemption, and identity." "Maybe things like YouTube," he adds, "should be meant to share with all audiences around the world to different art and different video—to share the news and to not worry about the economics."[102]

REFORM

It remains uncertain how a sustainable music ecosystem can be achieved absent new laws that govern the industry. There is, however, a model for artistic leadership in Bonnie Raitt. Kathy Kane says the Rhythm and Blues Foundation (which Raitt supported since its 1987 inception): "...was so instrumental in making some of these record labels change their contracts to pay artists more fairly, in helping so many musicians who had fallen on hard times and in honoring these pioneers through awards ceremonies. There was lots of royalty reform work going on with these labels. The organization really forced these labels to go back to their contracts and pay artists equitably for their artistic contributions."[103] Rosanne Cash recommends today: "One thing people can do is to support the Fair Play, Fair Pay Act of 2015, sponsored by Music First."[104] This would create a standard market value for royalty payments for all broadcasting. Michael Bracy concludes: "Most musicians, if you told them that they can make enough money from their art to pay a mortgage, and have health insurance for their family, and maybe get on local radio—they would take that deal."[105]

Part IV

ROCKIN' THE FREE WORLD

Chapter Nine

Ripple in Still Water

AMERICA ROCKED THE WORLD

Rock and roll has empowered and amplified progress on freedom, equality, human rights, and peace rippling across generations. Rock and rollers have educated and engaged in activism, while advancing fairness in industry. What is next for the rock and roll revolution? Dennis McNally says: "Dylan encapsulated that challenge that the '60s represented and he stimulated it as well. I mean, a whole lot of people listened to 'Highway 61' and decided they weren't going to follow any conventional paths. It's a progression. It's a progression that goes all the way back to Thoreau."[1] Bob Dylan looks even further, saying: "These songs of mine, they're like mystery stories, the kind that Shakespeare saw when he was growing up. I think you could trace what I do back that far. They were on the fringes then, and I think they're on the fringes now. And they sound like they've been on the hard ground."[2] The sources of the rock and roll ethic and the power to advance progress run deep. As Graham Nash asked: "How far can the ripples go once you throw that stone into the pool?"[3]

POWER TO DO GOOD THINGS

People across generations and around the world have been impacted by rock and roll. David Gans suggests this is achieved with intent and as part of an evolution:

The Beatles began with juvenile romantic dribble like everybody else did and got really, really, good at it—and musically adventurous at it. Then, when they had everybody's attention, they started making music that said something. They took advantage of the opportunity to try to change the world. They made the world safe for more sophisticated music and for more directed messages. At the same time, Bob Dylan was doing that. Bob Dylan went into the socially conscious folk music and sort of kicked it open to rock and roll and hedonism in a way, while maintaining serious themes. And the Beatles went from this hedonistic, juvenile romantic rock and roll to a much more sophisticated musical and socially conscious presentation. And between those two paths, opened up this entire universe of possibility for the rest of us.[4]

Paul McCartney said in 1968, there is "...a desire to get power in order to use it for good. When you've got power, you've got to use it for the good."[5]

"A Platform for People to Amplify their Voices"

The impact of rock and roll advancing progress in America is varied, but clear. Danny Goldberg explains:

Though there's certainly a country-folk element in rock and roll, it was mostly black music at the origin of it. Definitely, that's one of the defining political changes in America in the last fifty years, sixty years, whatever it is. So clearly rock and roll played a big role in that. It also clearly played a role in terms of loosening sexual mores. That had some reverberations on some political issues such as the gay rights movement and feminism and free speech—broadening what was acceptable in terms of speech.[6]

Goldberg sees these influences present today—though with some limitations: "Miley Cyrus is experimenting with activism in the context of a pop career. She's a real, modern, pop star. There's nothing 'old' about her—she's only 22 or 23 and she's hosting the *MTV* awards and having hit singles and an extremely active presence on the web and YouTube and things like that." Taylor Swift's forcing a change in Sony policy on royalties from its streaming plans was an important demonstration of influence. But, Goldberg says: "I think that's a different thing. I mean, first of all, she is arguably the biggest pop superstar at the moment and, secondly, that was a pretty narrow issue. That wasn't about changing the tax rate or commenting on carbon tax. It was commenting on a particular practice within the music business. I think artists don't have a lot of clout within the music business because stars do. The big stars can move the needle. But that's a little different than trying to end the war in Vietnam or stop nuclear power."[7]

Danny Goldberg is, in addition to working with legendary artists, a progressive activist, taking inspiration from his No Nukes experience:

> More than thirty-five years later, Bonnie, CSN, Jackson—who were the main leaders of it—completely undiminished in terms of their beliefs and their willingness to talk about them publically. No Nukes was the turning point for Springsteen. It was the first political thing he ever did. I think it felt good to him and he's been, in his own way, a much bigger star in recent years. But he's been seen consistently taking positions on things politically as part of his public role. I think one thing you've got to say about those artists is that they really were sincere and committed and sort of contradicted any cliché of any faddishness or flavor of the month or anything like that. There's nothing particularly commercially valuable to them about having done that. It's just who they are as people; I think really the heirs of the previous generation of folk activists such as Belafonte—Pete Seeger. I think they really took the torch from them and carried it with the same level of sincerity.[8]

As manager for Nirvana, Danny Goldberg saw what happens when artistic genius achieves mass appeal: "There was a pent up yearning for something that had a feeling of authenticity. Already Jane's Addiction had addressed that, the Pixies had addressed that, R.E.M. had addressed that. But, Nirvana was the one that had the song; that they had a mass appeal thing. In that respect they didn't try to copy the hit records at the time and make a record that sounded like the latest Aerosmith record or Bon Jovi or Whitesnake or whatever the big rock hits were. They made their own kind of music and it became popular and that created a new current of commercial space for other artists."[9] Sinéad O'Connor, who also hit big in the early 1990s, says: "What I do is actually a little dangerous in that I came along, people like myself and Kurt Cobain, we were the first people to talk about being survivors of child abuse that weren't blocked out and shut out. That made us slightly dangerous. We were writing about and singing about, the sound of our voices having that—all the pain of that. And that perhaps was dangerous—at that time it was quite fucking dangerous. We were hot potatoes."[10] Still, Danny Goldberg points out: "You've always got to put an asterisk next to anything to do with Nirvana because Kurt Cobain was a one-in-a-million genius. A once in a generation genius."[11] Today the ripples from Nirvana continue to flow. Nirvana's bassist Krist Novoselić is an advocate for election reform. Novoselic combines technological access and social networking as the basis for a new "Open Source" political party. Novoselic writes: "Organizing for change has traditionally been the way to rein in the abuse of power. Social networking is connecting people as never before. The key with the party is to fuse two similar concepts—social networking and political association."[12] Novoselic's political philosophy reflects the connections that rock and roll provides: "The biggest motivation for Open Source is to provide a platform for people to amplify their voices."[13]

Jann Wenner was correct to identify Bob Dylan as the nexus that reinforced American principles—a new vision of America that could be personal and shared; local and universal. But there are many tributaries fueling the power of rock and roll. "I can see how someone said 'Dylan gave voice to his America,'" says Liberty Devitto. But, he adds:

> There's people that think and see the whole pie. There's people like me that take a slice out that's closest: that's in your neighborhood. So I would have to say, maybe, the Young Rascals, because they started talking about 'People Got to be Free'and also the Motown artists, when Marvin Gaye started going 'What's Going On?' It was more of like, 'What's going on in this neighborhood? What's happening right here?' I believe if I'm going to do something, its going to do with the guy that's in the street right in front of my house right here. That's where I'm going to start and hope it will grow out from there. If you're going to take on the whole country, it's like, 'Whoa!' And you become an example and you just, hopefully, pass it on. When I see kids, [I say] 'It's always nicer to be nice. It takes less energy to be nice than it does to be mean.'[14]

"Music," Christine Havrilla says, "people can tap into. They get sucked in musically. But then they start really hearing what an artist might be saying about the government, or about homelessness, about equal rights. I'm not a big political person. For me it's subtle and for me it's all about communicating first—individually, family, community, city, state. I think when everybody takes care of themselves in their communities, it's going to trickle up."[15]

David Gans reflects on the artist as a connector: "One way that I like to describe the purpose of art is to personalize the universal and to universalize the personal. If all you're doing is telling your own story, it's not going to be very interesting. You find ways of telling your story that other people hear themselves in. You tell a personal story that describes the whole world and you can tell a global story that relates to a specific person. That to me, the tension between the personal and the universal, is where all that creativity lives."[16]

Dar Williams traces the evolution of these forces as they connect artistic vision with progress:

> I think the effects of the '60s and the '70s —and the singer songwriters—not just Pete [Seeger] and Peter [Yarrow], but like John Prine, Bonnie Raitt. These were the songwriters who influenced everything from Silicon philanthropy to kids now just having automatically sort of 'reflective language' about understanding their own flaws, sharing self-reflection and self-critique, finding respectful language for one another, really understanding the invisible dynamics of race, class, and sex. I think that the effect was to, at the end of the day, carry on that expanding consciousness. They introduced something very basic through poetry.

Bob Dylan shakes President Barack Obama's hand following his performance at the In Performance At The White House: A Celebration Of Music From The Civil Rights Movement concert in the East Room of the White House, February 9, 2010. Official White House photo by Pete Souza.

I really see it reaching through into the way kids believe they should grow food to the way they believe they should treat other countries. Kids who've been rinsed through with this poetry—which music has a unique opportunity to do— have a pretty natural vernacular about how we can live side-by-side.[17]

Bill Payne sees the common bond of rock and roll as a foundation for progress: "When you take it to different communities around the United States and the world, you see that you're bringing together people that politically have oceans between them. Yet this music brings them together and they're like—'You know what, that's cool, I like 'Oh Atlanta.'" Payne adds: "Music has that power to get people to think. And, thinking is critical to solving problems, to observing who we are and how we view others."[18]

El Norte Tears

Rock and roll artists have the power to amplify and spread the path to progress while creating space for activism. Graham Nash points out: "I don't want to preach to people. I don't want to tell people what to do. What I do want is to have them think about shit that they may not be aware of or that they might not want to think about."[19] Billy Bragg says: "That's what you do. You challenge your audience. Sometimes you are confirming the things that they support. I don't like the phrase 'preaching to the choir'—but you are 'recharging their batteries'—by reminding them; they're standing in the room and everybody in the room sees there's power in union together."[20] Sometimes just the telling of a story can generate empathy and thus become a transcendent force for progress. For example, in "El Norte Tears," Bruce Schmidt tells a heartbreaking tale of unwanted separations among immigrants with the mournful cry—"Angelina! Angelina! What have I done?" "My father was a general contractor," Schmidt says: "So, from day one I worked on the jobs—cleaning up the jobs and sweeping. He was very close to his Mexican help and there were a lot of guys up here, illegal immigrants, I heard for years the stories of what those guys sacrificed to be here, to support their families. Their dream was to keep their families well-fed and warm. And they had this dream about saving up enough money and going home and buying some land." Bruce Schmidt says: "I knew individuals who worked for me for years who were that character. I had stories of guys who had to go home because their wife's died. They'd have to go home for emergencies for their kids, or they'd want to go home for Christmas and they didn't have enough money. I loaned them money. I loved these guys."[21]

PROGRESS

Rock and roll evolved along with society's embrace of freedom to explore and create new things—to innovate. Dennis McNally reflects on the Grateful Dead: "Improvisation is the fundamental signifier of freedom in this country." He says: "Sometimes the band would jump off the cliff and fly. And sometimes they ended up on the rocks below—and giant train wrecks. Musically, that's the whole point—within that risk that you have the potential for magic; the potential for things that are simply dazzling, that stimulate you in ways that you don't even know. It is that implicit risk at the root of improvisation that makes it so potent a signifier." McNally says:

That's the exact point that Thoreau understood intuitively, that Twain understood intuitively—all their successors. Here you have this country in which the original ideals are still given lip service to this day. Going back to Alexander Hamilton, you have a situation in which the notion of freedom that the entire Founding Fathers, Constitutional era espoused became the freedom to make large sums of money. That is the history of the 19th century and since. And Thoreau watched this. He watched it, literally watched this by rowing a canoe through Lowell, Massachusetts, the birthplace of the American industrial revolution.[22]

Cameron Sears says: "You can get kind of philosophical about it, but when you look at the intersection of what society was going through—music, alternative viewpoints, social change, environmental awareness—I mean what did Rachel Carson and the Grateful Dead have in common? More than you might think." Sears reflects: "I think that consciousness evolved over time. The earlier songs definitely have a strong link to—if you want to really stretch the connection to people like Emerson and Thoreau—I mean strong, rooty, American notions; wilderness, outlaw, freedom." To Sears:

> It's steeped in kind of that Emersonian/Thoreau along with the—sort of—wide-open western frontier. People come to California for a reason—and the West in general. Everyone has their various preconceptions about it, but one of the things that this area is good at is open-mindedness in a lot of ways—and possibility. And I think the Dead represent a lot of what's good about creative possibilities—and risk-taking. The music was taking risk. They encouraged people to go out and explore through that sense of risk at the shows—and did it in a non-preachy way.[23]

Dennis McNally says of his friend Jerry Garcia: "When you have a half a million people telling you that you're the greatest, that you're Beethoven, Jerry would just say, 'Shit, man, I was just trying to stay in tune up there.' Jerry wanted to be Huck Finn with a joint in his mouth and a guitar floating down the river."[24]

How Things Get In

Dar Williams sees music as "how things get in" as ideas permeate and shape people's views of themselves, their community, and their world.[25] And, that community can show up in the most unlikely of places. Michael Stanley recalls having a rare early-1980s day off and finding a gig in Texas playing mainly for one fan from Chagrin Falls, Ohio—a village in northeast Ohio:

> So we're driving to San Antonio and we're getting closer to San Antonio. There's all these things on the radio:'Going to be the first snowstorm in San Antonio in, like, thirty years; it's going to be horrible, stay off the roads.' And we're driving, getting closer and closer. There's nothing. We get to the club, there's nobody there. We set up and all the sudden the door opens and a kid walks in with a Chagrin Falls T-Shirt—takes a chair and puts it in the middle of the thing. We played the whole show to this kid in a Chagrin Falls T-Shirt.[26]

Bob Gross describes a similar sharing of the rock and roll connection:

> They'll hire rock and roll bands to play parties for deaf people, because they can feel the beat and dance to it. One of my friends has a sister who's deaf and blind.

I've known her since she was a little girl. She was totally blind when I first met her. I did a special gig where I played a party for that family. On the break, I went up to Judy—and she's with somebody—I can talk to her through them. They have to do it a special way since she can't see signs. She has to actually feel the hands that spell things out. So I went over and said, 'Tell her big Bob is here,' and she did. Judy gives me a big hug and then through her interpreter said, 'Tell him I can feel him playing.' And that meant the world to me.[27]

Matt Busch shows how small acts of rock and roll kindness spread progress: "If the guy next to you looks like he's having a hard time at whatever it was you've done—give 'em a hand, you know? If you've got an extra ticket that night, hand it off to someone that really needs it—and you'll probably get one a week down the road. I try to do that every single night."[28]

It can also be the artist's job to challenge people—"preaching from the stage." Still, Sinéad O'Connor says: "We milk life for songs, that's what we do. All of these feelings that we've musically expressed, they were there before we came along. They may have become part of our feelings, but they came from a whole swoosh of people before us." She cautions: " I think we ought to be careful about assuming that we're dreadfully powerful because that can just be a temptation—there are all manner of vanity and temptations, there really are."[29] The path to progress is also slow. David Crosby says they thought that they could end the Vietnam War "in a year—it took us ten."[30] Crosby explains: "There is societal inertia and it makes the accomplishment of change far more difficult. That's why it took so long for civil rights to change and for black people to be able to vote in the South. It took a long fucking time. That's why it took twenty years from when Sinéad O'Connor rang the bell." Crosby also says: "I'm not saying that it couldn't change. And, I'll tell you why. Because there are human beings; this is a truth—an act of exemplary humanity can change everything; you can stand up and speak truth to power and change everything."[31]

David Wish believes: "You challenge society because you want to shake up notions that don't make sense. The music itself and even the rebelliousness of the music itself makes society a better place because it is the embodiment of the freedoms that are embodied by the Constitution. Often times the music directly speaks to how short we're falling against our own ideals. And, it can be really unpopular: 'Four dead in Ohio'—there's a real toe tapper, you know?" Wish reflects on the impact of Steven Van Zandt's anti-Apartheid work:

I was in high school, I was so moved, and so motivated. I wrote letters and when I got to college I joined the divestment movement and we got our college to divest. It just felt like, 'We can do this thing!' And it was the first time I felt in my life, the tremors of something I still believe—my favorite saying which is: 'We are the people we've been waiting for.' Us. Us long hairs, us pierced, tattooed, whatever we are, ducktailed if that was your generation. We're the ones. We're the rebels without a cause. We're going to shake up the status quo and make it a better place.[32]

Jack Healey recalls Amnesty International rocked the world to a better place: "We did two days in Chile. We were live on television through Latin America—Mexico, Spain for 10 hours, two days in a row. We got 20 hours of live television where all those disappearances and torture were occurring. It's no wonder they cleaned up. Seriously. It wasn't just us. I'm just saying it affects the culture when you do things like that."[33]

"Think About What I Said"

David Crosby says the potential for progress is always there, waiting for the creative spark: "One human being, one act of exemplary humanity can change the whole ballgame. And that's where I hang my hat." At the same time, Crosby reveals: "I'm pretty discouraged, truth be to tell. Country's fucked. Democracy's not happening any more. Being stand-up human beings? I don't do it because I think I'm going to win. I do it because it's the only way I can be proud of myself. I do it because that's who I am and I'm not ashamed of that. I want to be that person." Crosby cautions, "Do I think that we're going to make a difference? Do I think we're going to change things? I think we've already lost. I'm very discouraged. I not only don't think we're going to win, I think we've already lost. Think about what I said."[34]

THEY'VE ALL COME TO LOOK FOR AMERICA

In the darkest hours, the promise of America has stood the test of time and rock and roll has been a part of its modern resilience. By reinforcing American values, rock and roll helps America lead by example. David Wish says:

> With the shifting world order, the United States still has what I would say almost uncontested primacy in the field of culture and innovation. The iPad was invented here. They are making it in China, [but] these technologies come from American entrepreneurial creativity. China is trying to get their minds around, 'Why do they [the Americans] get all the good ideas?' Well, a lot of it has to do with the culture and—what is the soundtrack of planet Earth right now? If there were a dominant soundrack—it's still American popular music, uncontested.[35]

As Paul Simon and Art Garfunkel sang in 1968: "Counting the cars on the New Jersey Turnpike—they've all come to look for America."

Greetings from Asbury Park

Asbury Park, New Jersey, is a small city steeped in history. Like America, it has risen, fallen, and been rebuilt—and with a rock and roll story. Inside the Asbury Park Music Heritage Foundation is a poster that hung after Hurricane Sandy devastated the region in 2012: "In the aftermath of Super Storm Sandy, we realized that as we rebuild the bricks and mortar and construct our future landscape, it is our music, the soul of the Jersey Shore that will carry us through: indomitable, resolute, optimistic." The president of the Asbury Park Music Heritage Foundation, Tom Gilmour, is also director of Economic Development for the city. He says: "I've always believed that arts are just a great economic engine. There's plenty of cities that can give you a great example of how they turned their city around embracing the arts."[36] A hub for vacationers and traveling musicians in the early twentieth century, racial riots in 1970 deeply affected Asbury Park. Gilmour says:

> People that lived here really were packing their suitcases and leaving. They were afraid. It burned half the town down on the West side, which was terrible. What happened with that was, a whole corrupt political era happened. The bad guys got elected, pretty much shut the city down—all sorts of corruption going on. Basically, the bad guys took over the city and as they did, bad things happened in the city. One of the bad things that happened, and one of the most difficult things, was that all the bad guys came into the city because they knew this was a place they could operate. We had a tremendous drug trade and everything that came with that—prostitution, burglaries, and everything like that. The county, shame on them, sort of went, 'You know, it's sort of good that all the drug dealers are in one place' —so they became very lenient. The drug dealers knew that they could come here, they could operate here. And the people who were buying drugs knew that they could come here and get their drugs. The city just went down. It went down very quickly. Slum lords came in here and bought the property up, took these beautiful Victorian houses and single family homes and made twelve apartments out of them.[37]

Eventually, Asbury Park began a turnaround. People from New York City continued to visit the beach and boardwalk during the summer and some began to buy cheap property in a diverse community on the ocean, sparking resurgence.

In 2008, just as Asbury Park looked again to be getting back on its feet and build on these assets, economic recession hit America. "Here we go again," says Tom Gilmour.[38] Gilmour says he met with a person who proposed a Smithsonian "Museum on Main Street." The exhibit was called "New Harmonies—Celebrating American Roots Music." "It was amazing. This exhibit was about how our ancestors came to the United States and everyone brought music with them and depending on where they settled, that became America's music." The Smithsonian exhibit was housed in the library over six weeks and had over 14,000 visitors in 2011. Asbury Park subsequently received a grant to do oral histories of local musicians. They trained local high school kids to do the videography and interviews. That was followed by concerts, book signings, and other events associated with the city's musical heritage. At the end of 2011, Gilmour recalls: "I'm saying: 'This is working. People are coming to the city in droves because they're loving what we're doing.' Even Springsteen showed up," Gilmour remembers:

> One day we had a panel discussion and we invited Bruce to come. Daniel Wolff, he wrote a book called *4th of July, Asbury Park*—which is a great read—he was the moderator. We had it in one of the churches. The day of the event, Bruce shows up, doesn't get up on the panel—sits in the audience. So Dan Wolff's up there and he's starting the panel discussion and there's about fifty people there. He's like, 'So Bruce, we invited you to be part of this panel, so come up and sit on the panel.' He very reluctantly gets up and sits down on the panel. Doesn't say anything for fifteen minutes. Just sort of checking this whole thing out. And then one of the musicians who was on the panel started talking about how he knew Bruce when Bruce was like fourteen years old, and he'd recognized that he had great talent. He used to sneak him in when they were playing on the west side clubs and every once in a while they'd let him get up on the stage.[39]

These experiences were a success for Asbury Park and that led them to create a nonprofit foundation, Gilmour says: "To figure out some way to really promote this music—let people really know what the music was all about."[40]

As the foundation built on the Smithsonian exhibit, they had planned for some kind of exhibit space and youth initiative. Then, Tom Gilmour says: "Sandy comes." Gilmour recalls: "We were in a really bad way here because we were in the dead of winter and we lost the whole Christmas season. All our businesses were just in a very bad way. We needed to scramble, and to get something. And the other things is, we needed to let people know that Asbury Park was open. Because what they were seeing was these houses down there—floating in the bays and all this other stuff. Meanwhile, our downtown's up and running. Our restaurants are open." Gilmour recalls: "At our November [2012] board meeting for the Music Heritage Foundation, one board member says, 'You know, you've been talking about opening a space. We should do it now.' I go like, 'Really?' We had no plan. We had no money. Like, 'Why would we do this?' And he says, 'Well, you know, we've got to get people to get back to the city.'"[41] They signed a lease December 1, 2012, and opened for their first exhibit—photography of various "Light of Day" benefit concerts—on January 15.

Marc Swersky grew up ten miles from Asbury Park and now brings artists to places like the Stone Pony and the Wonder Bar. Swersky says: "What's happening there is unbelievable and it's even mirroring Brooklyn in the sense of rock and roll at this point. There's such a vibrant scene there. But, let's face it, all the wonderful things that happened in Asbury Park musically never would have happened if it wasn't for the success of Bruce Springsteen."[42] And that, he says, is a mixed blessing:

> There's a potential for even a more vibrant music scene. I think that society in this day and age doesn't help the vibrancy of the music scene because everybody's just looking for a quick hit. Everybody's looking for something instant. The costs of everything make it prohibitive to go see music all the time. The venues have to charge so much money to keep their doors open. But the deep underbelly of it is still based on rock and roll. If the people would just notice that even Bruce is out there looking for new things. He's just out there looking for this stuff. He's not living in the past so much. And that's the only problem I see with Asbury Park is, it still lives in the past.[43]

Christine Martucci carries Asbury Park's torch forward with her song "Ocean Avenue." She uses the setting of Asbury Park's main drag to offer hope, spirit, a hunger to be free, and an abandonment of fear: "Found me an angel on Ocean Avenue, she's going to make it right, make all my dreams come true." Martucci says:

> I think that a lot of musicians come in with a song and a dream and whatever instrument they play. I don't know if it's the ocean or the 'Ghost of Bruce Springsteen' — though he's still alive. It's still that: 'Is he going to show up to one of our shows?' That kind of thing. It really just attracts a lot of young musicians from all over New Jersey. I guess a feeling here is: if you can make a name for yourself here, you can make it anywhere.[44]

She says Asbury Park allows artists to thrive: "I would say that if people coming in off the street stop and talk to the musician with the guitar around his back, he's got a lot to say. I mean, it took him a long time to get here, trust me. It's not easy to play this stage [the Stone Pony]. It's not easy to play anywhere, really. There's heroes here. We take care of our own here, we really do."[45]

"Local Pride, Global Embrace"

America was built around communities where citizens discuss, debate, disagree—and find democratic pathways to advance the common good. Dar Williams believes: "Music can be central to this." She talks of Lowell, Massachusetts, where they have a common green space in the center of town: "There's this awesome stage, the whole town comes out, they pay

$10.00 a person, huge green right in between two museums that are very popular."[46] The question is how can that model be built further? In the town of Delaware, Ohio, in early 2014 the local community bookstore—Beehive Books—closed, going out of business. It was at the heart of the town. It was where people gathered to talk, where they sat and contemplated life, and where music and books coexisted. The closing came just after Pete Seeger died— and the musicians performing played "Where Have All the Flowers Gone?" The packed store was filled with people from all walks of life—and with the silence of empty bookshelves. They stopped to gather in communion and sang. They sang for Pete Seeger and they sang for their community with the warmth of the moment and uncertainty over what came next. Dar Williams observes:

> Beehive Books—the fact that it was the bookstore and the heart of the community—you do need to replace that because the conversations that you had in that space, where you say, 'You know, the school system really sucks here lately, let's enrich it with…You know: 'Our school system's working on it.' So all these people kept on seeing each other in the farmer's market and they would say well, 'Look, we can't raise the taxes, because you know, there are a lot of people hurting in this town, but we want it better. So I'll teach French, you teach cooking, you teach science, you get involved, you do a musical.' Like all these parents just step up in the most incredible way and then we all meet at those events that we put together. We laugh and we talk and then we say, 'You know, the waterfront's a mess, why don't we clean it up?' It really requires common spaces and we don't have enough of them.[47]

"If we had a bookstore that was the heart of the community," Dar Williams says, "I think we would have a much greater chance of standing up against the Barnes & Nobles, the Roger Ailes, the crack epidemic, whatever."[48]

Dar Williams sees clear correlation between acting locally and having an impact globally by integrating common spaces with music:

> The other thing that happens when music comes through communities—I call it 'Local Pride, Global Embrace.' So you have the local pride of being proud of your theater and being proud of your town and showing off your town to artists who come through. And they're impressed and they like it and they want to hang out in the morning and meet people after their shows. Then, you have that other sort of trade wind, that wonderful trade wind thing of Jimmy Dale Gilmore or Shawn Colvin or Patty Griffin or me coming through. And if you've been on the road for a while, you're just weird. I don't care how normal you are, you're just weird because you travel. And so it's like we bring our weirdness, our new ideas, our different ways of being.[49]

Dar Williams is talking about the creative foundations of progress: "Having a great model of democracy that works." She says: "What's a coffeehouse but local governance? I mean, 'With this permit I can do this.' Suddenly you have something that you value and you put your time and energy into it. And you have to sort of bicker with one another and have your hierarchies. But, at the end of the day, you really keep it together and the longer it's there, the stronger it gets." "I give the musical movement a ton of credit for that," Williams adds: "It's always expanding, but it's always going to be invisible. You're always going to have the commerce outstrip the speed of human dialogue." And she says: "That's why I believe in Beehive Books—and finding a replacement—and simple spaces; all these places where we can meet one another. Because, I think that we have a lot of knitting up to do. I think that musical events, musical coordination, musical careers, musical performances, and the music itself – all help to bring the green space back to the downtowns. And [they] help people grow as community members, from the town center out into the world, as opposed to be sucked out to the perimeter where they feel this instability affects their global politics."[50]

Joe McDonald tells a similar story of Berkeley, California—where in 2010 Eugene Yamashita announced he was closing Mr. Mopps' Toy Store, which was founded in 1962. The local newspaper reported: "The news surprised and dismayed hundreds of people who had spent time in the toy store and many of them rallied to keep it open. Many *Berkeleyside* readers shared their memories of the store in the Comments section and the story went viral—accumulating an astonishing 905 Facebook 'Likes.' It wasn't long before a 'Let's Buy Mr. Mopps' page was formed on Facebook."[51] Mr. Mopps' remains the epitome of the community toy store—thanks to Devon McDonald and his wife Jenny Stevenson who bought it. Devon is the son of Joe McDonald. Joe McDonald says:

> The story of Mr. Mopps' is also quite incredible—and a war story. I knew the Yamashita family. The Yamashita family were interned in a Japanese concentration camp here during World War II, and, two brothers were born. The younger brother Yashita was born in an internment camp in the United States during World War II. Then they got out and moved to Japan to live—three sisters and two brothers. And during the Vietnam War era, the two brothers moved back to the United States and were drafted. One brother didn't even speak English really, and he was killed in Vietnam in the tank corps in the invasion of Cambodia. The mother asked for him to be buried in Japan. Nixon refused and had him buried in San Francisco in a military cemetery. So the whole family moved back to the Bay Area to be with the grave. As a result of that, [they] started a restaurant in Berkeley and Mr. Mopps' Toy Store.[52]

Today, McDonald says, "It's great! They've got all kinds of stuff in there now."[53] In 2013, the owners opened up something just as exciting a few doors down: Mr. Mopps' Children's Books.

Sacred Honor

Mark Karan says when he talks to some people in small towns in New England, he finds: "They want society to be off the hook because they kind of don't want there to be a society. That's at least my take on it: 'Thank you very much, we would like our society to be our small town, and leave us alone.'" He contrasts that with the idealism that formed the beginning of the Haight Asbury scene in San Francisco fifty years ago: "That's an example of when it works, and it's a beautiful thing when it works. But I also see human nature. If the last few hundred years are any example, left to our own devices, there's a lot of humans who will choose greed and self-service."[54] Still, he says his ex-wife turned him on to a different understanding of playing rock and roll. Karan says she told him: "'Honey, when you go somewhere where the windows are boarded up and it's been winter for six months and whatever, you're bringing the rainbows. You're bringing these people joy. Joy they wouldn't otherwise have in their lives. So you are bringing a gift—it's not a selfish thing.'" "It's the positive version of the NIMBY [not in my back yard] thing," Karan laughs: "How 'bout BIMBY?—'be in my backyard.' The NIMBY thing is very anti-community—it's like, 'Fuck you, I got mine!"[55] Mark Johnson, of Playing for Change, concludes that values need to triumph through cooperation: "Sacred honor is really what we need to get back to in America here, like a collective pride in what we're building together—not individually."[56]

POLITICS

What is the place for rock and roll in politics? Perhaps it matters a lot, perhaps at the margins, perhaps because it mainly reminds us of our obligation to each other. Michael Franti observes:

> I really feel that, at the end of the day, if you can't be connected with the people that you love—and be close to them and celebrate with them and dance with them and cry with them and laugh with them, that all the things that we do politically to try to change the world are meaningless. The whole reason that any of us should be concerned about the great issues of the day—climate change, economics, war, renewable energy, education for all people—the only reason anyone should be concerned about that is because it helps us to have the space in our life for the freedom to love each other.[57]

"Sometimes," Franti adds, "that gets lost when we see congressional hearings hijacked by corporate deniers of environmental issues and climate change…It gets so baffling that things become so twisted. Music is one of those things that remind us of why we do it, and why we stay in the fight. And that's ultimately when it's most powerful."[58] Serj Tankian cautions that politics can clash with artistic integrity. He says: "It's like being on stage. When you're on stage, it's like a truth-telling. If you're fearful an audience feels it. If you're powerful an audience feels it. If you're inspired, an audience feels it. For artists, we have that moment where we have to be truthful. There's no escaping it. Politicians don't. They should, but they don't." Tankian adds: "If you're always telling the truth, you can't have a side. You can't be partisan in any way. People are always asking me the same question: 'Why don't you run for politics? Why don't you ever do that since you care so much?' And I'm like, 'Well then I can't always be traditional in this way,' it's hard."[59]

Democracy

Rock and roll is one among many broader social and cultural institutions that can make modern democracy accountable to the people. At one level, those bridges are being advanced—for example with cultural shifts that have moved faster than politicians. The lack of responsiveness in Washington, D.C., however, can take a toll on citizen engagement. Graham Nash concludes: "The American public are getting tired, and they're beginning to realize that their power is the power of unification—of getting people that think like-mindedly together to put pressure on their congressmen and their senators and their presidents. The American people are getting completely pissed."[60] Glen Ballard says: "Nobody's listening to the politicians anymore man. They're not. I can tell you they're not; including me. I used to, and I just at a certain point went: 'Really?'" "Musicians," Ballard says, "have an obligation to speak the truth because everybody else has to prevaricate."[61]

As rock and roll emerged and progressed, its artists renewed and advanced an American vision of freedom, equality, human rights, and peace—all goals of the nation's founding. David Crosby says of America's founders: "They were smart guys. Oh my God man, intelligent discourse? It's like a lost art. They talked about real stuff, man. Franklin, Adams, Jay—all those guys. They were smart and committed. They were believers. They were courageous men." Now, Crosby says, courage has been replaced with a politics of fear: "Fear now is a tool for people who are running things. And what are their names? It's a very good point—because you don't know. You know the most obvious, most egregious ones—the Koch Brothers, people like that. But we don't know the names of the guys on the boards of the companies that own this country now. What is it—158 people or something own most of the wealth in the world?"[62]

Michael Stanley says: "It's like the political situation is just completely out of control. As long as they keep everybody worried about whether they can pay the bills or their mortgage is going down or how are they going to afford college, they're not going to pay attention to what the congressmen are doing." Stanley adds regarding education: "The 'intellectual elite'?—might as well call them child molesters. There's this thing like: 'Do I get you right, you want your child to grow up stupid?'"[63] Kate Pierson says: "There's so many things out there—AIDS and Lyme disease, shootings in schools and everything—there's a lot of fear."[64] George Clinton offers a similar assessment—speaking in the context of Ferguson, Missouri, in summer 2014:

> It's horrible, but this is the world we live in. It's the species. We can fool ourselves into thinking that we are still in progress for real, evolving. We are animals and endless intellect, trying to figure its way in too. That brain has got a lot of space to learn new shit than we ain't even begun to know what it's up there for. So we have to really just be careful. Like blame; it could be our problem. Love, the one we know is consistent. I don't give a fuck what you say, that was consistent all the time. Blame and fear is the enemy. Fear is natural, we know that from the old. That's going to be there to protect us, somewhere. Blame is that problem of intellect intersecting with animal, trying to figure shit out. Blame for shit, that's when the shit started to get deep.[65]

That can be countered by democracy that embraces the values of community, says George Clinton: "Real values, all of that. If you are talking about a democracy, those things you have to be able to really want for everybody like you want for yourself."[66]

Rock and roll can narrow political divides derived from fear and unite people around principles. When Michael Stipe stood up for gay rights in the 1980s, it was a career risk. Today, it sells records for Katy Perry and Macklemore and marriage equality rules the land. Bertis Downs reflects on R.E.M.'s impact:

> It was kind of like—some people put up yard signs, this is our yard sign. You do what you can. You do what you can as a citizen. You do what you can as a donor. Different people have different skills and different ways of helping. In their case, they had a pretty big platform, a pretty big microphone - where it made sense. They tried not to overdo it and they took some heat from it sometimes. But where it made sense they tried to weigh in on things they thought—whatever the cliché would be—'lead by example' or 'be a force for good.' I think they did it well.[67]

While some of these issues are associated with "left" or "right" partisan views, in reality, they are neither. David Crosby says: "In some ways, I'm a conservative. I don't think welfare is a good idea. I'll step right up and put myself on the target, right there. I think it's built some bad kind of people, to raise them on the dole." Crosby goes further: "I'm in favor of smaller government. I'm in favor of states' rights. I'm in favor of fiscal responsibility. I'm not in favor of us having national debt that we have. All of those are conservative bellwether issues."[68] While issues may resonate one way or another, the power of rock and roll is not partisan—it is, in effect, democratic, with a "small d."

In contemporary America, the rock and roll community shines a light on the quality of democracy—from protecting voting rights advocated by R.E.M. and others to the pervasive influence of money in politics. Danny Goldberg says: "There's very dark forces that are very scary to me—and the influence of money in politics is the scariest factor because it can pull things or put you in an insane direction whether it's on climate change or wars or other things." "Voter suppression is very dangerous," Andy Bernstein says: "And money in politics is very dangerous. But, the counterbalance to all of these things is just people being engaged. And that is where HeadCount comes in and it is what we are trying to do. But it's definitely difficult. We'll keep fighting the good fight."[69]

HeadCount volunteers at Participation Row during the Grateful Dead's Fare Thee Well concerts in Chicago in 2015. Photo courtesy of HeadCount.

From protesting the Vietnam War to advocating for veterans; from advancing nuclear safety to the advent of ecological touring, rock and roll artists and their associates have made a difference. At the top end, the Beatles undoubtedly changed the world. Jann Wenner observes:

> They were revolutionary. John was a very political person—deeply involved and all that kind of stuff. It was really him doing it—of the four. But no doubt that they and the music that flowed behind them was a powerful liberating force, I think particularly in the Western countries—and under the Soviet Union. Or just the society—just, the society of England; they helped liberate and change that from that stratified hard-down system. I mean, they gave voice to—same in America—all this youth and rebelliousness and the desire for economic opportunity.[70]

The potential to change hearts is perhaps the most powerful tool rock and roll artists have. Given the record of influence across issues and societies, are there best practices for rock and rollers?

Kathy Kane says: "Everything seems case-by-case with me, which potentially could be an argument for why it might be so difficult to try and make change happen because there is no 'across the board' situation. Every venue is different, every city's different with their recycling policies. Every utility company handles things differently. Each situation seems to be so different." "Just changing over the cleaner products alone would stop pollution in the runoff in all these venues—with the pesticides in the lawns," Kane says, adding: "It would just be an amazing thing to have venues do an overhaul of this magnitude." Kathy Kane is regarded among peers for doing extensive research about what an artist wants to achieve and how to achieve it:

> That was one of the reasons I set up ARIA—to help artists focus in on the type of non-profits they want to work with: 'Well, I'm into animal rights'—'O.K. — what kind of animal rights are you into? Are you into helping rescue animals and locally, or nationally? Are you into stopping animal testing?' What is it that interests you? Are you wanting to work with one small organization that you really can help them—that's in your community? Or are you thinking of trying to do something national? Are you thinking of a PETA that's really on the forefront of stopping cruelty to animals, or are you wanting to work with the Humane Society and focus on rescuing animals and finding them new homes? What focus is a match for you?' But, those decisions are made, the most important part of the hunt is looking at the financials of the organization to make sure they have low administration costs and the majority of the funds are actively being used for the campaigns.[71]

"The nonprofit world is like any industry," Kane observes, "you've got your spectrum from those with integrity to those with not so much. And that's when looking at those financials and analyzing where the money goes is so important." Kathy Kane explains: "You don't want egg on your face. If all of the sudden you find out that the organization spends 50 percent of its yearly budget on administration, it's worth a little more investigation. I do believe that becoming informed should be one of the top priorities for making any sort of decision. By becoming informed you hope that you will bring the inspiration for activism out of you because the more you learn, the more you realize there's an injustice going on. Whatever department it could be—from royalty reform to environmental and social justice issues—you usually will find that there's some sort of injustice happening that requires attention. And to sleep at night—be at peace with yourself—and to try and make a difference is something that really has to come from the inside."[72]

Danny Goldberg also emphasizes: "Every situation is different, every artist is different, every moment is different, and every issue is different. I think you start with the Hippocratic Oath of first do no harm. You just make sure people are informed correctly and thinking about things in a way that's going to advance what they believe and not be a distraction from it." Goldberg continues: "You just try to figure out what the artist wants and to get them connected by the best people, to avoid people that are assholes, to put them in a position where they're going to be supported and not disrespected. Then once you get all those things in place you try to find the biggest megaphone you can find—and it varies from moment to moment." Goldberg adds:

> Occasionally, I do have a predisposition to be connected with current people that share some of those ideas. I mean, Steve Earle is unique. I've worked with him for fifteen years so I've had a different relationship with him than I've had with any other artist—a longer relationship with him. And he's a political guy. He's gone through a few years of not doing anything political because just, as an artist, he wants to do what comes, what feels right and not just be didactic. But then, he just did a song about the Mississippi confederate flag that we put up online last week. I love being able to be his manager and help figure out how to make the most of those moments and have impact. I worked with Morello for four years. I don't work with him anymore. Seventy percent of what he wanted to do was political. It was during the Occupy period. And Peaches did a song about Pussy Riot that was on the end credits for the *HBO* documentary about them. So those things still come up from time to time with certain artists. It's fun for me to do. Most of the time, it's not the case. It's not what people pay me to do. I believe art and music has its own value in the world. I bridle when political people pressure artists into writing a song for them or doing something for them

and don't treat them correctly. I think music is just as important as politics is. To many people it's more important.[73]

Goldberg explains: "I'm not a political person who also works with musicians. But the two do collide every once-in-a-while and when it works, it's fun. I mean, this little thing with Steve's song ['Mississippi, It's Time']. It's just one song. It's an issue that just applies really to one place. But it's been kind of cool to be a part of that. And, I think it's been useful to the Southern Poverty Law Center—200,000 people have seen the video."[74]

"Artists come in every flavor and every size and every shape," Erin Potts says, and with a wide range of views of progress:

> Some artists get worried when one fan says, 'Hey, I don't like what you said.' And then there's some artists who just don't give a fuck. And so we are going to help all of them. That's part of the beauty of what we are able to do and how we are able to work. We do see almost groupings of artists. There's, 'We don't give a fuck; we're going to play and we're going to say what we want.' Then there's those that are more timid or nervous about what their fans think about. And we may find other strategies that are a little bit less abrasive or advocacy-oriented for those types of artists because we want them to be true to what they are.[75]

For artists looking to advance progress, Potts says: "We're trying to provide as much 'DIY [do it yourself] and DIT [do it together]—that type of resource, as possible knowing that with a staff of six, trying to resource over a thousand artists and their managers is impossible. We have to give them the tools to be able to become strategic on their own. And so [RPM is] trying to put out as much information as possible, while still doing lots of training, briefings, and other sort of resource capacity building." Potts adds: "It's always interesting, the wide variety of things that artists and managers, once they get into a room, will talk about. I've realized over the last ten years there are actually not a lot of venues for artists to have conversations with one another. They see each other at festivals, they're there playing music so things become very much about that, or just chilling out—not having intense conversations."[76] Uniting the rock and roll community and looking for places of common cause beyond the live benefit experience into an integrated and sustained effort can be a critical mass.

As America and the world head further into the twenty-first century, the need for the rock and roll ethic is great—and it is simultaneously at risk. In his 1969 song "Long Time Gone," David Crosby called on people to "speak out, speak out against the madness—you've got to speak your mind—if you dare." Hope remains—because the darkest hour, he sings, "is always just before the dawn." "Yeah, that's me out there," Crosby says, "Peace! Tie-dye!" Crosby says:

> It's still alive. I do still believe. And I do still think it's possible. But I'm *really* discouraged. We wrote it in these songs; I can't see a way that it doesn't get worse. It's like one good thought getting lost in an angry verse. There's so much going in the wrong direction. There's so much greed and so much ignorance, and so much short-sightedness, and so much stupidity. And so much greed—did I mention greed? And then ignorance, and racism, and fear mongering—and fear used as a way to manipulate people.[77]

The troubadours are trying to tell us something. Yet, as Damien Dempsey observes, they can be harder to find. Dempsey laments: "It's getting harder and harder for artists, for anyone to get to hear them. On the other end of it now, they're out there. The people are out there who are speaking these truths. It's frightening that it's getting hard to find them, I suppose. But if you're looking for, if you want to find them, they're there."[78]

"A More Perfect Union"

Bill Payne observes about the American ideal: "It's one of horizons that seem endless."[79] That sense of newness, exploration, and freedom is ever present in rock and roll. Erin Potts reflects: "It's that Langston Hughes poem—'Let America be America Again.' I think that's the struggle that artists and others are undertaking; it is extremely patriotic. My favorite line [in the U.S. Constitution] is toward 'a more perfect union'—but we haven't gotten there yet. We'll never get there. It's always in striving for it. I think that's what making change is all about."[80] Jackson Browne says: "The solutions lie in our individual choices, the way we live our lives, and what we decide to do in the world. But I think that corresponds to each person's own understanding. I'm not trying to just write another broadside or polemic. I'm just trying to refer to these things that everybody's going through, and to refer to them in a way that show that at the heart of it is the idea that I'm glad to be alive now when these problems need to be solved."[81] Christine Martucci is on board—on board the "Tucci Train" (as her fans are called): "Let's go there!" she says, adding: "I like to tell stories—and it's always good to have an optimistic, happy ending. No one wants to hear a sad story. I mean, you've got to have the sad to appreciate and to feel that. You've got to feel sad to get to the good. I get that. I mean, me of all people know. Many people too. But, yeah, let's go there! Let's go to the stories about the happy ending. I think we can do it. I still believe in the goodness of humanity."[82]

Christine Martucci rocks for her fans—"The Tucci Train" at the Stone Pony in Asbury Park, New Jersey. Photo by Arielle Dawn Friedman, courtesy of Christine Martucci.

A MIRROR TO OUR SOCIETY

President Barack Obama said at an event celebrating the National Endowment for the Arts and Humanities in October 2015: "It is our artists who hold up a mirror to our society, reminding us of our common purpose and our collective obligations. Our music in particular has always been an honest reflection of who we really are—a reflection of our successes and our shortcomings; of our diversity, our imagination, our restlessness; of our stubborn insistence on blending the old with the new, tradition with experimentation." President Obama added the: "…quintessentially American creative spirit—sowed in our own soil, defined by our own experience, flavored by each new wave of immigrants that reaches our shores—that may be our greatest export: the American soundtrack." The President concluded: "We've got to support our artists and celebrate their work, and do our part to ensure that the American creative spirit that has defined us from the very beginning will thrive for generations to come."[83] And yet Washington, D.C. has been uninclined to provide much money. As journalist Mike Boehm wrote: "The total federal arts allocation would be somewhat less than the Air Force would expect to pay for two new long-range bombers, which carry an estimated price tag of $810 million each."[84] One survey done by researchers at the University of Chicago shows that between 1982 and 2008, students receiving any arts education in public schools fell from 65 to 50 percent. The number of African American children who received any exposure to arts education fell from 51 percent in 1982 to 26 percent and for Hispanics from 47 to 28 percent.[85]

The Rock and Roll Ethic

There are steps the government can take to promote a more sustainable rock and roll ecosystem. First, a new political imperative that sees the rock and roll emphasis on freedom, equality, human rights, and peace as advancing the national interest is needed. That requires the vocal and sustained activism of artists who can wield influence. This also requires advocacy for federal, state and local arts funding to compensate for how schools are funded, that is, for music education allowing equality of opportunity. Nonprofits like Little Kids Rock are doing all they can for music education—but society has to be on the hook for these programs. Second, if artists are to sustain their work, they need fair compensation. This can be helped by advancing and building on the "Fair Play Act," which was introduced by Congressman Jerrold Nadler (D-New York) with bipartisan support from Congresswoman Marcia Blackburn (R-Tennessee). Congresswoman Blackburn says: "The Fair Play Fair Pay Act will ensure that the intellectual property of artists can no longer be exploited by Big Radio without compensation. All radio platforms should be treated the same when they use music to draw in listeners and earn billions in revenue."[86] The government can support artists—and without new spending—by using the tax code to allow artists a level of tax-free income from sales of their products. This policy approach was pioneered in Ireland in 1969 when the country offered artists and musicians tax-free status for earnings under a certain level. Eventually, as acts like U2 grew in scale, pressure to limit this tax relief grew and thus was capped in 2009—although only 2 percent of those who qualified were at the U2 level. Most artists (67 percent) earned less than 10,000 euros from sales of their work—even with the tax incentive, not a sustainable wage.[87]

For the United States, this kind of rebalancing of the playing field would return market competition because popular demand is better served from the bottom up, not by poll-tested corporate priorities. The stakes are high, as Joan Jett said on her induction into the Rock and Roll Hall of Fame in 2015:

> I come from a place where rock and roll means something. It means more than music, more than fashion, more than a good pose. It's a language of a subculture that's made eternal teenagers of all who follow it. It's a subculture of integrity, rebellion, frustration, alienation, and the glue that set several generations free from unnatural societal and self-suppression. Rock and roll is political. It is a

meaningful way to express dissent, upset the status quo, stir up revolution, and fight for human rights. Think I'm making it sound more important and serious than it is? 'It's only rock and roll,' right? Rock and roll is an idea, and an ideal. Sometimes, because we love the music and we make the music, we forget the political impact it has on people around the world. There are Pussy Riots wherever there is political agitation. We've become so conditioned to measuring our music's impact in dollar signs only, we can forget what it's really about—the music, emotion, expression…giving a voice to those who aren't satisfied to be put into whatever box they were given. The rock and roll ethic is my entire life.

That rock and roll ethic also applies to the audience. How can citizens invest in their own future by engaging in rock and roll?

Some straightforward investments by individuals can payoff. First, pay for music. The temptation to take it for free is significant, but paying is an investment in future music. Second, diversify away from the corporate radio and let corporate power know that locally valued music sells meaningful advertising. Disc jockeys too can make a difference—even in restricted formats. You work for a classic rock station owned by a massive corporation? Play classic rock— but incorporate the B-Sides, the more obscure songs, the back catalogue of classic artists. Educate people about these artists and what they accomplished. Even better, include contemporary music by classic artists. On streaming services, build playlists around the influences of groups one likes (i.e., you like the Grateful Dead—then better check out Don Rich or Ornette Coleman) or to cross reference lyrical interests amid genres. Third, get out to a local bar or coffee house and hear music, especially supporting artists that are trying to make it performing original material. If they are selling merchandise and you like what they are doing—buy a t-shirt and a CD because often that is the only way the band is getting paid. For sure, do not go up to a local bar and say, "Oh, there's a cover charge, I'm not going in" —support live music. Or, reach out to a favorite artist—some perform "House Concerts"—literally in your living room—and it costs nothing but voluntary donations from friends.

If your favorite artist is advocating a cause, learn about it and, if interested, engage. Organize a fundraiser—ask local musicians to play. For example, Los Angeles-based "Law Rocks" features lawyers playing rock and roll at battle-of-the-bands fundraisers with the motto "Rock Globally, Give Locally" raising about $550,000 for charities. Cofounder and president of Law Rocks, Ted Scott, says: "The bands pick their own charities. We don't have any set charity. The only requirement we have is we like it to be a local charity with an operating budget of $10 million or less—a small, local charity so it really makes an impact."[88] For artists and average citizens, activism can be personal. As Tom Petersson of Cheap Trick said on his Rock and Roll Hall of Fame induction in 2016: "Thanks to my son Liam, we have discovered that music can help children who have autism and find their voices. With my wife Alison and my daughter Lilah, we created Rock Your Speech to help kids with autism communicate and practice speech with rock and roll music." Petersson concluded: "We are truly honored to be here. Music does matter. Music has value. Let's keep rock and roll alive for future generations making sure people can continue making a living following their creative dreams."

The Blessings of Liberty

Rock and roll—and its many tributaries—can help Americans count the blessings of liberty. George Clinton says that as he travels and sees America's places: "I'm enjoying them now more than ever. You know, I've seen them under the influence over the years, and you have your picture of everything. Now, I can take a look and go, 'Wow! This shit looks like my kindergarten books—in Europe; Switzerland, the Alps and all that shit.' You look at the side of the mountains in Colorado! I was just in Maui, and it's like, 'Shit!' The moon sometimes! It's the most beautiful place you've ever seen in your life."[89] Joe McDonald contemplates: "I'm grateful that I live in America which has freedom and I'm grateful that I can play my music and that I have an audience—and music makes me feel good. And that's what I have. I mean, there are times when I despair. But personally, if I was in Iran it would be impossible for me legally to play rock and roll or perform—and in North Korea. I've learned over the years that I can't change the world—I can just do my thing."[90]

BLOWIN' IN THE WIND

"We really don't know what our art, what effect it has," David Crosby concludes: "I even wrote a song about it somewhere back there in ancient history, called 'Paper Glider.' What we do is make a piece of art and it's like writing it down on a piece of paper—and folding it up into a glider and tossing it out a high-rise window. We have no fucking idea where it lands."[91] It is clear that rock and roll landed with a bang—and in turn, America rocks the world. Bob Dylan gave voice to ideas from the nation's founding that are now embedded globally—united via music. Credit is much owed to, as Graham Nash says: "Especially Bob Dylan, because he seems to be totally plugged into the pulse of American society at one level, but worldwide on another level. When you write 'Blowin' in the Wind'—Holy Toledo! That's a great American song, but it applies worldwide."[92] In the end, Bob Dylan—and so many other artists—used their voice as a tool of power advancing progress and a hope for the future. "Hope," Jann Wenner concludes: "that's a good message."[93]

Sources

BOOK LIST

Aretha Franklin, *From These Roots* (New York: Villard, 1999).

Bill Graham and Robert Greenfield, *Bill Graham Presents: My Life Inside Rock and Out* (Boston: De Capo Press, 2004).

Bill Kreutzman, *Deal* (New York: St. Martin's Press, 2015).

Blair Jackson and David Gans, *This is All a Dream we Dreamed: An Oral History of the Grateful Dead* (New York: Flatiron Books, 2015).

Bob Dylan, *Chronicles*, Volume One (New York: Simon & Schuster, 2005).

Daniel Wolff, *4th of July, Asbury Park: A History of the Promised Land* (New York: Bloosmbury, USA, 2005).

Danny Goldberg, *Bumping into Geniuses: My Life Inside the Rock and Roll Business* (New York: Avery, 2009).

David Crosby and David Bender, *Stand and Be Counted: Making Music, Making History* (New York: HarperCollins, 2000).

Dennis McNally, *On Highway 61: Music, Race, and the Evolution of Cultural Freedom* (Berkeley, CA: Counterpoint, 2014).

Dick Weissman, *Talkin' 'Bout a Revolution: Music and Social Change in America* (New York: Backbeat Books, 2000).

Dorian Lynesky, *33 Revolutions* (New York: HarperCollins, 2001).

Erik Kirschbaum, *Rocking the Wall: The Untold Story of a Concert in East Berlin that Changed the World* (Berlin: Berlinica Publishing, 2013).

Evelyn McDonnell and Ann Powers, eds. *Rock She Wrote: Women Write about Rock, Pop, and Rap* (London: Dell Publishing, 1995).

Graham Nash, *Wild Tales* (New York: Crown Archtype, 2013).

Jack Healey, *Create Your Future: A Memoir* (Los Angeles: Snail Press, 2015).

Jann Wenner, *Rolling Stone Interviews* (New York: Back Bay Books, 2007).

John Covach and Andrew Flory, *What's That Sound?: An Introduction to Rock and Its History*, 4th edition (New York: W.W. Norton, 2015).

Jonathan R. Piestack, *Sound Targets: American Soldiers and Music in the Iraq War* (Bloomington, IN: Indiana University Press, 2009).

Joseph G. Bilby and Harry Ziegler, *Asbury Park Reborn* (London: History Press, 2012).

Larry Nager, *Memphis Beat: The Lives and Times of America's Musical Crossroads* (New York: St. Martin's Press, 1998).

Leslie Woodhead, *How the Beatles Rocked the Kremlin* (New York: Bloomsbury USA, 2013).

Peter Brown and Steven Gaines, *The Love You Make: An Insider's Story of the Beatles* (London: NAL, 2002).

Robert Rosenthal and Richard Flacks, *Playing for Change: Music and Musicians in Service of Social Movements* (New York: Routledge, 2012).

Robin Wright, *Rock the Casbah: Rage and Rebellion Across the Islamic World* (New York: Simon & Schuster, 2012).

Russell Myrie, *Don't Rhyme for the Sake of Riddlin': The Authorized Story of Public Enemy* (Edinburgh: Canongate Books, 2008).

Sara Marcus, *Girls to the Front: The True Story of the Riot Grrrl Revolution* (New York: Harper Perennial, 2010).

Timothy W. Ryback, *Rock around the Bloc: A History of Rock Music in the Eastern Bloc and the Soviet Union* (Oxford: Oxford University Press, 1990).

INTERVIEWS

Artists

Graham Nash (Crosby, Stills, Nash, and Young/The Hollies)—May 2014—telephone

David Crosby (Crosby, Stills, Nash, and Young/The Byrds)—June 2014—Santa Ynez, California

Liberty Devitto (Billy Joel Band)—June 2014—telephone

Christine Havrilla (Christine Havrilla and Gypsy Fuzz)—June 2014—Asbury Park, New Jersey

Christine Martucci (Christine Martucci)—June 2014—Asbury Park, New Jersey

David Gans (Independent artist, author, and radio host)—June 2014—Oakland, California

Mark Karan (the Rembrandts, Paul Carrack, Huey Lewis, the Other Ones, Ratdog)—June 2014—Fairfax, California

John Barlow (The Grateful Dead-lyricist)—June 2014—San Francisco, California

Bob Gross (Delaney Bramlet, Jemimah Puddleduck)—June 2014—telephone

Serj Tankian (System of a Down)—July 2014—telephone

Rasoo, The Muckers—July 2014—Skype

Sinéad O'Connor (Sinéad O'Connor)—July 2014—Skype

Michael Stanley (Michael Stanley Band)—August 2014—Cleveland, Ohio
Dar Williams (Dar Williams)—September 2014—telephone
Michael Franti (Michael Franti and Spearhead)—September 2014—telephone
Billy Bragg (Billy Bragg)—September 2014—telephone
George Clinton (Parliament/Funkadelic)—September 2014—Columbus, Ohio
Joe McDonald (Country Joe and the Fish)—November 2014—telephone
Lukas Nelson (Lukas Nelson and Promise of the Real)—November 2014—telephone
Bill Payne, Little Feat, December 2014—telephone and Chicago, Illinois
Gedeon Luke, Gedeon Luke and the People/American Idol, December 2014—telephone
Johanna Fateman (Le Tigre)—January 2015—Skype
Damien Dempsey (Damien Dempsey), February 2015—telephone
Bruce Schmidt (Ruben Lee Dalton Band)—March 2015—telephone
George Gecik (performer, instructor)—March 2015—e-mail
Kate Pierson (the B-52s)—June 2015—telephone

Industry

Glen Ballard (Producer/Writer—Michael Jackson, Alanis Morrisette, Dave Matthews, Wilson Phillips, etc)—June 2014—Los Angeles, California
Cameron Sears (Manager, the Grateful Dead, Rex)—June 2014—Mill Valley, California
Bertis Downs (Manager/Adviser R.E.M.)—July 2014—telephone
Dennis McNally (former Publicist, Grateful Dead, historian, author)—July 2014—telephone
Chris McCutcheon (Tamalpias Research Institute)—July 2014—telephone
Marc Swersky (Producer/Writer—Joe Cocker, Hillary Duff)—August 2014—telephone
Matt Busch (Manager/Bob Weir)—September 2014—telephone
Carianne Brinkman (Blackheart Records)—January 2015—telephone
Kathy Kane (Manager/Bonnie Raitt)—January 2015—telephone
Danny Goldberg (former Publicist/Led Zepplin, Manager/Nirvana, former Chairman and CEO of Warner Bros. Records and Atlantic Records, President of Gold Village Entertainment Management)—October 2015—telephone

Journalism

Jann Wenner, *Rolling Stone*—June 2014—New York City
Thom Shanker, *New York Times*—November 2014—telephone
Jonathan Landay, *McClatchy News*—March 2015—telephone

Foundations

David Wish (Founder/Director of Little Kids Rock)—June 2014—Verona, New Jersey

Tom Gilmour (President, Asbury Park Musical Heritage Society)—June 2014—Asbury Park, New Jersey

Andy Bernstein (Founder/Director of Headcount)—June 2014 and October 2015—telephone

Erin Potts (RPM)—June 2014—telephone

Michael Bracy (Future of Music Coalition)—June 2014—telephone

Sara Wasserman (Founder, Executive Director, Music Heals International)—June 2014—Mill Valley, California

Ruthie Moutafian (Associate Director, Milagro Foundation—Carlos Santana)—June 2014—Mill Valley, California

Kaitlin Stuebner (Director, Grammy Education Program)—June 2014—Los Angeles, California

Ted Scott (Law Rocks USA)—August 2014—telephone

Mark Johnson (Founder, Director—Playing for Change)—August 2014—telephone

Willie Dixon Blues Heaven Foundation (Keith Dixon)—December 2014—Chicago, Illinois

Jack Healey (former Director USA of Amnesty International)—February 2015—telephone

Paul Riechkoff (Director, Iraq and Afghanistan Veterans Association)—March 2015—telephone

Lauren Onkey (Vice-President for Education and Programs, Rock and Roll Hall of Fame and Museum)—June 2015—Cleveland, Ohio

Related

Sini Anderson (Director—*The Punk Singer*—Documentary on Kathleen Hanna)

Richard Combs (Deputy Chief of Mission, US Embassy Moscow at end of Cold War—e-mail), September 2014

Notes

CHAPTER ONE

1. Interview with Sinéad O'Connor, Skype, July 2014.
2. Interview with David Crosby, Santa Ynez, California, June 2014.
3. Interview with Jann Wenner, New York City, June 2014.
4. Ibid.
5. Interview with Serj Tankian, telephone, July 2014.
6. Interview with Graham Nash, telephone, June 2014.
7. For further details, see Dennis McNally, *On Highway 61: Music, Race, and the Evolution of Cultural Freedom* (Berkeley, CA: Counterpoint, 2014).
8. David Crosby and Graham Nash, interview with Keith Olberman, MSNBC, October 24, 2011, available at https://www.youtube.com/watch?v=o_BP5HFrOxs (accessed in October 2014).
9. Interview with David Crosby, Santa Ynez, California, June 2014.
10. Ibid.
11. "Springsteen Honors Pete Seeger," *Billboard*, May 4, 2009.
12. Interview with Kate Pierson, telephone, June 2015.
13. Interview with Billy Bragg, telephone, September 2014.
14. Ibid.
15. "Concert for Newtown," Public Broadcasting Service, 2013, available at https://www.youtube.com/watch?v=OOUG_K0AVBo (accessed in October 2014).
16. Interview with Dar Williams, telephone, September 2014.
17. Ibid.
18. Interview with Jann Wenner, New York City, June 2014.
19. Interview with Kate Pierson, telephone, June 2015.
20. See *The Punk Singer*, directed by Sini Anderson, 2013.
21. Interview with Sini Anderson, Delaware, Ohio, October 2014.
22. Interview with David Crosby, Santa Ynez, California, June 2014.
23. Interview with Graham Nash, telephone, June 2014.

24. Interview with Glen Ballard, Los Angeles, California, June 2014.

25. Ibid.

26. Ibid.

27. Interview with Glen Ballard, Los Angeles, California, June 2014.

28. Ibid.

29. Interview with George Clinton, Columbus, Ohio, September 2014.

30. Ibid.

31. Ibid.

32. Interview with Mark Karan, Fairfax, California, June 2014.

33. Interview with Michael Stanley, Cleveland, Ohio, August 2014.

34. Ibid.

35. Ibid.

36. Interview with Serj Tankian, telephone, July 2014.

37. Interview with Erin Potts, telephone, June 2014.

38. Ibid.

39. Ibid.

40. Interview with Jann Wenner, New York City, June 2014.

41. Interview with Sinéad O'Connor, Skype, July 2014.

42. Ibid.

43. Press Conference, The Grateful Dead, October 1967, available at http://www.bing.com/videos/search?q=grateful+dead+interview+pot+bust+1967&FORM=VIRE1#view=detail&mid=DDD3122CB1576B87FD37DDD3122CB1576B87FD37 (accessed in October 2014).

44. Interview with Jerry Garcia, "History of Rock Interview" available at https://www.youtube.com/watch?v=NVkkbJ_KI2Y (accessed in October 2014).

45. Ibid.

46. Interview with Jann Wenner, New York City, June 2014.

47. Interview with Cameron Sears, Mill Valley, California, June 2014.

48. Frank Zappa interview with Danish Television, September 1987, available at https://www.youtube.com/watch?v=k3J0X8WaC4c (accessed in October 2014).

49. Interview with Jann Wenner, New York City, June 2014.

50. Richard Leiby "Alice Cooper's Political Makeup," *Washington Post*, August 24, 2004.

51. Interview with Jann Wenner, New York City, June 2014.

52. Interview with George Clinton, Columbus, Ohio, September 2014.

53. Ed Bradley, 60 Minutes, interview with Bob Dylan, 2004, available at https://www.youtube.com/watch?v=gKkZcgrec8A#t=297 (accessed in October 2014).

54. Interview with Graham Nash, telephone, June 2014.

55. Bob Dylan, Interview in *Booklet* for *Biograph*, 1985.

56. Bob Dylan, Interview, *Playboy*, March 1978.

CHAPTER TWO

1. "Abbie Hoffman Remembers John Lennon," *PBS Arts* (1980), available at https://www.youtube.com/watch?v=2CInfsZZG04 (accessed in November 2014).

2. John Lennon, "Interview," *Playboy*, January 1981.

3. Interview with Serj Tankian, telephone, July 2014.

4. Interview with Graham Nash, telephone, June 2014.

5. Timothy W. Ryback, *Rock around the Bloc: A History of Rock Music in the Eastern Bloc and the Soviet Union* (Oxford: Oxford University Press, 1990), 3.

6. Interview with David Crosby, Santa Ynez, California, June 2014.

7. Beatles Interview, available at https://www.youtube.com/watch?v= XxAR1n6WoOk (accessed in November 2014).

8. Ed Vulliamy, "For Young Soviets, the Beatles were a First, Mutinous Rip in the Iron Curtain," *The Guardian*, April 20, 2013.

9. Ibid. Also see Leslie Woodhead, *How the Beatles Rocked the Kremlin* (New York: Bloomsbury USA, 2013).

10. Mikhail Safonov, "The Beatles: 'You Say You Want a Revolution'," *History Today*, 53:8, available at http://www.historytoday.com/mikhail-safonov/beatles-%E2%80 %98you-say-you-want-revolution%E2%80%99 (accessed in November 2014).

11. Interview with Thomas Shanker, telephone, November 2014.

12. See Peter Rutland, "Rock and Roll and the End of Soviet Socialism," *Transitions Online*, 11 April 2011, available at http://prutland.web.wesleyan.edu/ Documents/Rock%20and%20roll%20and%20the%20end%20of%20communism.pdf (accessed in November 2014).

13. Pedro Ramet and Sergei Zamascikov, *"The Soviet Rock Scene,"* Woodrow Wilson International Center for Scholars, Washington, D.C., 1987.

14. Interview with Thomas Shanker, telephone, November 2014.

15. Interview with Liberty Devitto, telephone, June 2014.

16. Ibid.

17. "Billy Joel's Historic Soviet Concert Tour," available at http://historyofrussia. org/billy-joels-historic-soviet-concert-tour/ (accessed in January 2015).

18. Thomas Shanker, "Was Billy Joel Rock's Best Rep to USSR?", *Chicago Tribune*, August 9, 1987.

19. "30 Days Out: Exclusive Interview with Liberty Devitto," available at http:// 30daysout.wordpress.com/2008/07/24/30-days-out-interview-liberty-devitto-former-drummer-for-billy-joel/ (accessed in November 2014).

20. Interview with Liberty Devitto, telephone, June 2014.

21. Interview with Thomas Shanker, telephone, November 2014.

22. Interview with Liberty Devitto, telephone, June 2014.

23. Billy Joel interview, *Today Show*, available at https://www.youtube.com/watch ?v=YIVrrof6ODA&feature=player_embedded (accessed in November 2014).

24. Interview with Liberty Devitto, telephone, June 2014.

25. Interview with Liberty Devitto, telephone, June 2014.

26. Billy Joel interview, *Today Show*, available at https://www.youtube.com/watch ?v=YIVrrof6ODA&feature=player_embedded (accessed in November 2014).

27. Sally McGrane, *"An Unwanted Reprise Riles a Soviet Rocker,"* New York Times, April 25, 2014.

28. Interview with Bill Payne, telephone, December 2014.

29. James Sullivan, "How a Revolutionary Czech Rock Band Inspired Vaclav Havel," *Rolling Stone*, December 19, 2011.

30. Michael Weiss, "Vaclav Havel: Rock'n'Roll and the Power of the Powerless," *World Affairs*, available at http://www.worldaffairsjournal.org/article/vaclav-havel-rock-%E2%80%99n%E2%80%99-roll-and-power-powerless (accessed in November 2014).

31. "Queen Live in Budapest 1986," Eagle Rock Entertainment, 2012. Also see references to Australian television interview from 1985, with Freddie Mercury available at http://www.queenlive.ca/queen/86-07-27.htm (accessed in November 2014).

32. Greg Mitchell, "As Berlin Marks Fall of the Wall: The Secret Police Document on Bob Dylan," *Huffington Post*, October 30, 2014.

33. "Fearing the Moonwalk Revolution: East German Stasi Spied on Michael Jackson," *Spiegel Online*, July 21, 2009, available at http://www.spiegel.de/international/germany/fearing-the-moonwalk-revolution-east-german-stasi-spied-on-michael-jackson-a-639520.html (accessed in December 2014).

34. Ibid.

35. Kate Connolly, "The Night Bruce Springsteen Played East Berlin—and the Wall Cracked," *The Guardian,* July 5, 2013. Also see Erik Kirschbaum, *Rocking the Wall: The Untold Story of a Concert in East Berlin that Changed the World* (Berlin: Berlinica Publishing, 2013).

36. Interview with David Crosby, Santa Ynez, California, June 2014.

37. Interview with Graham Nash, telephone, June 2014.

38. Ibid.

39. Interview with Sinéad O'Connor, Skype, July 2014.

40. Ibid.

41. "The Wall—Live in Berlin" available at http://www.rogerwaters.org/about_berlin.html (accessed in November 2014).

42. Linda Mastalir, "Frank Zappa's Connection to Prague," *Radio Prague*, May 23, 2006.

43. "From Velvet Underground to Velvet Revolution," *The Economist*, October 30, 2013.

44. "Lou Reed and Vaclav Havel I," available at https://www.youtube.com/watch?v=qM4zO2q-gzI (accessed in November 2014).

45. Interview with Richard Combs, e-mail, November 2014.

46. Interview with Thomas Shanker, telephone, November 2014.

47. "Harry Belafonte Remembers Miriam Makeba," *National Public Radio,* November 11, 2008.

48. Ibid.

49. John Harris, "The Sins of Freddie Mercury," *The Guardian*, January 14, 2005.

50. "Nelson Mandela at Live 8," July 2, 2005, available at http://www.thelive8concert.com/nelsonmandela.htm (accessed in November 2016).

51. "Artists United Against Apartheid, 'Sun City'," *Rolling Stone: 100 Best Albums of the Eighties* available at http://www.rollingstone.com/music/lists/100-best-albums-of-the-eighties-20110418/artists-united-against-apartheid-sun-city-20110330 (accessed in December 2014).

52. Dave Marsh, "Talking Sun City with Steven Van Zandt," January 24, 2014.

53. Ibid.

54. Dave Marsh, "Talking Sun City with Steven Van Zandt," January 24, 2014.

55. Robin Denselow, "Paul Simon's Graceland: The Acclaim and the Outrage," *The Guardian,* April 19, 2012.

56. Paul Simon, "Remembering Days of Miracle and Wonder," *New York Times*, December 13, 2013.

57. Dave Marsh, "Talking Sun City with Steven Van Zandt," January 24, 2014.

58. Alex Seitz-Wald, "O'Reilly Laments that You Can't Make fun of Arabs Anymore," *Think Progress*, January 19, 2010, available at http://thinkprogress.org/politics/2010/01/19/77937/oreilly-arabs/ (accessed in December 2014).

59. Joe Jervis, "Bono Turns Up the Volume for Social Enterprise," *The Guardian*, November 14, 2012.

60. Cordelia Hebblethwaite, "Is Hip Hop Driving the Arab Spring?", *British Broadcasting Corporation*, July 24, 2011.

61. Lauren E. Bohn, "Rapping the Revolution," *Foreign Policy*, July 22, 2011.

62. "A Modern Revolution: Hip Hop Shines Over the Arab Spring," *Soundcheck*, March 18, 2013, available at http://soundcheck.wnyc.org/story/275290-hip-hop-arab-spring/ (accessed in December 2014).

63. "Middle East: Hip Hop is a Soundtrack to the North African Revolt," *Freemuse,* available at http://freemuse.org/archives/1732 (accessed in December 2014).

64. Interview by Margaret Warner with Robin Wright, July 21, 2011, available at http://video.pbs.org/video/2064921024/ (accessed in December 2014). Also see Robin Wright, *Rock the Casbah: Rage and Rebellion Across the Islamic World* (New York: Simon & Schuster, 2012).

65. "U.S. Diplomacy: Hitting the Right Notes," *CBS News*, July 4, 2010.

66. Hishaam Aidi, "Leveraging Hip Hop in U.S. Foreign Policy," *Al Jazeera,* November 7, 2011.

67. Ryan Reed, "Iran's 'Happy' Dancers Sentenced to 91 Lashes," *Rolling Stone*, September 19, 2014.

68. Thomas Erdbrink, "Rapper Faces Death Threats in Iran," *New York Times*, May 15, 2012.

69. "Life as an 'Illegal' Rock Star in Iran's Islamic State," *British Broadcasting Corporation*, March 10, 2014.

70. Gil Kaufman, "Meet Iran's Hypernova," *MTV*, April 5, 2007.

71. Interview with Rasoo, the Muckers, Skype, August 2014.

72. Interview with Rasoo, the Muckers, Skype, August 2014.

73. Interview with Rasoo, the Muckers, Skype, August 2014.

74. Interview with Rasoo, the Muckers, Skype, August 2014.

75. Interview with Rasoo, the Muckers, Skype, August 2014.

76. "The Universal Sound of Protest," *The Rock and Roll Hall of Fame*, October 13, 2011, available at http://rockhall.com/blog/post/6660_protest-music-in-2011/ (accessed in December 2014).

CHAPTER THREE

1. Interview with Billy Bragg, telephone, September 2014.
2. Interview with Billy Bragg, telephone, September 2014.
3. Interview with Graham Nash, telephone, June 2014.
4. Interview with Serj Tankian, telephone, July 2014.
5. Interview with Michael Stanley, Cleveland, Ohio, August 2014.
6. Ibid.
7. "Real Time with Bill Maher," *HBO*, September 23, 2011.
8. "Interview with Tom Morello," *Bill Moyers' Journal, Public Broadcasting Service*, May 18, 2012.
9. Jim Tankersley, "Why America's Middle Class Is Lost," *Washington Post*, December 12, 2014.
10. "Interview with Tom Morello," *Bill Moyers' Journal, Public Broadcasting Service*, May 18, 2012.
11. David Bauder, "Occupy Wall Street: Music Central to Protest," Associated Press, November 13, 2011.
12. James C. McKinley Jr., "At the Protests, the Message Lacks a Melody," *New York Times,* October 18, 2011.
13. Interview with Johanna Fateman, Skype, January 2015.
14. Interview with Dar Williams, telephone, September 2014.
15. Christine Martucci, "Working Man," The Wonder Bar, December 7, 2011, available at https://www.youtube.com/watch?v=LL9J83fd680 (accessed in December 2014).
16. Interview with Christine Martucci, Asbury Park, NJ, June 2014.
17. Ibid.
18. Interview with David Crosby, Santa Ynez, California, June 2014.
19. Cory Grow, "Bob Dylan: The Government's Not Going to Create Jobs," *Rolling Stone*, January 22, 2015.
20. "Stax Records – Jim Stewart," February 13, 2008, available at https://www.youtube.com/watch?v=M_17yWmvofQ (accessed in June 2014).
21. Larry Nager, *Memphis Beat: The Lives and Times of America's Musical Crossroads* (New York: St. Martin's Press, 1998), 177.
22. Interview with Liberty Devitto, telephone, June 2014.
23. Interview with Lauren Onkey, Cleveland, Ohio, June 2015.
24. Interview with Bill Payne, telephone, December 2014.
25. Interview with George Clinton, Columbus, Ohio, September 2014.
26. Ibid.
27. D.L. Chandler, "Race Riots Explode in Georgia, Rock City of Augusta in 1970," available at http://newsone.com/3009368/race-riots-augusta-ga/ (accessed in December 2014).
28. Larry Kane, "The Beatles Fight Bigotry in America," *CBS News*, January 30, 2014.
29. Audie Cornish, "The Beatles: Fab Four AND Civil Rights Activists," *National Public Radio*, September 18, 2011.

30. See "About: Quincy Jones," available at http://www.quincyjones.com/about/ (accessed in December 2014).

31. Interview with Glen Ballard, Los Angeles, California, June 2014.

32. Ibid.

33. Interview with Glen Ballard, Los Angeles, California, June 2014.

34. Ibid.

35. Interview with Gedeon Luke, telephone, December 2014.

36. Michael Powell, "Blacks in Memphis Lose Decades of Economic Gains," *New York Times,* May 30, 2010.

37. U.S. Census, "State and County Quick Facts," available at http://quickfacts. census.gov/qfd/states/47/4748000.html (accessed in December 2014).

38. Wendi C. Thomas, "Inequality in Memphis: A Tale of Two Neighborhoods," *Commercial Appeal*, April 25, 2014.

39. Interview with Gedeon Luke, telephone, December, 2014.

40. Ibid.

41. Ibid.

42. Interview with Gedeon Luke, telephone, December,2014.

43. Interview with Gedeon Luke, telephone, December 2014.

44. Ibid.

45. Interview with Glen Ballard, Los Angeles, California, June 2014.

46. Aretha Franklin, *From these Roots* (New York: Villard, 1999), 112.

47. Interview with Kate Pierson, telephone, June 2015.

48. Institute for Women's Policy Research, "About Pay Equity and Discrimination," available at http://www.iwpr.org/initiatives/pay-equity-and-discrimination (accessed in December 2014).

49. Billboard, *"Music's Top Money Makers,"* available at http://www.bill-board.com/articles/list/5930326/music-s-top-40-money-makers-2014-the-rich-list (accessed in December 2014).

50. "Women Who Rock: In the Pages of Rolling Stone," available at http://www. rollingstone.com/music/pictures/women-who-rock-in-the-pages-of-rolling-stone-20120622/madonna-0166625 (accessed in December 2014).

51. Interview with Sinéad O'Connor, Skype, July 2014.

52. Interview with Sinéad O'Connor, Skype, July 2014

53. Ibid.

54. Alana Horowitz, "Sinéad O'Connor: Why I Wrote the Miley Letters," *Huffington Post*, 14 November 2013.

55. Suzannah Ramsdale, "I Could Be a Housewife..." Marie Claire, November 6, 2014, available at http://www.marieclaire.co.uk/blogs/suzannah-ramsdale/545782/debbie-harry-chris-stein-blondie-and-the-advent-of-punk.html#eF55zXObdetMsyge.99 (accessed in December 2014).

56. Amy Wallace, "Miss Millennium: Beyoncé," *Gentlemen's Quarterly,* February 2013.

57. Elias Leight, "Annie Lennox: 'Twerking is not Feminism,'" *Billboard*, October 21, 2014.

58. "Women Who Rock: In the Pages of *Rolling Stone*," available at http://www. rollingstone.com/music/pictures/women-who-rock-in-the-pages-of-rolling-stone-20120622/madonna-0166625 (accessed in December 2014).

59. Ibid.

60. Jancee Dunn, "Q&A with Bonnie Raitt," *Rolling Stone*, April 21, 1994.

61. Interview with Kathy Kane, telephone, January 2015.

62. Touré, "Adele Opens Up About Her Inspirations, Looks and Stage Fright," *Rolling Stone,* April 28, 2011.

63. "Joan Jett and Cherie Currie talk The Runaways," available at https://www. youtube.com/watch?v=fukr8hy0NPw (accessed in January 2015).

64. Brian Ives, "Q&A: Joan Jett on Her Own All-Star Tribute Concert," October 25, 2014, available at http://radio.com/2014/10/25/joan-jett-interview-all-star-tribute-concert/ (accessed in December 2014).

65. Interview with Carianne Brinkman, telephone, January 2015.

66. Interview with Sini Anderson, Delaware, Ohio, October 2014.

67. Kathleen Hanna Papers, Series I, Box 1 Folder 12, "Bikini Kill Zine # 2" [1991], Fales Library, New York University, accessed in June 2014.

68. Kathleen Hanna Papers, Series I, Box 1 Folder 12, "Bikini Kill Zine # 2" [1991], Fales Library, New York University, accessed in June 2014.

69. Kathleen Hanna Papers, Series I, Box 1 Folder 10, "Bikini Kill Zine # 1" [1991], Fales Library, New York University, accessed in June 2014.

70. Kathleen Hanna Papers, Series I, Box 1 Folder 10 ,"Bikini Kill Zine # 1" [1991], accessed at Fales Library, New York University, June 2014.

71. Tracy McVeigh, "Paul McCartney: Yoko Ono Did Not Break Up the Beatles," *The Guardian*, October 27, 2012.

72. Interview with Kate Pierson, telephone, June 2015.

73. Interview with Johanna Fateman, Skype, January 2015.

74. Erik Ernst, "Dar Williams Talks about the Significance of Lilith Fair," *Milwaukee Journal Sentinel*, September 27, 2001, available at http://archive.jsonline. com/blogs/entertainment/130608398.html (accessed in September 2015).

75. "VH1 Top Ten," July 27, 1997, available at https://www.youtube.com/ watch?v=XBhUjdHv7-I (accessed in December 2014).

76. Interview with Carianne Brinkman, telephone, January 2015.

77. Interview with Carianne Brinkman, telephone, January 2015.

78. Interview with Sini Anderson, Delaware, Ohio, October 2015.

79. Interview with Carianne Brinkman, telephone, January 2015.

80. "Joan Jett Talks – The Runaways," available at https://www.youtube.com/ watch?v=T_-oJxtV080 (accessed in January 2015).

81. Interview with Carianne Brinkman, telephone, January 2015.

82. Interview with Johanna Fateman, Skype, January 2015.

83. Ibid.

84. "Taylor Swift On Feminism, Famous Friends, and Single Girl Freedom," *Cosmopolitan*, December 2014.

85. Taylor Swift, "For Taylor Swift the Future of Music is a Love Story," *Wall Street Journal,* July 7, 2014.

86. Erin Strecker, "Watch Taylor Swift Talk Feminism & Girl Fights in Media," *Billboard,* September 30, 2014.

87. Kimberly Dadds, "Taylor Swift: 'You Have To Make Sure That No One Can Call You A Crazy Bitch," *Buzzfeed*, November 26, 2014.

88. "Totally Biased: Kamau Interviews Kathleen Hanna," November 13, 2013, available at https://www.youtube.com/watch?v=WozprgZeCmo (accessed in December 2014).

89. Katie Van Syckle, "Kathleen Hanna: I Don't Want Men to Validate Me," *Rolling Stone*, November 27, 2013.

CHAPTER FOUR

1. Amnesty International, Press Release, "World's Top Rock Stars Join Amnesty International in Saluting Landmark Human Rights Anniversary," December 3, 2013, available at http://www.amnestyusa.org/news/press-releases/world-s-top-rock-stars-join-amnesty-international-in-saluting-landmark-human-rights-anniversary (accessed in January 2015).

2. "Who is Bill Graham?" available at http://www.billgrahamfoundation.org/bio.html (accessed in January 2015). Also see Bill Graham and Robert Greenfield, *Bill Graham Presents: My Life Inside Rock and Out* (Boston: De Capo Press, 2004).

3. Michael Goldberg, *Rolling Stone*, December 1991 available at http://www.billgrahamfoundation.org/about.html (accessed in June 2016).

4. Interview with Jack Healey, telephone, February 2015.

5. Ibid.

6. Interview with Jack Healey, telephone, February 2015.

7. Ibid.

8. Andy Greene, "How Amnesty International Rocked the World: The Inside Story," *Rolling Stone*, October 25, 2013.

9. Interview with Jack Healey, telephone, February 2015.

10. Interview with Jack Healey, telephone, February 2015.

11. *SPIN Magazine*, November 1991, p. 9.

12. Interview with Jack Healey, telephone, February 2015.

13. Interview with Bob Gross, telephone, July 2014.

14. Interview with Damien Dempsey, telephone, February 2015.

15. Interview with Jack Healey, telephone, February 2015.

16. Peter Crutchley, "Give Ireland Back to the Irish: Paul McCartney's Forgotten Protest Song," *British Broadcoasting Corporation*," August 7, 2013.

17. Bono, "Psalm Like It Hot," *The Guardian*, October 30, 1999.

18. Adam Block, "Bono Bites Back," *Mother Jones*, May 2, 1989.

19. Joshua Busby, "Is There a Constituency for Global Poverty? Jubilee 2000 and the Future of Development Advocacy," *The Brookings Institution*, 2007 available at http://www.brookings.edu/~/media/Events/2007/8/01sustainable%20development/2007busby.PDF (accessed in February 2015).

20. Ibid.

21. "About One" available at http://www.one.org/us/about/ (accessed in February 2015).

22. Busby, "Is there a Constituency..."

23. "Stop Picking on the Rich, Says U2 Drummer Larry Mullen," *The Independent*, June 22, 2009.

24. *Irish Times*, July 6, 2012.

25. Ian Lovett, "U2 Guitarist's House Plan Rejected by California Board," *New York Times*, June 17, 2011.

26. Sean Michaels, "U2 Criticized for World Tour Carbon Footprint," *The Guardian*, July 10, 2009.

27. Interview with Damien Dempsey, telephone, February 2015.

28. Interview with Damien Dempsey, telephone, February 2015.

29. Ed Moloney, *A Secret History of the IRA* (New York: W.W. Norton, 2002), Introduction.

30. Adam Block, "Bono Bites Back," May 1989.

31. U2 concert, Denver, Colorado, November 8, 1987.

32. "The Day Bono 'Interfaced' with Trimble and Hume," *Belfast Telegraph*, June 9, 2004.

33. Tom Shales and James Andre Miller, *Live from New York* (Boston: Backwater Books, 2002), 390.

34. Shales and Miller, *Live...*, 392.

35. Sinéad O'Connor, "To Sinéad O'Connor, the Pope's Apology for Sex Abuse in Ireland Seems Hollow," *Washington Post*, March 28, 2010.

36. John Pareles, "Why Sinéad O'Connor Hit a Nerve," *New York Times*, November 1, 1992.

37. Interview with Sinéad O'Connor, Bray, Ireland, June 2010.

38. Interview with Sinéad O'Connor, Skype, July 2014.

39. Interview with Sinéad O'Connor, Bray, Ireland, June 2010.

40. "Statement by the Taoiseach," July 20, 2011, available at http://www.rte.ie/news/2011/0720/303965-cloyne1/ (accessed in January 2015).

41. Interview with Sinéad O'Connor, Bray, Ireland, June 2010.

42. Interview with David Crosby, Santa Ynez, California, June 2014.

43. Interview with Damien Dempsey, telephone, February 2015.

44. "Interview to Russia Today TV Channel: President of Russia," *Russia Today*, September 6, 2012.

45. "Pussy Riot Sentencing a 'Bitter Blow' to Freedom in Russia," *Amnesty International*, August 17, 2012, available at http://www.amnestyusa.org/news/press-releases/pussy-riot-sentencing-a-bitter-blow-to-freedom-in-russia (accessed in January 2015).

46. "Paul McCartney Voices Support of Jailed Russian Band Pussy Riot," *Rolling Stone*, August 16, 2012.

47. Erin Coulehan, "Paul McCartney Supports Pussy Riot in Letters to Russian Authorities," *Rolling Stone*, May 23, 2013.

48. "Madonna Calls for Pussy Riot's Release at Moscow Show," *Rolling Stone*, August 8, 2012.

49. "Amnesty International and Sting Call for Release of Pussy Riot Band Members in Moscow," July 25, 2012, available at http://www.sting.com/news/title/amnesty-international-and-sting-call-for-release-of-pussy-riot-bandmembers-in-moscow (accessed in January 2015).

50. Sean Michaels, "Franz Ferdinand and Red Hot Chili Peppers Voice Support for Pussy Riot," *The Guardian*, July 24, 2012.

51. "Adele, Yoko Ono, U2, Madonna, Radiohead, Kesha, Sir Paul McCartney Unite with More Than 100 Musicians to Call for Release of Pussy Riot," *Amnesty International Press Release*, July 22, 2013.

52. "Approaching the 2014 Sochi Olympics: Human Rights in Russia," *Amnesty International's Brief*, 2013, available at http://www.amnestyusa.org/sites/default/files/ai_brief_-_human_rights_in_russia_2013_0.pdf (accessed in January 2015).

53. Patrick Reevell, "Pussy Riot's Maria Alyokhina: 'I Was Always Free Because I Felt Free,'" *Rolling Stone*, December 24, 2013.

54. Diana Magnay, Steve Almasy, and Ben Brumfield, "Freed Pussy Riot Rockers Say they will Continue to Rock Russian System," *CNN,* February 18, 2014.

55. "Interview: Freed Pussy Riot Member Says Outside Support was a 'Miricle'," *Radio Free Europe/Radio Liberty,* December 23, 2013.

56. Matthias Schepp, "Interview with Pussy Riot Member," *Spiegel Online*, December 30, 2013.

57. "Pussy Riot First European T.V. Show," *RTE*, February 1, 2014, available at https://www.youtube.com/watch?v=b0zgRhyrHo4 (accessed in January 2015).

58. Interview with Sinéad O'Connor, Skype, July 2014.

59. Micheal Idov, "Pussy Riot: The Jailhouse Interview," *Gentleman's Quarterly*, November 2012.

60. Luke Morton Britton, "Patty Smith and David Lynch Discuss Pussy Riot," *NME,* November 20, 2014.

61. Interview with Johanna Fateman, Skype, January 2015.

62. Rick Gladstone, "Pussy Riot Members Take Tour to New York," *New York Times*, February 5, 2014.

63. Anonymous Members of Pussy Riot, "We Wish Nadia and Masha Well—But They're No Longer Part of Pussy Riot," *The Guardian,* February 6, 2014.

64. Lindsay Zoladz, "Pussy Riot's Nadya Tolokonnikova and Masha Alyokhina," April 10, 2014, available at http://pitchfork.com/features/interviews/9374-nadya-tolokonnikova-and-masha-alyokhina-of-pussy-riot/ (accessed in January 2015).

65. Ibid.

66. Kathy Belge, "Dusty Springfield," available at http://lesbianlife.about.com/od/lesbianmusicians/p/Dusty-Springfield.htm (accessed in February 2015).

67. Interview with Kate Pierson, telephone, June 2015.

68. "Elton's Frank Talk," *Rolling Stone*, October 1976.

69. "Elton John Talks Coming Out," *Huffington Post*, July 18, 2012.

70. Henry Rollins, "Gay Marriage is Punk Rock," *LA Weekly*, December 20, 2012.

71. Interview with Dar Williams, telephone, September 2014.

72. Julian Barnes, "Joint Chiefs Chairman Mullen Supports Rights of Gays to Serve in Military," *Los Angeles Times*, February 2, 2010.

73. Interview with Christine Martucci, e-mail, March 2015.

74. Ibid.

75. Ibid.

76. Interview with Jann Wenner, New York City, June 2014.

77. Bill Werde, "Lady Gaga 'Born this Way' Cover Story," *Billboard*, March 4, 2011.

78. Zach Rosen, "Katy Perry: The New Gay Interview," June 10, 2008, available at http://thenewgay.net/2008/06/katy-perry-new-gay-interview.html (accessed in August 2016).

79. Cavan Sieczkowski, "Katy Perry on 'I Kissed A Girl': It Was A Bit Radical To Sing about Bisexuality," *Huffington Post,* October 22, 2013.

80. Mark Brown, "Chart-Topping Lesbian Love Song Divides Gay Community," *The Guardian*, August 7, 2008.

81. Ibid.

82. Abby Goodman, "The Original Riot Grrrl on Katy Perry, '90s Revival," *CNN*, June 7, 2011.

83. "Katy Perry Lately!" available at http://www.katyperrylately.com/post/25446671375/interview-katy-perry-talks-marriage-madonna (accessed in February 2015).

84. Interview with Glen Ballard, Los Angeles, California, June 2014.

85. Interview with Kate Pierson, telephone, June 2015.

86. Interview with David Crosby, Santa Ynez, California, June 2014.

87. Ibid.

88. Stacy Lambe, "The Making of Macklemore," *Out Magazine* May 8, 2013.

89. James C. McKinley, Jr., "Stars Align for a Gay Marriage Anthem," *New York Times*, June 30, 2013.

90. See Jamie Cooper Holland, "An Open Letter to Kate Pierson," *Huffington Post*, December 5, 2014.

91. Interview with Kate Pierson, telephone, June 2015.

92. "Bob Weir Talks Pot Legalization," available at http://videos.huffingtonpost.com/healthy-living/bob-weir-talks-pot-legalization-and-the-peril-of-drugs-518207190 (accessed in February 2015).

93. The Editorial Board, "Repeal Prohibition—Again," *New York Times*, http://www.nytimes.com/interactive/2014/07/27/opinion/sunday/high-time-marijuana-legalization.html (accessed in February 2014).

94. Interview with David Crosby, Santa Ynez, California, June 2014.

95. Ibid.

96. Interview with David Crosby, Santa Ynez, California, June 2014.

97. Joshua Tucker, "Is Pot the New Gay Marriage?," *Washington Post*, October 22, 2013.

98. Mark Schiff, "15 Surprising Advocates for Marijuana in the Music Industry," *AXS*, July 9, 2014.

99. "Carlos Santana: Obama Should Legalize Pot," *CBS News*, April 3, 2009.

100. "John Legend, Marijuana Community Member and Proud of It," *Huffington Post*, June 21, 2013.

101. Sting, "Let's End the War on Drugs," *Huffington Post*, May 31, 2010.

102. Cory Grow, "Willie Nelson: Obama 'May Be Happy' With Weed Legalization," *Rolling Stone*, November 8, 2014.

103. Interview with Lukas Nelson, telephone, November 2014.

CHAPTER FIVE

1. Jonathan R. Piestack, *Sound Targets: American Soldiers and Music in the Iraq War* (Bloomington, IN: Indiana University Press, 2009), 82.

2. Tim Jonze, "Britney Spears Music Used by British Navy to Scare Off Somali Pirates," *The Guardian*, October 29, 2013.

3. Justin Sharrock, "The Torture Playlist," *Mother Jones*, February 22, 2008.

4. Kelsey McKinney, "How the CIA used Music to 'Break' Detainees," *VOX*, December 11, 2014.

5. Ibid.

6. Ibid.

7. Interview with Billy Bragg, telephone, September 2014.

8. Interview with Jonathan Landay, telephone, March 2015.

9. Ibid.

10. Ibid.

11. Ibid.

12. Clay Tarver, "The Rock 'n' Roll Casualty Who Became a War Hero," *New York Times*, July 2, 2013.

13. Interview with Bruce Schmidt, telephone, March 2015.

14. Interview with Paul Rieckhoff, telephone, March 2015

15. Interview with Paul Rieckhoff, telephone, March 2015.

16. Interview with Jann Wenner, New York City, June 2014.

17. Interview with Joe McDonald, telephone, November 2014.

18. Ibid.

19. Interview with Jann Wenner, New York City, June 2014.

20. George W. Bush and Merle Haggard are quoted in Greg Mitchell, "Ten Years Ago Today a Dixie Chick Dared to Hit Bush on War—and a Hate Campaign Began," *The Nation*, March 10, 2013.

21. Chris Parton, "Natalie Maines Is Still Not Ready to Make Nice," *CMT News,* March 11, 2015.

22. Interview with Serj Tankian, telephone, July 2014.

23. Ibid.

24. Interview with Serj Tankian, telephone, July 2014..

25. Interview with Serj Tankian, telephone, July 2014.

26. Ibid.

27. Interview with Serj Tankian, telephone, July 2014.

28. Gary Graff, "System of a Down Open to Writing New Music," *Billboard*, April 1, 2014.

29. See System of a Down, Armenia concert, April 2015, available at http://www. rollingstone.com/music/videos/system-of-a-down-armenia-live-stream-20150423 (accessed in May 2015).

30. Interview with Serj Tankian, telephone, July 2015.

31. Interview with Graham Nash, telephone, June 2014.

32. Ibid.

33. Interview with Sinéad O'Connor, Skype, July 2014.

34. Interview with David Crosby, Santa Ynez, California, June 2014.

35. Interview with Graham Nash, telephone, May 2014.

36. Interview with David Crosby, Santa Ynez, California, June 2014

37. Dorian Lynskey, "Neil Young's Ohio—The Greatest Protest Record," *The Guardian,* May 6, 2010.

38. Interview with George Gecick, e-mail, March 2015.

39. Ibid.

40. Interview with Kate Pierson, telephone, June 2015.

41. Interview with Michael Stanley, Cleveland, Ohio, August 2014.

42. Interview with David Crosby, Santa Ynez, California, June 2014.

43. Ibid.

44. Transcript, "VH-1 Behind the Music," available at http://www.may4archive. org/vh1.shtml (accessed in March 2015).

45. Ibid.

46. Interview with David Crosby, Santa Ynez, California, June 2014.

47. In spring 1968, Walter Cronkite, the venerable news anchor for *CBS* ended a broadcast by editorializing that at best America could claim a stalemate and that it was time to negotiate the best possible departure from Vietnam. For detail see Douglas Brinkley, *Cronkite* (New York: Harper, 2013)

48. Interview with Bill Payne, telephone, December 2014.

49. Ibid.

50. Interview with Liberty Devitto, telephone, June 2014.

51. Ibid.

52. Ibid.

53. Interview with Michael Franti, telephone, September 2014.

54. Interview with Johanna Fateman, Skype, January 2015.

55. Interview with Lukas Nelson, telephone, November 2014.

56. Interview with Joe McDonald, telephone, November 2014.

57. Ibid.

58. Interview with Joe McDonald, telephone, November 2014.

59. Interview with Joe McDonald, telephone, November 2014.

60. Interview with Joe McDonald, telephone, November 2014.

61. Ibid.

62. "America Meets the Rag," available at http://www.countryjoe.com/frost.htm (accessed in March 2015).

63. Interview with Bruce Schmidt, telephone, March 2015.

64. Ibid.

65. Interview with Christine Martucci, e-mail, March 2015.

66. Bureau of Labor Statistics, "Employment Situation of Veterans Survey," March 18, 2015 available at http://www.bls.gov/news.release/vet.nr0.htm (accessed in March 2015).

67. Peter Baker, "Obama Signs Suicide Prevention for Veterans Act into Law," *New York Times,* February 12, 2015.

68. "Veteran's Statistics: PTSD, Depression, TBI, Suicide," available at http://veteransandptsd.com/PTSD-statistics.html (accessed in March 2015).

69. "Musiccorps," background information available at http://www.musicorps.net/About.html (accessed in March 2015).

70. Marissa Calhoun, "How the Healing Power of Music Helps Wounded Warriors," *CNN,* December 17, 2014.

71. "Guitars for Vets to Launch Nashville Chapter," October 21, 2013, available at http://www.visitmusiccity.com/media/pr_GuitarsforVets (accessed in March 2015).

72. Leo Shane, III, "Veteran Wins Chance to Rock and Roll All Night," *Stars and Stripes,* May 23, 2012.

73. Interview with Paul Rieckhoff, telephone, March 2015.

74. Ibid.

75. Ibid.

76. Interview with Paul Rieckhoff, telephone, March 2015.

77. Ibid.

78. Kory Grow, "John Fogerty Addresses 'Fortunate Son' Concert for Valor Controversy," *Rolling Stone*, November 13, 2014.

79. Ethan Epstein, "Anti-Military Anthem Played at 'Concert for Valor,'" *The Weekly Standard*, November 11, 2014.

80. Interview with Paul Rieckhoff, telephone, March 2015.

81. Interview with Paul Rieckoff, telephone, March 2015.

82. Interview with Joe McDonald, telephone, November 2014.

83. Ibid.

84. Ibid.

85. Interview with Paul Rieckoff, telephone, March 2015.

CHAPTER SIX

1. Interview with Serj Tankian, telephone, July 2014.

2. Albert Einstein, et al., *Ultimate Quotable Einstein* (Princeton, NJ: Princeton University Press, 2011), 100–101.

3. "Interviw with Jerry Dipizzo," *All Sides with Ann Fischer, WOSU*, December 19, 2014, available at http://wosu.org/2012/allsides-archive/sides-weekend-best-local-music-2014/ (accessed in May 2015).

4. Interview with Liberty Devitto, telephone, June 2014.

5. Interview with Bill Payne, telephone, December 2014.

6. Ibid.

7. Interview with Michael Stanley, Cleveland, Ohio, August 2014.

8. Ibid.

9. Interview with Damien Dempsey, telephone, February 2015.

10. Ibid.

11. Interview with Bertis Downs, telephone, July 2014.

12. Interview with Kate Pierson, telephone, June 2015.

13. Ibid.

14. David Remnick, "Bob Dylan: Extending the Line,"*New Yorker*, February 9, 2015.

15. Interview with David Crosby, Santa Ynez, California, June 2014.

16. Interview with Dar Williams, telephone, September 2014.

17. Project Noise, "Tom Morello – From Harvard to Hollywood," July 16, 2009, available at https://www.youtube.com/watch?v=4cjZzoSz2bw (accessed in December 2014).

18. Interview with David Crosby, Santa Ynez, California, June 2014.

19. Ibid.

20. Interview with Kathy Kane, telephone, January 2015.

21. Interview with Matt Busch, telephone, September 2014.

22. Ibid.

23. Interview with Cameron Sears, Mill Valley, California, June 2014.

24. Ibid.

25. Interview with Cameron Sears, Mill Valley, California, June 2014.

26. Information and data provided to the author by Katherine Dunn of the Southern Education Foundation, June 2015.

27. Interview with Bertis Downs, telephone, July 2014.

28. Bertis Downs, "Parent to Obama: Why Don't Private Schools Adopt Your Test-Based School Reforms?" *Washington Post*, March 5, 2014.

29. Interview with Bertis Downs, telephone, July 2014.

30. Interview with Johanna Fateman, Skype, January 2015.

31. Interview with Dar Williams, September 2014.

32. Ibid.

33. "Rock and Roll: An American Story," available at http://www.rockandrollfor-ever.org/ (accessed in May 2015).

34. Ibid.

35. Data provided by Little Kids Rock, available at http://www.littlekidsrock.org/ (accessed in August 2016).

36. Interview with David Wish, Verona, New Jersey, June 2014.

37. Ibid.

38. Interview with David Wish, Verona, New Jersey, June 2014.

39. Interview with David Wish, Verona, New Jersey, June 2014.

40. Ibid.

41. Ibid.

42. Ibid.

43. Ibid.

44. Ibid.

45. Ibid.

46. Interview with David Wish, Verona, New Jersey, June 2014.

47. Ibid.

48. Interview with Liberty Devitto, telephone, June 2014.

49. Data made available from Little Kids Rock, e-mail, May 2015.

50. Interview with David Wish, e-mail, May 2015.

51. "Joan Jett and Little Kids Rock," *Little Kids Rock*, October 24, 2014, available at http://www.littlekidsrock.org/news-events/press-releases/joan-jett-and-little-kids-rock/ (accessed in May 2015).

52. Brian Ives, "Q&A: Joan Jett on her Own All-Star Tribute," *Radio.com*, October 25, 2014, available at http://radio.com/2014/10/25/joan-jett-interview-all-star-tribute-concert/ (accessed in May 2015).

53. Central Intelligence Agency, *CIA World Fact Book,* 2015.

54. See Classbase—Haiti, available at http://www.classbase.com/Countries/Haiti/Education-System (accessed in May 2015).

55. Interview with Sara Wasserman, Mill Valley, California, June 2014.

56. Ibid.

57. "Music Heals Project," available at https://www.youtube.com/watch?v=UnliAcJSIVs&app=desktop (accessed in May 2015).

58. Interview with Sara Wasserman, Mill Valley, California, June 2014.

59. Ibid.

60. Ibid.

61. "Origin! Rock and Roll Camp for Girls," available at http://rockpowerforgirls.org/origins.php (accessed in June 2015).

62. See Girls Rock Camp Alliance, available at http://girlsrockcampalliance.org/about-2/impact/ (accessed in June 2015).

63. Kathleen Hanna, "Girls Rock Camp Alliance," March 4, 2013, available at http://www.kathleenhanna.com/girls-rock-camp-alliance/ (accessed in June 2015).

64. Education Mission and Program Goals, Grammy Museum, available at http://www.grammymuseum.org/education/mission-program-goals (accessed in June 2015).

65. Interview with Kaitlyn Steubner, Los Angeles, California, June 2014.

66. Ibid.

67. Interview with Kaitlyn Steubner, Los Angeles, California, June 2014.

68. Ibid.

69. Ibid.

70. Rock and Roll Hall of Fame and Museum, "History and Overview," available at http://rockhall.com/visit-the-museum/learn/history-and-overview/ (accessed in June 2015).

71. Rock and Roll Hall of Fame and Museum, "Education" available at http://rockhall.com/education/#sthash.wFx2naUd.dpuf (accessed in June 2015).

72. Interview with Lauren Onkey, Cleveland, Ohio, June 2015.

73. Interview with Lauren Onkey, Cleveland, Ohio, June 2015.

74. Ibid.

75. Rock and Roll Hall of Fame and Museum, "Bill Haley and His Comets," available at http://www.rockhall.com/education/distance-learning/online-professional-development/bill-haley/ (accessed in June 2015).

76. Rock and Roll Hall of Fame and Museum, "Country Music and Rock and Roll," available at http://www.rockhall.com/education/distance-learning/online-professional-development/bill-haley/bill-haley-objective-1/ (accessed in June 2015).

77. Rock and Roll Hall of Fame and Museum, "Bill Haley: Objective Three" available at http://www.rockhall.com/education/distance-learning/online-professional-development/bill-haley/bill-haley-objective-3/ (accessed in June 2015).

78. Interview with Lauren Onkey, Cleveland, Ohio, June 2015.

79. John Covach, "Why No Yes in Rock Hall?" *Cleveland Plain Dealer*, December 29, 2010.

80. Lauren Onkey, "A Response to 'Why No Yes in the Rock Hall?'" available at http://rockhall.com/blog/post/5442_a-response-to-why-no-yes-in-t/ (accessed in June 2015).

81. Interview with Lauren Onkey, Cleveland, Ohio, June 2015.

82. See "Future Rock Legends," available at http://www.futurerocklegends.com/blog_files/Women_in_the_Rock_Hall.html (accessed in June 2015).

83. Chuck Arnold, "'There Should Be More Women' in the Rock and Roll Hall of Fame," *Billboard*, April 6, 2015.

84. Interview with Lauren Onkey, Cleveland, Ohio, June 2015.

85. Interview with Glen Ballard, Los Angeles, California, June 2014.

86. Interview with Michael Stanley, Cleveland, Ohio, August 2014.

CHAPTER SEVEN

1. David Johnston, "Bangladesh: The Event that Almost Wasn't," *Los Angeles Times*, June 2, 1985.

2. Graham Nash, *Wild Tales* (New York: Crown Archtype, 2013), 270.

3. Interview with David Crosby, Santa Ynez, California, June 2014.

4. Graham Nash, *Wild Tales*, 271.

5. "Live Aid 1985: How It Happened," *British Broadcasting Corporation*, available at http://www.bbc.co.uk/music/thelive8event/liveaid/history.shtml (accessed in July 2015).

6. David Rieff, "Cruel to be Kind?," *The Guardian*, June 23, 2005.

7. Alan Cowell, "Celebrities' Embrace of Africa Has Critics," *New York Times*, July 1, 2005.

8. Interview, Erin Potts, telephone, June 2014.

9. David Crosby and David Bender, *Stand and Be Counted: Making Music, Making History* (HarperCollins: New York, 2000), 132.

10. Adam Yauch, interview, available at https://www.youtube.com/watch?v=DDwCoEuU4u4 (accessed in July 2015).

11. Interview with Erin Potts, telephone, June 2014.

12. Live 8, "Make Promises Happen," available at http://www.live8live.com/makepromiseshappen/# (accessed in June 2014).

13. Fuse ODG, "Why I Had to Turn Down Bob Geldoff," *The Guardian*, November 19, 2014.

14. Majewski, "Inside Band Aid 30."

15. Interview with Graham Nash, telephone, June 2014.

16. Interview with Erin Potts, telephone, June 2014.

17. Interview with Matt Busch, telephone, September 2014.

18. Interview with Kathy Kane, telephone, January 2015.

19. Interview with Lukas Nelson, telephone, November 2014.

20. "Bonnie Raitt Video Q&A, *Billboard*, December 28, 2011.

21. Interview with David Crosby, Santa Ynez, California, June 2014.

22. Interview with Kathy Kane, telephone, January 2015.

23. Ibid.

24. Interview with Kathy Kane, telephone, January 2015.

25. Interview with Kathy Kane, telephone, January 2015.

26. Interview with Kathy Kane, telephone, January 2015.

27. Ibid.

28. Interview with Kathy Kane, telephone, January 2015.

29. Ibid.

30. Interview with Kathy Kane, telephone, January 2015.

31. Ibid.

32. Julia Wasson, "REVERB Greens Rock Concert Scene," November 6, 2009, available at http://www.blueplanetgreenliving.com/tag/bonnie-raitt/ (accessed in July 2015).

33. Interview with Lauren Sullivan, telephone, September 2014.

34. Interview with Lauren Sullivan, telephone, September 2014.

35. Ibid.

36. Ibid.

37. Interview with Lauren Sullivan, telephone, September 2014.

38. Ibid.

39. REVERB, "Environmental Impact," available at http://REVERB.org/ (accessed in July 2015).

40. Interview with Cameron Sears, Mill Valley, California, June 2014.

41. Ibid.

42. Interview with Cameron Sears, Mill Valley, California, June 2014.

43. Ibid.

44. Ibid.

45. Ibid.

46. Do It for the Love Foundation, "Mission," available at http://doitforthelove.org/pages/mission (accessed in July 2015).

47. Interview with Michael Franti, telephone, September 2014.

48. Ibid.

49. Interview with Michael Franti, telephone, September 2014.

50. Ibid.

51. Ibid.

52. Interview with Michael Franti, telephone, September 2014.

53. Ibid.

54. "Do It For the Love Foundation Promotional Video," available at https://www.youtube.com/watch?v=VyByUqZ2jGs (accessed in July 2015).

55. *Milagro Foundation*, "Milagro at a Glance," available at http://milagrofoundation.org/Content/About_Milagro.pdf (accessed in July 2015).

56. Ibid.

57. *See Milagro Foundation: Partners*, available at http://www.milagrofoundation.org/partners.asp (accessed in August 2015).

58. Interview with Ruthie Moutafian, Mill Valley, California, June 2014.

59. Ibid.

60. Interview with David Wish, e-mail, August 2015.

61. Ibid.

62. Interview with Ruthie Moutafian, Mill Valley, California, June 2014.

63. Mimi Towell, "Santana Opens Doors," *Marin Magazine*, available at http://www.marinmagazine.com/August-2010/Santana-Opens-Doors/ (accessed in August 2015).

64. Interview with Ruthie Moutafian, Mill Valley, California, June 2014.

65. Interview with Jann Wenner, New York City, June 2014.

66. Ibid.

67. Kurt Loder, "Bruce Springsteen: The Rolling Stone Interview," *Rolling Stone*, December 6, 1984.

68. Eveline Chao, "Stop Using My Song," *Rolling Stone*, July 8, 2015.

69. Randy Lewis, "Neil Young Expands on His Response to Donald Trump's Use of 'Free World' Song," *Los Angeles Times*, August 28, 1999.

70. "Really Randoms," *Rolling Stone*, 28 August 1999.

71. Interview with David Crosby, Santa Ynez, California, June 2014.

72. Letter to Joe Walsh, available at http://reporter.blogs.com/files/walsh-walk-away-0001.pdf (accessed in August 2015).

73. Tom Morello, "Tom Morello: 'Paul Ryan is the Embodiment of the Machine Our Music Rages Against,'" *Rolling Stone*, 16 August 2012.

74. Ibid.

75. Interview with Matt Busch, telephone, September 2014.

76. Ibid.

77. Ibid.

78. Ibid.

79. Dorian Lynesky, *33 Revolutions* (New York: Harper/Collins, 2001), 424.

80. Interview with Bertis Downs, telephone, July 2014.

81. Ibid.

82. 99 Percent Invisible and Whitney Jones, "Why R.E.M.'s *Out of Time* is the Most Politically Significant Album in U.S. History," *Slate*, July 25, 2014.

83. Rock the Vote, available at http://www.rockthevote.com/ (accessed in August 2015).

84. Mary McGuirt, "Young Black Turnout a Record in 2008 Election," *ABC News*, July 21, 2009.

85. Interview with Bertis Downs, telephone, July 2014.
86. About HeadCount, available at http://www.HeadCount.org/about-HeadCount/ (accessed in August 2015).
87. Interview with Andy Bernstein, telephone, June 2014.
88. Interview with Andy Bernstein, telephone, June 2014.
89. Interview with Andy Bernstein, telephone, June 2014.
90. Interview with Andy Bernstein, telephone, June 2014.
91. Ibid.
92. Ibid.
93. Interview with Andy Bernstein, telephone, September 2015.
94. Ibid.
95. Revolutions Per Minute, "Results" available at http://revolutionsperminute. net/results/ (accessed in August 2015).
96. Ann Charters, *The Beat Reader* (New York: Viking, 1992), xxxi.
97. Interview with Erin Potts, telephone, June 2014.
98. Ibid.

CHAPTER EIGHT

1. Interview with Billy Bragg, telephone, September 2014.
2. David Vandivier, "Rock and Roll, Economics, and Rebuilding the Middle Class,"*Council of Economic Advisers*, June 12, 2013, available at https://www.white-house.gov/blog/2013/06/12/rock-and-roll-economics-and-rebuilding-middle-class (accessed in August 2015).
3. Bertis Downs, "Lecture at the Terry College of Business: University of Georgia," available at https://www.YouTube.com/watch?v=UpFNF8GJQcM (accessed in August 2015).
4. Kristin Thompson, "Mythbusting: Data Driven Answers to Four Common Assumptions About How Musicians Make Money," *Future of Music Coalition*, December 2, 2012, available at http://money.futureofmusic.org/mythbusting/ (accessed in August 2015).
5. Ibid.
6. Interview with Dar Williams, telephone, September 2014.
7. David Goldman, "Music's Lost Decade: Sales Cut in Half,"*CNN Money*, February 3, 2010.
8. Downs, "Lecture at the Terry School of Business."
9. Ashley Lutz, "These 6 Corporations Control 90% of the Media in America," *Business Insider*, June 14, 2012.
10. Future of Music Coalition, "False Premises, False Promises," December 13, 2006, available at https://www.futureofmusic.org/article/research/false-premises-false-promises (accessed in August 2015).
11. Federal Communications Commission, "Telecommunications Act of 1996," available at https://transition.fcc.gov/telecom.html (accessed in August 2015).
12. Future of Music Coalition, "False Premises."

13. Future of Music Coalition, "False Premises."

14. Interview with Michael Bracy, telephone, June 2014.

15. Interview with Glen Ballard, Los Angeles, California, June 2014.

16. Ibid.

17. Common Cause, "Fallout From the Telecommunications Act of 1996: Unintended Consequences and Lessons Learned," May 9, 2005, available at http://www.commoncause.org/research-reports/National_050905_Fallout_From_The_Telecommunications_Act_2.pdf (accessed in August 2015).

18. Interview with Michael Bracy, telephone, June 2014.

19. Interview with Michael Stanley, Cleveland, Ohio, August 2014.

20. Interview with Michael Stanley, Cleveland, Ohio, August 2014.

21. Vandivier, "Rock and Roll…"

22. Vince Calio, "The 10 Most Expensive Concert Tickets,"*24/7 Wall Street*, March 8, 2014, available at http://247wallst.com/special-report/2014/03/08/the-10-most-expensive-concert-tickets/2/ (accessed in August 2014).

23. Ray Waddell, "Grateful Dead Concerts Made $52 Million, Set Record for Biggest Music PPV Event Ever,"*Billboard*, July 23, 2015.

24. Joe Coscarelli, "As Grateful Dead Exit, A Debate Will Not Fade Away,"*New York Times*, July 2, 2015.

25. Interview with Danny Goldberg, telephone, October 2015.

26. Ibid.

27. Johnson, "The Creative Apocalypse…"

28. Future of Music Coalition, "The Data Journalism that Wasn't," August 21, 2015, available at http://futureofmusic.org/blog/2015/08/21/data-journalism-wasnt (accessed in August 2015).

29. Ryan Waniata, "Taylor Swift is Right: Music Can't Survive if You Don't Pay for It," April 25, 2015, available at http://www.digitaltrends.com/music/how-spotify-and-pandora-are-hurting-artists/ (accessed in August 2015).

30. Interview with Glen Ballard, Los Angeles, California, June 2014.

31. Interview with Michael Stanley, Cleveland, Ohio, August 2014.

32. Interview with David Crosby, Santa Ynez, California, June 2014.

33. Interview with Cameron Sears, Mill Valley, California, June 2014.

34. Bill Kreutzman, *Deal* (New York: St. Martin's Press, 2015), 326.

35. Interview with Matt Busch, telephone, September 2014.

36. Interview with Michael Bracy, telephone, June 2014.

37. Interview with Bertis Downs, telephone, July 2014.

38. Joe Coscarelli, "Few Dollars, but Maybe Career Sense, for Struggling Bands at SXSW," *New York Times*, March 16, 2015.

39. Ibid.

40. Ibid.

41. Jack Conte, "Pomplamoose 2014 Tour Profits (or Lack Thereof)," November 24, 2014, available at https://medium.com/@jackconte/pomplamoose-2014-tour-profits-67435851ba37#.i9rlliafb (accessed in August 2015).

42. Interview with Glen Ballard, Los Angeles, California, June 2014.

43. Steve Albini, "The Internet Has Solved Music's Problem," *The Guardian*, November 16, 2014.

44. See Allison Keyes, "George Clinton Fights for his Right to Funk," *National Public Radio*, June 6, 2012.

45. Eriq Gardner, "George Clinton Can't Prevent Sound Recordings from Being Sold," *Billboard*, June 23, 2014.

46. Interview with George Clinton, Columbus, Ohio, September 2014.

47. Ibid.

48. Interview with Michael Stanley, Cleveland, Ohio, August 2014.

49. Ibid.

50. Ibid.

51. Interview with Carianne Brinkman, telephone, January 2015.

52. Ibid.

53. Ibid.

54. Ibid.

55. Interview with Chris McCutcheon, telephone, July 2014.

56. Ibid.

57. Interview with Christine Havrilla, Asbury Park, New Jersey, June 2014.

58. Interview with Bruce Schmidt, telephone, March 2015.

59. Interview with Glen Ballard, Los Angeles, California, June 2014.

60. Ibid.

61. Ibid.

62. Interview with Danny Goldberg, telephone, October 2015.

63. Interview with Matt Busch, telephone, September 2014.

64. Interview with Kathy Kane, telephone, January 2015.

65. Interview with Glen Ballard, Los Angeles, California, June 2014.

66. Glenn Peoples, "Spotify Now Paying Sound Exchange for Mobile Radio Streams in U.S., Lowers Royalty Bill,"*Billboard*, September 24, 2012.

67. *British Broadcasting Corporation*, "Spotify Reveals Artists Earn $0.0007 Per Stream," December 4, 2013.

68. Nate Rau, "'All About That Bass' Writer Decries Streaming Revenue,"*The Tennessean*, September 22, 2015.

69. Andy Swartz, "Rosanne Cash: I've Always Been a Union Member," available at http://www.local802afm.org/2015/08/rosanne-cash-ive-always-been-a-union-member/ (accessed in June 2016).

70. Interview with Bill Payne, telephone, December 2014.

71. *The Graham Norton Show*, October 25, 2014.

72. David Carr, "Chasing Relevancy at Any Cost, Even Free,"*New York Times*, November 9, 2014.

73. Christopher Williams, "Apple Tie-up with U2 Branded a 'Dismal Failure' by Music Retailers,"*The Telegraph*, September 16, 2014.

74. Chris Richards, "U2, Apple and Rock-and-roll as Dystopian Junk Mail,"*Washington Post,* September 10, 2014.

75. Taylor Swift, "For Taylor Swift, the Future of Music is a Love Story,"*Wall Street Journal*, July 7, 2014.

76. Brian Anthony Hernandez, "Taylor Swift's YouTube views doubled after pulling music from Spotify,"*Mashable*, November 20, 2014.

77. Hernandez, "Taylor Swift's YouTube views..."

78. Jon Healey, "Taylor Swift fans stymied on Spotify but not on YouTube," *Los Angeles Times*, November 26, 2014.

79. Joshua P. Fiedlander, "News and Notes on 2014 Mid-Year RIAA Shipment and Revenue Statistics," available at http://riaa.com/media/1806D32F-B3DD-19D3-70A4-4C31C0217836.pdf (accessed in August 2015).

80. David Byrne, "Open the Music Industry's Black Box," *New York Times*, July 31, 2015.

81. Ben Sisario, "Sony Terms with Spotify Uncovered in Contact," *New York Times*, May 24, 2015.

82. Alex Stedman, "Taylor Swift Slams 'Shocking, Disappointing' Free Apple Music Trial,"*Variety*, June 21, 2015.

83. Billy Bragg on Taylor Swift, U2 and The Smiths - Gigwise Interview," available at https://www.YouTube.com/watch?v=Ze5Sk07394c#t=148 (accessed in August 2015).

84. Interview with Sinéad O'Connnor, Skype, July 2014.

85. Ibid.

86. James Grebey, "Dave Grohl: Not an 'American Idol' Fan," *Spin*, October 29, 2014.

87. Interview with Damien Dempsey, telephone, February 2015.

88. Interview with David Crosby, Santa Ynez, California, June 2014.

89. Interview with Glen Ballard, Los Angeles, California, June 2014.

90. Interview with Gedeon Luke, telephone, August 2014.

91. Ibid.

92. Interview with Danny Goldberg, telephone, October 2015.

93. Interview with Marc Swersky, telephone, August 2014.

94. Ibid.

95. Ibid.

96. Interview with Danny Goldberg, telephone, October 2015.

97. Ibid.

98. Interview with Mark Johnson, telephone, September 2014.

99. Ibid.

100. Ibid.

101. Interview with Mark Johnson, telephone, September 2014.

102. Ibid.

103. Interview with Kathy Kane, telephone, January 2015.

104. Swartz, "Rosanne Cash..."

105. Interview with Michael Bracy, telephone, June 2014.

CHAPTER NINE

1. Interview with Dennis McNally, telephone, July 2014.

2. "Bob Dylan's Full MusiCares Speech," February 7, 2015, available at http://www.latimes.com/entertainment/music/posts/la-et-ms-grammys-2015-transcript-of-bob-dylans-musicares-person-of-year-speech-20150207-story.html (accessed in October 2015).

3. Interview with Graham Nash, telephone, June 2014.

4. Interview with David Gans, Oakland, California, June 2014.

5. "Paul McCartney Interview," *British Broadcasting Corporation*, May 23, 1968, available at http://www.beatlesinterviews.org/db1968.0523.beatles.html (accessed in October 2015).

6. Interview with Danny Goldberg, telephone, October 2015.

7. Ibid.

8. Interview with Danny Goldberg, telephone, October 2015.

9. Ibid.

10. Interview with Sinéad O'Connor, Skype, July 2014.

11. Interview with Danny Goldberg, telephone, September 2015.

12. Krist Novoselić, "Open Source Party," December 30, 2013, available at http://kristnovoselic.blogspot.com/2013/12/open-source-party.html (accessed in October 2015).

13. Krist Novocelić, "Open Source Party: Part II," December 30, 2013, available at http://kristnovoselic.blogspot.com/2013/12/open-source-party-part-ii.html (accessed in October 2015).

14. Interview with Liberty Devitto, telephone, June 2014.

15. Interview with Christine Havrilla, Asbury Park, New Jersey, June 2014.

16. Interview with David Gans, Oakland, California, June 2014.

17. Interview with Dar Williams, telephone, September 2014.

18. Interview with Bill Payne, telephone, December 2014.

19. Interview with Graham Nash, telephone, June 2014.

20. Interview with Billy Bragg, telephone, September 2014.

21. Interview with Bruce Schmidt, telephone, March 2015.

22. Interview with Dennis McNally, telephone, July 2014.

23. Interview with Cameron Sears, Mill Valley, California, June 2014.

24. Geoff Edgers, "The Strange Story of the Grateful Dead's Path to the Summer's Hottest Ticket," *Washington Post*, June 12, 2015.

25. Interview with Dar Williams, telephone, September 2014.

26. Interview with Michael Stanley, Cleveland, Ohio, August 2014.

27. Interview with Bob Gross, telephone, July 2014.

28. Interview with Matt Busch, telephone, September 2014.

29. Interview with Sinéad O'Connor, Skype, July 2014.

30. Interview with David Crosby, Santa Ynez, California, June 2014.

31. Ibid.

32. Interview, with David Wish, Verona, New Jersey, June 2014.

33. Ibid.

34. Interview with David Crosby, Santa Ynez, California, June 2014.

35. Interview with David Wish, Verona, New Jersey, June 2014.

36. Interview with Tom Gilmour, Asbury Park, New Jersey, June 2014.

37. Ibid.

38. Interview with Tom Gilmour, Asbury Park, New Jersey, June 2014.

39. Ibid.

40. Ibid.

41. Interview with Tom Gilmour, Asbury Park, New Jersey, June 2014.

42. Interview with Marc Swersky, telephone, August 2014.

43. Ibid.
44. Interview with Christine Martucci, Asbury Park, New Jersey, June 2014.
45. Ibid.
46. Interview with Dar Williams, telephone, September 2014.
47. Ibid.
48. Ibid.
49. Interview with Dar Williams, telephone, September 2014.
50. Ibid.
51. Francis Dinkelspiel, "Berkeley Couple Buys Mr. Mopps' Toy Store," *Berkeleyside*, October 15, 2010.
52. Interview with Joe McDonald, telephone, November 2014.
53. Ibid.
54. Interview with Mark Karan, Fairfax, California, June 2014.
55. Ibid.
56. Interview with Mark Johnson, telephone, September 2014.
57. Interview with Michael Franti, telephone, September 2014.
58. Ibid.
59. Interview with Serj Tankian, telephone, July 2014.
60. Interview with Graham Nash, telephone, June 2014.
61. Interview with Glen Ballard, Los Angeles, California, June 2014.
62. Interview with David Crosby, Santa Ynez, California, June 2014.
63. Interview with Michael Stanley, Cleveland, Ohio, August 2014.
64. Interview with Kate Pierson, telephone, June 2015.
65. Interview with George Clinton, Columbus, Ohio, September 2014.
66. Ibid.
67. Interview with Bertis Downs, telephone, July 2014.
68. Interview with David Crosby, Santa Ynez, California, June 2014.
69. Ibid.
70. Interview with Jann Wenner, New York City, June 2014.
71. Interview with Kathy Kane, telephone, January 2015.
72. Ibid.
73. Interview with Danny Goldberg, telephone, October 2015.
74. Ibid.
75. Interview with Erin Potts, telephone, June 2014.
76. Interview with Erin Potts, telephone, June 2014.
77. Interview with David Crosby, Santa Ynez, California, June 2014.
78. Interview with Damien Dempsey, telephone, February 2015.
79. Interview with Bill Payne, telephone, December 2014.
80. Interview with Erin Potts, telephone, June 2014.
81. Jeff Slate, "Jackson Browne, 'Standing in the Breach'—the Interview," available at http://www.rockcellarmagazine.com/2014/10/07/jackson-browne-standing-in-the-breach-the-interview/#sthash.eSgesTKX.dpbs (accessed in October 2014).
82. Interview with Christine Martucci, Asbury Park, New Jersey, June 2014.
83. "President Obama Hosts 'In Performance at the White House,'" October 14, 2015, The White House, Washington, D.C.

84. Mike Boehm, "Obama Budget: Good for D.C. Museums, Not for NEA and Arts Grants," *Los Angeles Times*, March 5, 2014.

85. Eric Robelen, "Arts Education Sees Decline, Especially for Minorities, Report Suggests,"*Education Week*, February 28, 2011.

86. "Reps. Nadler and Blackburn Introduce the Fair Play Fair Pay Act of 2015," April 13, 2015, available at http://nadler.house.gov/press-release/reps-nadler-and-blackburn-introduce-fair-play-fair-pay-act-2015 (accessed in October 2015).

87. Julie Kirby, "Tax Free Era for Irish Artists May End," *British Broadcasting Corporation,* September 9, 2009.

88. Interview with Ted Scott, telephone, August 2014.

89. Interview with George Clinton, Columbus, Ohio, September 2014.

90. Interview with Joe McDonald, telephone, November 2014.

91. Interview with David Crosby, Santa Ynez, California, June 2014.

92. Interview with Graham Nash, telephone, June 2014.

93. Interview with Jann Wenner, New York City, June 2014.

Index

activism, 1, 5, 22, 79, 153–54, 231–32;
  AIDS, 90–91;
  aid to Africa, 154–57;
  antiracism, 40–41;
  antiwar, 9, 157–58. *See also* war,
    protest against;
  civil rights, 9;
  environmental, 163–66;
  life-threatening diseases, 167–69;
  nonprofit, 158–71, 176–77;
  political, 171–79;
  risk of, 17–18;
  for underserved and vulnerable
    children, 169–71;
  voting rights, 175–77
Adams, Bryan, 35, 74, 75
Adkins, Adele Laurie Blue, 65
Afghanistan war, 45, 103, 107–8,
  115–16, 122–23, 125
African Americans, 53, 56, 57, 230
African National Congress, 38
Ahmadinejad, Mahmood, 44
Ahmed, Asif, 189
AIDS activism, 90–91
Albini, Steve, 190
Alex Kapranos, 86–87
Allman Brothers, 53, 171

all-women rock groups, 65, 66
Alyokhina, Maria, 2, 85, 87–88, 90
American Idol, 57, 59, 199, 200, 201
American values, 215–21
Amnesty International, 73–77, 215;
  "Conspiracy of Hope" tour
    (1986), 74–75;
  "Human Rights Now" tour
    (1988), 75–76;
  on Pussy Riot's imprisonment, 86, 87
Anderson, Laurie, 50
Anderson, Sini, 12, 65–66, 68
Apartheid, 37–41, 134, 214–15
Arab Spring, 41, 42
Arcade Fire, 202
Armenian genocide, 111, 112
Artists United Against Apartheid, 39
arts education, 229–30
Asbury Park, 216–18
Asbury Park Music Heritage
  Foundation, 216
audience, and rock and roll
  ethic, 231–32

Baez, Joan, 6, 8, 9, 103, 153–54, 155
Balzary, Michael Peter. *See* Flea
Baker, Arthur, 39

Baker, James, 36
Balkans, nationalist mobilization of war
    in, 106
Ballard, Glen, 13, 56, 60, 184, 187, 189,
    195–96, 200;
  on democracy, 222;
  independent label, 193–94;
  and Jackson, 56;
  on music education, 152;
  on Perry, 95;
  and Starr, 14
Band, the, 35
Band Aid, 154–55, 157
Beach Boys, 12, 13, 38
Beastie Boys, 156
Beatlemania, 27
Beatles, 13, 26–27, 67;
  Ballard on, 13–14;
  and Crosby, 13;
  and drug use, 97;
  and politics, 225;
  tour in America (1964), 54–55
Beehive Books, 219, 220
Belafonte, Harry, 8, 38
Bernstein, Andy, 176–77, 179, 224
Berry, Chuck, 52, 138
Bikini Kill, 65, 66, 67, 89, 145
Biko, Steve, 38
Bill Haley and His Comets, 5, 149
Billy Joel Band, 28, 29, 30, 117
Blackburn, Marcia, 230
Blackheart Records, 65, 68, 191–92
Bloom, Arthur, 122
Blues Brothers, 104
Boehm, Mike, 229
Bono, 41–42, 78–79, 81–82, 171
Booker T., 52
Boomtown Rats, 78
Bowie, David, 90
Bracy, Michael, 183, 184, 188
Bragg, Billy, 10–11, 47–48, 106, 181,
    199, 211–12
Brinkman, Carianne, 65, 68, 191–92

Broadus, Cordozar Calvin. *See*
    Snoop Dogg
Brown, James, 15, 54
Browne, Jackson, 39, 50, 109, 153,
    202, 228
Brownstein, Carrie, 145
Brownstein, Marc, 176
Bruce Springsteen and the E. Street
    Band, 34, 39, 53
B-52s, 10, 12, 61, 67, 90, 96, 114,
    133, 150
Burroughs, William S., 179
Busby, Joshua, 79
Busch, Matt, 173–74, 194–95;
  on benefits of concerts, 158;
  education of, 135–36;
  and Obama campaign, 174;
  on progress and rock and roll, 214;
  on sponsorships, 194–95;
  on touring, 188
Byrds, 6, 13, 26, 34, 98
Byrne, David, 173, 198

"Call To Action against
    Poverty," 156–57
Campbell, Tom, 162
Campus Consciousness Tour
    (2015), 166
careers, sustainable, 194, 195–96
Carrack, Paul, 16, 35
Casale, Gerald, 114
Cash, Rosanne, 196, 204
Celtic Tiger, 79, 80–81, 84
Charter 77, 33
Chaz, Washboard, 202
Ciccone, Madonna Louise, 63, 64, 91
civil rights movement, 9, 10, 46, 52–53,
    54, 61, 78, 147, 214
Clancy Brothers, 78
Clapton, Eric, 15, 53, 155, 186
Clash, 5, 10, 11, 25, 41
Clayton, Adam, 78, 80
Clayton, Sam, 53

About the Author

Sean Kay is Robson Professor of Politics and Government at Ohio Wesleyan University. His previous books include *America's Search for Security: The Triumph of Idealism and the Return of Realism; Celtic Revival? The Rise, Fall, and Renewal of Global Ireland; Global Security in the Twenty-first Century: The Quest for Power and the Search for Peace; NATO and the Future of European Security*; and the co-edited volumes *NATO after Fifty Years and Limiting Institutions: The Challenge of Eurasian Security Governance*. In addition to his work as a political scientist and policy adviser, born in the San Francisco Bay Area in the "Summer of Love" and coming of age in America's heartland in Ohio, Sean Kay has long played guitar and sung rock and roll in the United States and Europe.